PRENTICE-HALL

Foundations of Economic Geography Series
NORTON GINSBURG, *Editor*

GEOGRAPHY OF MANUFACTURING, *Gunnar Alexandersson*

GEOGRAPHY OF MARKET CENTERS AND RETAIL
DISTRIBUTION, *Brian J.L. Berry*

GEOGRAPHY OF NATURAL RESOURCES, *Ian Burton* and
Robert W. Kates

GEOGRAPHY OF AGRICULTURE, *Howard Gregor*

GEOGRAPHY OF ENERGY, *Nathaniel B. Guyol*

GEOGRAPHY OF URBAN LAND USE, *Harold Mayer*

GEOGRAPHY OF WATER RESOURCES, *W.R. Derrick Sewell*

GEOGRAPHY OF TRANSPORTATION, *Edward J. Taaffe* and
Howard L. Gauthier, Jr.

GEOGRAPHY OF INTERNATIONAL TRADE, *Richard S. Thoman*
and *Edgar C. Conkling*

GEOGRAPHY OF WHOLESALING, *James E. Vance, Jr.*

A PROLOGUE TO POPULATION GEOGRAPHY, *Wilbur Zelinsky*

Foundations of Economic Geography Series

Geography

of

Transportation

EDWARD J. TAAFFE

Professor of Geography
The Ohio State University

HOWARD L. GAUTHIER

Professor of Geography
The Ohio State University

PRENTICE-HALL, INC., Englewood Cliffs, N.J.

Library of Congress Cataloging in Publication Data

TAAFFE, EDWARD JAMES.
    Geography of transportation.

    (Prentice-Hall foundations of economic
geography series)
    Bibliography: p.
    1.–Transportation.   I.–Gauthier, Howard L.,
joint author. II–Title.
HE151.T3   380.5   72–8995
ISBN 0–13–351395–5
ISBN 0–13–351387–4 (pbk)

PRENTICE-HALL INTERNATIONAL, INC., *London*
PRENTICE-HALL OF AUSTRALIA, PTY. LTD., *Sydney*
PRENTICE-HALL OF CANADA LTD., *Toronto*
PRENTICE-HALL OF INDIA PRIVATE, LTD., *New Delhi*
PRENTICE-HALL OF JAPAN, INC., *Tokyo*

to Robert S. Platt—
pioneer in the use of a
spatial perspective in
geographic research

Contents

preface   xiii

transportation   CHAPTER **1**

and spatial processes   1

The Functional Region • *Linkages* • *Nodes* • *Diagrammatic Representation of Hinterland Structure* • *Hinterland Studies* • *Hierarchies* • *Summary*

transportation   CHAPTER **2**

and spatial structure   34

Regional Specialization • *Transportation Costs* • *Agglomeration Economies* • *An Idealized Process of Transportation Development* • *The Development of U.S. Transportation as a Spatial Process* • *Summary*

CHAPTER 3   *the gravity model*   73

The Basic Gravity Model • The Gravity Model and Traffic • The Gravity Model and Hinterland Analysis • The Gravity Model and Potential Maps • Ullman's Triad • Complementarity • Intervening Opportunity • Weaknesses of the Gravity Model • Summary

CHAPTER 4   *structural analysis of*

transportation networks: aggregate measures   100

The Network as a Graph • Connectivity • Stages in Network Growth • Network Structure and the Region • Summary

CHAPTER 5   *structural analysis*

of transportation networks:

measures of nodal accessibility   116

Nodal Accessibility • Nodal Accessibility: A Southeastern U.S. Example • The Shortest Path Matrix • Networks as Valued Graphs • A Graph-Theory Interpretation of Hierarchies • Summary

CHAPTER 6   *allocation models*   159

The Transportation Model • Empirical Examples of the Transportation Problem • Flows in a Capacitated Network • Empirical Studies • Variations of the Basic Transportation Problem • Summary

CHAPTER 7   *summary and*

some unanswered questions   192

Transport Analysis of a Hypothetical Region • Unanswered Questions

some statistical **APPENDIX A**
considerations 204

bibliography 211

index 223

Foundations of Economic Geography Series

Among the fields of geography, economic geography, perhaps more than any other, has experienced remarkable changes within the past twenty years—so many that it is almost impossible for one scholar to command all aspects of it. The result has been increasing specialization on the one hand and, on the other, a need for bringing the fruits of that specialization to students of economic geography.

The *Foundations of Economic Geography* Series consists of several volumes, each focusing on a major problem in economic geography. It is designed to bring the student, whether novice or more experienced, to the frontiers of knowledge in economic geography, and in so doing, to demonstrate the methodological implications of current research—but at a level comprehensible even to those just becoming aware of the fascinating problems in the field as it is developing today.

Each volume stands as a contribution to understanding in its own right, but the series as a whole is intended to provide a broad cross-section of on-going research in economic geography, in short, a conceptual inventory. On the other hand, the series should not be regarded as a complete synthesis of work in economic geography. The volumes do explore in depth certain major issues of keen interest to economic geographers to a degree impossible in textbooks that attempt to cover the entire field. At the same time, the student is brought face-to-face with the kinds of intellectual and conceptual problems that characterize economic geography in a way that no over-all survey can accomplish. Each volume thus provides a basis for an intensive exploration of issues that constitute the cutting edge of research in this dynamic and demanding field of knowledge.

As time goes on and new volumes appear in the series, the original volumes will be modified in keeping with new developments and orientations, not only in economic geography, but in the field of geography as a whole. The first volume to appear in the series, Wilbur Zelinsky's *A Prologue to Population Geography*, acts as a bridge between economic and cultural geography and as a means for exploring ideas and methods concerning a problem of increasing interest to geographers and social scientists alike: the growth, diffusion, and distribution of populations throughout the world.

Brian J. L. Berry's *Geography of Market Centers and Retail Distribution* attempts to fill a major lacuna in the literature of economic geography, as it lays down principles concerning the spatial distribution and organization of marketing in both advanced and lesser developed economies. In so doing, it provides bridges among the geographies of consumption, production, and cities.

Gunnar Alexandersson's *Geography of Manufacturing* reflects the need for considering the historical-ecological settings within which manufacturing enterprises originate and flourish. Though superficially nontheoretical, it contains flashing insights into the socioeconomic complexities that have resulted in the world pattern of manufacturing.

Richard E. Thoman and Edgar C. Conkling in their *Geography of International Trade* deal with a topic that has not been given the attention it deserves by economic geographers. By careful analysis of trade data and an imaginative use of graphic and tabular devices, they interpret the pattern and structure of international trade in terms of current monetary and economic blocs. The result is the first modern treatment of one of the basic types of international relations.

In his *Geography of Agriculture: Themes in Research,* Howard Gregor has imaginatively analyzed the intellectual history of this subdiscipline of economic geography. His bibliography alone is a substantial achievement. Even more important, he has presented with extraordinary clarity the major geographical problems relating to the study of agriculture at a level of intellectual discourse of as great value to professional geographers as to novices in the field.

Unusual for a series of this kind, James E. Vance, Jr.'s *The Merchant's World: The Geography of Wholesaling* makes a substantial contribution to knowledge of the principles which apply to the distribution and organization of wholesaling activities. Although readily comprehensible to literate neophytes in geography, Professor Vance's thesis suggests a major dimension in the study of economic activity, which has been seriously neglected so far. Moreover, he raises fundamental and demanding questions about the state of theory in economic geography, and his work illustrates the value of an historical–analytical approach to geographic problems.

In his *Energy in the Perspective of Geography,* N. B. Guyol defines energy as a focus for investigation in economic geography and for the comparative study of national economies in their world setting. He develops a system of energy accounting that makes it possible to compare energy supply and demand in various countries on a consistent basis, and he further relates this technique to the more general problem of economic development wherever it occurs. An example of the successful marriage between geography and economics, his book serves to further illustrate the diverse directions in which economic-geographic enterprise has been moving in recent years.

The latest volume in this Series, *The Geography of Transportation* by Edward Taaffe and Howard Gauthier, Jr., also makes valuable contributions through a review and analysis of fundamental concepts that relate transportation patterns and structures to other forms of human occupance. Like the others a conceptual inventory and a history of ideas, their study does not attempt to provide a synthesis of all work in a large and diverse field. Rather, it concentrates on the organization of area as a partial function of transportation networks and systems, through an appraisal of some of the more useful models for what they call "real-world applications."

Every editor likes to think that the volumes in his series do more than describe what is readily known; but not every editor is so fortunate as to have authors who distinguish so perceptively between the more and the less important, between what is and what might be. It is the authors of the volumes in this series who deserve the gratitude of their professional colleagues, as well as of the students who seek significance and relevance in their academic work. All of their contributions display bridging qualities that transcend the narrow limitations of ordinary descriptive handbooks. All are concerned with the fresh as well as the traditional, with the transformation of what had been a rather parochial field of scholarship into one that is intellectually innovative and pioneering.

NORTON GINSBURG

The University of Chicago and
The Center for the Study of Democratic Institutions

Preface

This book represents a survey of some ways in which geographers have approached the study of transportation. The first two chapters show how the geographer views a transportation system; how he looks for such structural elements as nodes and linkages, and the manner in which they are organized into hinterlands and hierarchies; and how he looks for the spatial processes associated with the development of a transportation system. The next four chapters focus on three ways in which the geographer has attempted to analyze transportation systems; the gravity model as an attempt to detect underlying forces; graph-theoretic methods of evaluating the accessibility both of entire networks and of individual nodes within a network; and allocation-model methods whereby flows in a network may be organized in a least-cost fashion.

Transportation geography is by no means a new field, and the problem in writing a short volume such as this is one of selection from a voluminous literature. No attempt was made to provide a summary either of the large geographic literature dealing with the substantive characteristics of different transport systems or of the many problems currently associated with the different modes of transportation. Our goal has been simply to provide the student with a skeletal framework of approaches to the geographic study of transportation. We have selected certain models and attempted to supply enough detail to illustrate the reasoning and assumptions underlying them. This should permit the student to assess the strengths and limitations of these models for actual or potential real-world applications.

A course in transportation geography along these lines has been taught by both authors for several years, and we feel that this volume can serve as a text if supplemented by articles chosen according to the interests of the instructor. In fact, the book as here presented is quite compressed; and we, ourselves, have not been able to treat all the topics discussed within the confines of a single quarter—in part, perhaps, because of our tendency to become bemused with some favorite topics to the exclusion of others. At times, for example, we have devoted additional time to the more substantive earlier chapters, and eliminated some of the models. The more complex topics in the latter parts of Chapters 4, 5, and 6 have been casualties at different times. Conversely, we have sometimes emphasized the models in the latter chapters to the virtual exclusion of the earlier material, supplementing them with some of the indicated articles. In both approaches, we found it helpful to use the local region as a laboratory. Application of concepts or models to a familiar region is one of the most effective ways to enhance the student's understanding and to demonstrate a model's potential strengths and weaknesses in the consideration of local transportation problems.

We have also made an attempt in this book to show the continuum that exists between historical and descriptive studies, on the one hand, and abstract-theoretical studies, on the other. Sharp dividing lines between the two are neither possible nor desirable. Many of the questions dealt with in the earlier chapters are also dealt with in the later chapters. Such U.S. examples as air traffic and Interstate Highway patterns are used repeatedly to emphasize this continuity of concern. Effective work in transportation geography is today being carried on at many points in the continuum according to the inclinations of the investigator, the data available, and the nature of the problem. We hope that the sample of viewpoints and methods represented in this book will stimulate students toward both independent investigation and further study of a still-expanding literature.

We would like to express our deepest appreciation: to Dr. Carl Youngmann and Miss Sherry Barhorst for the preparation of many of the more difficult maps; to a long parade of transportation geography students at Northwestern and at Ohio State for serving as an articulate and willing set of critics; to our wives, Marialyce and Ginny, for their encouragement, patience, and tolerance; and to Norton Ginsburg and our colleagues in transportation geography for their continuing faith through the years that someday there would indeed be a transportation book in the Foundations of Economic Geography Series.

EDWARD J. TAAFFE
HOWARD L. GAUTHIER

CHAPTER 1 *transportation and spatial structure*

Geographers have traditionally studied transportation as part of a broad regional study or as a subject of study in itself. To understand the geographer's interest in transportation, one must consider geography more as a point of view than as a field dealing with particular types of phenomena. The point of view adopted by the authors in this volume is that of spatial organization. The geographer is not restricted to any one set of phenomena—economic, social, political, or geological—but considers these sets of phenomena separately or as they are interrelated. He does not consider *all* aspects of each—he focuses only on the aspects that have spatial expression. The geographer would not share the economists' concern with the fluctuations of the stock market or the operations of the banking system, but he would share a concern with the location of industry, which has a clear spatial expression.

There is an explicit spatial expression in the case of transportation also, in which the geographer studies transportation as an aspect of the *organization of area*. While economists may study the cost characteristics of the different modes of transportation, engineers may study the comparative operating characteristics of the modes, and political scientists may study the regulatory policies in each mode, the geographer focuses his attention on the spatial structures formed by these modes and attempts to understand the processes that have created them.

Therefore, the transportation geographer is concerned with (1) the particular linkages and flows that comprise a transportation network, (2) the centers, or nodes, connected by these linkages, and (3) the entire system of hinterlands and hierarchical relationships associated with the network. His analysis starts with these patterns, then moves to the processes that have brought these patterns about. At this point he finds himself working more closely with the transportation economist, the civil engineer, and the specialist in business logistics, since the disciplinary lines dividing processes into those that are explicitly spatial and those that are not become less clear. Students of transportation from any one of the disciplines find it increasingly necessary to acquaint themselves with the models of the other disciplines in order to contribute effectively to a better understanding of the fundamental processes and relations in any transport system. Regional geographers also find the study of transportation necessary because of its pervasive effects on any region studied. The organization of every region is reflected in its transportation network as well as in the less visible networks of trade, communications, political ties, and social orientation.

The emphasis in this chapter is on identifying the structure of a transportation network. What does the geographer look for as he examines a transportation network? First he looks at the linkages and flows between centers, their nature and size. Then he considers the centers, or nodes, themselves, especially their size, function, and accessibility to the rest of the network. Finally he studies the structures of dominance and competition among the nodes within each network of linkages and flows. In short, the geographer examines the transportation network for evidence of the organization of the area. For this reason we start our discussion of transportation and spatial structure with the idea of the functional region that was put forward in the literature of geography in the late twenties by Robert Swanton Platt as a way of viewing the region.[1]

The Functional Region

Two different points of view have been adopted by geographers in their examination of regions: uniformity and functional organization. When the geographer searches for uniformity in a region, he stresses the manner in which the different parts of the region are similar or dissimilar. When he examines the functional organization of a region, he stresses the manner in which the different points within the region are linked to each other or to other points outside the region. A visual symbol for the uniformity view might be the mosaic formed by a land-use map (Fig. 1.1A). Each piece in the mosaic has been judged homogeneous according to a specific set of criteria. The pieces have been shaded accordingly. When a functional region is being examined, the visual symbol might be a cobweb formed by the linkages among points, as shown on a traffic-flow map (Fig. 1.1B).

It is misleading to think that one view is more useful than the other, since both of these views of the region provide some insights into its nature. One might ask a resident of northeastern Illinois, for example, what region he lived in. If he were to reply that he lived in the Corn

[1] Robert S. Platt, "A Detail of Regional Geography: Ellison Bay Community as an Industrial Organism," *Annals*, The Association of American Geographers, 18, No. 2 (June 1928), 81–126.

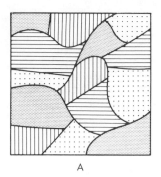
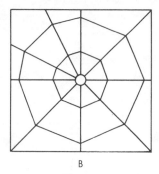

A   B

*Fig. 1.1.   Uniform and Functional Regions. Map A is based on criteria of uni-
formity, or homogeneity. Each section of the map has been classified as homogeneous in terms of a specified set of criteria and the map has been shaded
accordingly. A land-use map is a typical example. Map B shows a functional
region. It is based on linkages between points. Examples include traffic-flow
maps and maps of newspaper circulation areas.*

Belt, he would be using uniformity as his criterion. It is possible to delimit an area within which the crop-livestock mixes that are characteristic
of the Corn Belt are predominant. Uniformity would therefore be defined
in this case as a relatively narrow range of variation in agricultural activity, with the limits to the range arbitrarily set as part of a particular
classification scheme. If that same resident of northeastern Illinois were
to answer that he lived in the Chicago area, he would be using functional
organization as his criterion. In this case, he would probably be concerned with his own linkages to Chicago. The transportation system
focuses on Chicago, reflecting the movement of people and goods into
that metropolitan center. The same resident might consider himself
in the American Manufacturing Belt or in the Central Lowland. In both
cases, the regional identification would be based on uniformity. Any delimitation of the American Manufacturing Belt is based on a classification of cities, which provides a relatively homogeneous grouping.
Physiographic regions, such as the Central Lowland, are delimited by a
similarity of landforms according to specific criteria. Similarly, the functional organization of the area can be expressed in other ways. In addition
to being in the Chicago area, the individual may consider himself as
being in the market areas of certain shopping centers, or in the circulation area of a particular newspaper. He is thinking in both cases of a
particular set of linkages whereby his locality is organized into a system
along with a number of other localities. The Chicago area itself may be
thought of as a uniform or a functional region. If we look at the central
city, the Standard Metropolitan Statistical Area, or the urbanized area in
Figure 1.2, we are using criteria of uniformity. However, if we were to
consider the commuting contours in Figure 1.2 that represent the percentages of commuters to Chicago from each area, we would then be

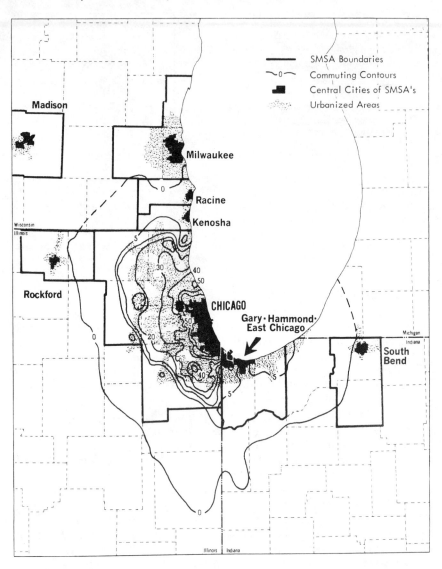

Fig. 1.2.   *The Chicago Region: Uniform and Functional Criteria. The delimitation of the central city, SMSA, and the urbanized area are based on criteria of uniformity. The contours show commuting percentages. These contours are thus based on linkages, and they represent a view of Chicago as a functional region. From Philip Reese,* "The Factorial Ecology of Metropolitan Chicago, 1960" *(M.A. thesis, University of Chicago), 1968.*

considering linkages and looking at Chicago in terms of its functional organization.

As we consider transportation geography and its relation to these and other geographic concerns, it is important to note one additional point. To say that the transportation geographer looks at an area from the point of view of functional organization, does not necessarily mean that he will attempt to *delimit* that area in terms of any set of linkages. In this connection, the term *nodal region* has given rise to much confusion.[2] For example, one might delimit an area around city A that is tied together by a set of relatively strong linkages. This functional region might be called "a nodal region centered on city A." Suppose, however, that one were studying an arbitrarily given area near but not including city A. The given area could still be studied in terms of its functional organization. Closer inspection would show that the area was organized around a few main lines of movement and a number of secondary lines. Nodes of varying significance would be located at different types of intersection points, and the entire given area would reflect a focus on an external center at city A. The emphasis of the study, however, would be on the structure of linkages within the area, not on the delimitation of city A's nodal region.

Although the distinction between uniform and functional regions has proven to be an historically useful one in geography—it redirected some of the geographer's research toward a more explicit concern with linkages —its present utility is questionable. The mosaics characterizing the uniform region and the cobwebs of linkages characterizing the functional region can both be considered aspects of a broader system of spatial organization. A change in a region's pattern of linkages brings about accompanying changes in its pattern of uniformity.

Linkages

A geographer considering a transport system tries first to determine its structure. The basic structural elements of a transportation system are linkages and nodes, or the transportation lines and centers themselves. The linkages are usually the object of the investigator's first concern in a structural study. He examines these linkages as they are displayed in map or tabular form, and he assesses their relative importance. In particular, he looks for *trunk lines*, or the most important lines in a region. The trunk lines may be evident in the physical characteristics of the linkages themselves, as in the case of four-lane highways, double-track railroads, and navigable waterways, or in the form of flow characteristics over the linkages, as in the case of high traffic densities. Once the trunk lines have

---

[2] The term *nodal region* was used in Derwent S. Whittlesey, "The Regional Concept and the Regional Method," in *American Geography: Inventory and Prospect,* ed. Preston E. James and Clarence F. Jones (Syracuse University Press, 1964), 19–69.

Fig. 1.3A. U.S. Railroads. This map of U.S. railroads, although generalized, shows too dense and un-differentiated a network of railroads to permit identification of trunk lines. From The Association of American Railroads, Railroads of America (Washington, 1970). p. 12.

been identified, the broad organizational framework frequently becomes apparent because the other routes are organized around these trunk lines.[3] Thus a distinction between trunk lines and other routes is often a helpful step in describing the spatial structure of a region.

The maps in Figures 1.3A and 1.3B show the railroads of the U.S. according to different criteria and can be used to illustrate a description of a region's trunk lines. Figure 1.3A is a generalized map of U.S. railroads. By no means complete, it still shows such a dense network of lines that it is virtually impossible to identify certain lines as trunk lines. One can note a generally denser network in the American Manufacturing Belt, that portion of the northeastern section of the country bounded roughly by Milwaukee, Chicago, and St. Louis on the west, and by Boston and Washington on the east.

The other map, from a railroad study made by Edward Ullman, is more useful simply because fewer railroads are shown, so it is possible to identify certain trunk lines. Figure 1.3B shows all multiple-track railroads in darker lines, as well as lines adapted for heavy traffic by centralized traffic control or automatic signals. The connections between Chicago and New York are particularly strong, both via the Mohawk–Hudson route (Buffalo–Albany–New York) and the Pittsburgh-Philadelphia route. To the south, a set of trunk lines connects the Manufacturing Belt to such southeastern cities as Jacksonville, Atlanta, and New Orleans. To the west, there are three transcontinental trunk lines: a northern line to Seattle and Portland, a central line to San Francisco, and a southern line to Los Angeles. The New York–Chicago trunk line would show up even more clearly on a map restricted to such highest-priority linkages as four-track rail lines, jet passenger travel, and maximum highway-traffic density.

The distinction between trunk lines and *feeder lines* may be used as an aid in describing the spatial structure of any arbitrarily delimited area. Figure 1.4, a highway map of Nevada, provides evidence of its organization. Two segments of the Interstate Highway System form trunk lines. Both represent segments of trunk lines between large centers outside of Nevada. The northern line is part of the central transcontinental route connecting Salt Lake City with San Francisco; the southern trunk line is part of the line connecting Salt Lake City with Los Angeles. The two largest Nevada cities are located on these trunk lines: Reno on the northern line and Las Vegas on the southern line. There is also a more developed network of major feeder highways connecting the two trunk lines. These highways emphasize the focus on Reno and Las Vegas, as well as the minor focus at Elko.

Bridge lines are another type of linkage related to traffic. The function of the bridge line is to carry through-traffic between two major transportation systems. An example of a railroad dominated by bridge-line traffic is the Richmond, Fredericksburg, and Potomac (Fig. 1.5), which

---

[3] Other terms, such as *main streets* or *magistral routes,* are also used to identify trunk lines.

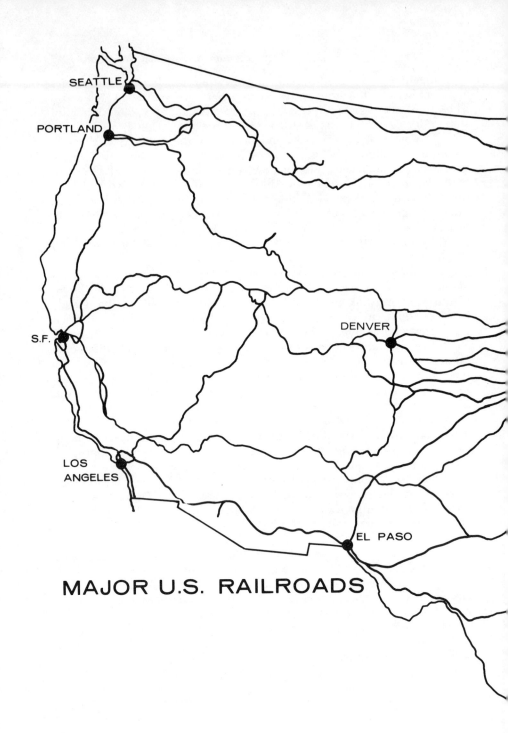

MAJOR U.S. RAILROADS

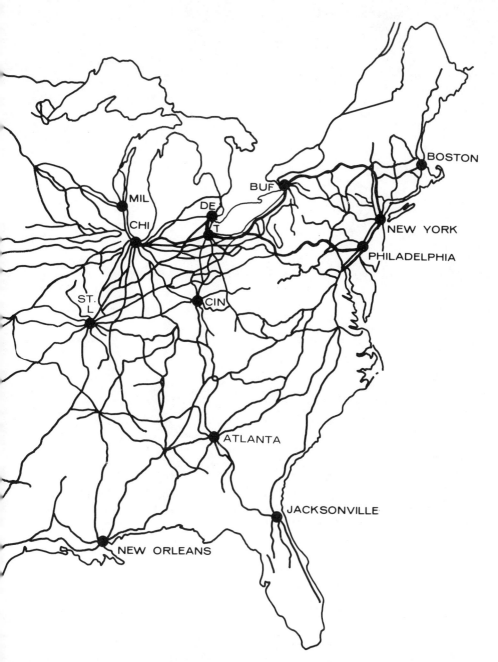

Fig. 1.3B. Major U.S. Railroads. In this map, Edward Ullman selected the major railroads of the U.S. on the basis of multiple trackage, electrification, and signaling systems. Certain trunk lines, such as Chicago–New York and the three transcontinentals, may now be identified. From Edward Ullman, "The Railroad Pattern of the U.S.," Geographical Review, 39 (1949), 244–45.

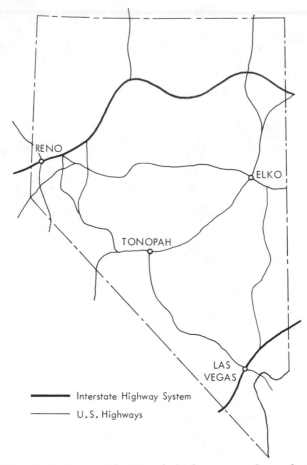

Fig. 1.4.   Nevada Highways. The Nevada highway map shows that the state's spatial organization is dominated by a northern and a southern trunk line, which are connected by a network of feeder lines.

carries traffic between the Southern railroads, most of which converge on Richmond, and the major railroads of the Northeast, which have connections in the Potomac Yard in Washington.[4]

[4] For a thorough discussion of a single bridge-line railroad, see Frank H. Thomas, *The Denver and Rio Grande Western Railroad: A Geographic Analysis,* Studies in Geography, No. 4 (Evanston, Ill.: Northwestern University Press, 1960). For a series of studies classifying railroads and railroad traffic, see William H. Wallace, "The Bridge Line: A Distinctive Type of Anglo-American Railroad," *Economic Geography,* 41 (1965), 1–38; "The Freight Traffic Functions of Anglo-American Railroads," *Annals,* The Association of American Geographers, 53 (1963), 312–31; "Railroad Traffic Densities and Patterns," *Annals,* The Association of American Geographers, 48 (December 1958), 352–74.

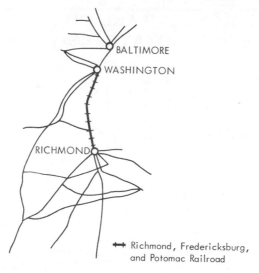

*Fig. 1.5.   Bridge Line: The Richmond, Fredericksburg, and Potomac Railroad.
The Richmond, Fredericksburg, and Potomac is an example of a bridge line
carrying traffic between the rail lines of the South and those of the American
Manufacturing Belt.*

Nodes

The cities that are connected by the linkages serve as *nodes* in the transportation system. A question of fundamental importance concerns the *relative accessibility* of these nodes. Some nodes are so situated in a transportation network that they have particularly easy access to all other nodes. Salt Lake City, for example, is well-connected to other major cities in the Interstate Highway System (Fig. 1.6). The System has been constructed to provide Salt Lake City with direct Interstate connections to Los Angeles, San Francisco, and the Pacific Northwest, as well as with major cities to the east. If, instead, direct links had been put in from Butte, Montana, for example, to San Francisco, and from Denver to Los Angeles, the relative accessibility of Salt Lake City in that part of the country would have been less impressive.

Another significant characteristic of nodes in a network is represented by the term *gateway*, which has been used frequently to represent one such class of cities.[5] The term is not a precise one, and it has been used in a variety of ways. The most frequent usage refers to a main entry-and-exit point for a region. Thus all major ports might be called

[5] For an interesting discussion of gateway cities and their function, see Andrew F. Burghardt, "A Hypothesis about Gateway Cities," *Annals,* The Association of American Geographers, 61, No. 2 (June 1971), 269–85.

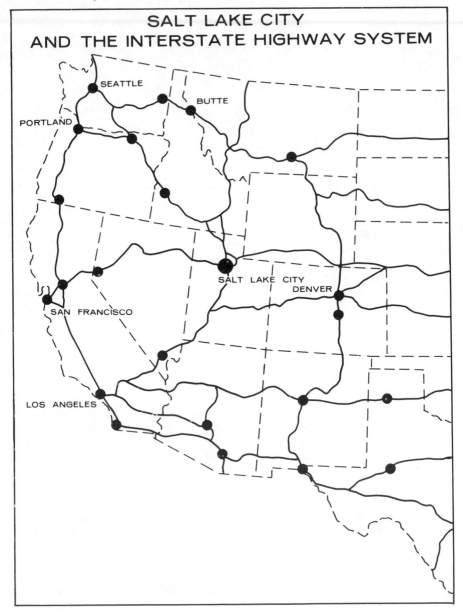

Fig. 1.6. Salt Lake City and the Proposed Interstate Highway System. The high relative accessibility of Salt Lake City among Western cities may be observed from its position in the proposed Interstate Highway System.

gateways—ocean routes converge on the port and land routes fan out from it. The idea of a gateway is much less clear-cut, however, if one is considering inland traffic patterns, where a variety of criteria might be

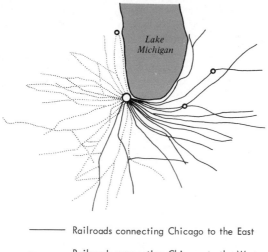

——————— Railroads connecting Chicago to the East

·············· Railroads connecting Chicago to the West

Fig. 1.7. Rail Gateways: Chicago. Chicago serves as a rail gateway in the sense that one set of railroads connects it to the East, and with only a few exceptions, an entirely different set connects it to the West.

employed. The term *gateway* might be attached to cities located in transitional zones between major regions, or to cities where routes fan out on one side and are concentrated on the other, or to cities where there is a break-of-bulk, change of carrier, or break in the freight-rate structure.

Chicago is a major rail gateway. Its location between two broadly defined regions allows it to serve as an entry point for the flow of Western and Midwestern agricultural commodities to the cities of the American Manufacturing Belt. There is a pronounced break at Chicago. As shown in Figure 1.7, one set of railroads connects Chicago to the West, and another set, almost entirely different, connects Chicago to the East. Chicago is also an important rate-break point, as are such other rail gateways as St. Louis and Cincinnati. Winnipeg is another type of gateway, although it is also located between two regions, the vast wheatfields of the Prairie Provinces to the west, the lakes and forests of the Canadian Shield to the east. Wheat is picked up on the elaborate trunk- and feeder-line network of the Canadian National and Canadian Pacific Railroads that converges on Winnipeg. East of Winnipeg there are relatively few lines, and there is heavy bridge traffic to Port Arthur and Fort William for transshipment via the Great Lakes.

New England provides an illustration of gateways, trunk lines, and feeder lines in a regional transportation network. Figure 1.8A shows the railroads of New England as they were in the 1950s. Figure 1.8B is a schematic diagram of the spatial organization of New England as expressed by its railroads. Three cities stood out as major gateways to New England: New York, Albany, and Montreal. In the New York area, rail-

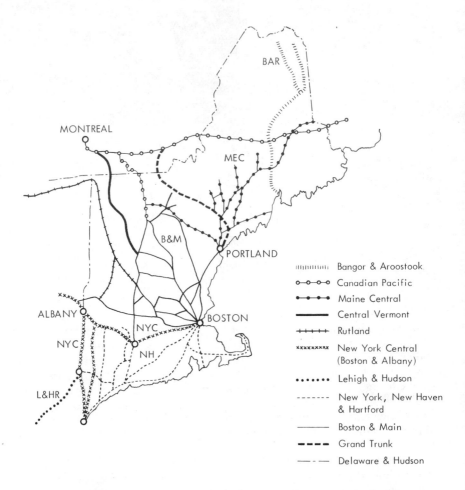

Fig. 1.8A.   Railroads of New England. This map shows a generalized version of the railroads operating in New England in the 1950s.

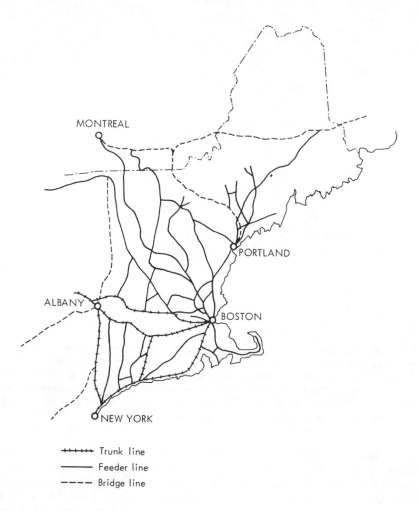

MONTREAL

PORTLAND

ALBANY

BOSTON

NEW YORK

┼┼┼┼┼ Trunk line

───── Feeder line

───── Bridge line

Fig. 1.8B. Railroads of New England: Schematic Diagram. This diagram shows a classification of New England's railroads into trunk lines, feeder lines, and bridge lines.

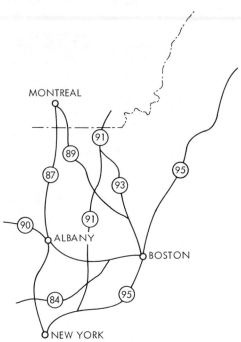

Fig. 1.9. Proposed Interstate Highway System for New England. The trunk lines between New York and Boston, Albany and Boston, and within the Connecticut Valley noted on the rail maps are still evident. The major differences between the highway and the rail map are in the northern extensions of the Interstate Highways, such as in Maine. For the most part, these are tourist-oriented and not indicative of the overall spatial organization of the area.

roads from the Manufacturing Belt converged and goods were transshipped into New England on the New York, New Haven, and Hartford (now Penn Central). Two railroads provided Albany with a connection to Boston from the Midwest via the Mohawk Valley. From Montreal a number of railroads diverged to different parts of New England. Consideration of schedule frequency and flow density suggested certain trunk lines, as shown on the diagram. The New York–Boston connection and the Boston–Albany connection were clearly trunk lines, as was the Connecticut Valley link between the two, from New Haven north through Hartford. There was a well-developed feeder pattern of routes focusing on Boston from northern New England, exemplified by the Boston and Maine Railroad. The Maine Central provided a less well-developed feeder-line pattern focused on Portland. Both of these patterns were connected to the Montreal gateway by segments of other railroads. The pattern was complicated further by a series of bridge lines. Two of these were international, providing Montreal with links to New Brunswick–Nova Scotia (Canadian Pacific) and to Portland (Grand Trunk or Canadian National), where connections were made with oceangoing vessels. Two other bridge lines (the Delaware and Hudson and the Lehigh and Hudson) connected the coal fields of eastern Pennsylvania with the major Albany gateway and with a smaller gateway near Poughkeepsie.

Figure 1.9 shows the Interstate Highway System as proposed for New England. As in the case of Nevada, there are close similarities to the rail pattern in general outline. New York, Albany, and Montreal again function as major gateways, with Poughkeepsie as a lesser gateway. The New York–Boston, Albany–Boston, and Connecticut Valley trunk lines are still evident. The major differences are the northern extensions to Maine, New Hampshire, and Vermont, primarily oriented to tourist travel. There is also a tendency for the highway gateways and nodes to bypass the major cities. They are located close to these cities, but seldom in them.

Hinterlands

Linkages and nodes may be organized into systems in a variety of ways. *Hinterlands*, or tributary areas of a particular port or retail center, may be defined by the linkages most clearly associated with that node. These hinterlands may, in turn, be organized into a system of hinterlands, including a number of nodes, each with its set of strongest linkages.

Diagrammatic Representation of Hinterland Structure

It is possible to represent in simple diagrammatic form some of the characteristics of linkages and nodes as they have been organized into hinterlands and systems of hinterlands.

The first distinction to make is between *field* and *hinterland*.[6] Figure 1.10A shows a field of influence around city A. The height of the vertical bar might be considered proportional to population, total traffic, or some similar measure of magnitude. Distance from the city is measured along the horizontal axis in either direction from A. The height of the lines extending from the vertical bar is proportional to the influence of city A. This influence might drop off at any number of different rates, and it might be measured in terms of such indicators as commuters, phone calls, or bus traffic. The field of city A extends as far in all directions as city A has influence.

The same idea is often expressed diagrammatically in terms of transportation costs, as shown in Figure 1.10B. In this case the height of the vertical bar represents production costs and the upward-sloping lines represent transportation costs. Ordinarily the transportation cost curve will be inversely related to the influence curve. Influence will tend to decline rapidly if transport costs are high, gradually if they are low.

When city A is surrounded by other cities with similar influence fields, the result is a pattern such as that shown in Figure 1.11A. The in-

---

[6] The distinction is based on one made in Sven Godlund, *The Function and Growth of Bus Traffic Within the Sphere of Urban Influence*, Lund Studies in Geography, No. 18 (Lund, Sweden: C. W. K. Gleerup, 1956). Godlund uses the term *umland* rather than *hinterland*.

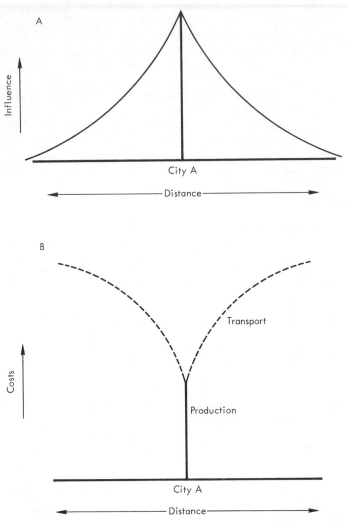

Fig. 1.10.   Influence Fields and Transport Cost. Figure A shows a field of influence declining in all directions around city A. Figure B shows transport costs from city A increasing in all directions.

fluence divide between city A and city B is represented by point x, midway between the two cities; the influence divide between city A and city C is represented by point y, also at the midpoint. The zone between x and y delimits the hinterland of city A, the zone within which city A's field of influence overrides the influence fields of B and C. Highway traffic from this zone would more likely be directed to city A than to B or C. A map of hinterland structure may be obtained by rotating the influence curves shown in the diagram. Figure 1.11B represents a hypothetical

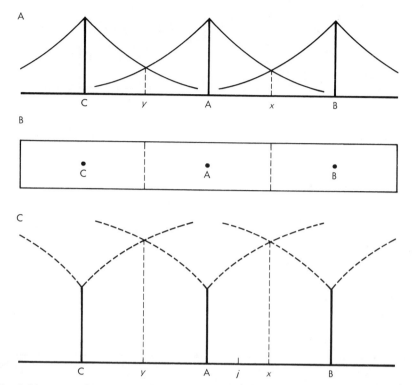

Fig. 1.11.   *Equidistant Hinterlands. Figure A represents divides between cities of equal influence with equal declines as distance increases. The divides are equidistant between the centers. Figure B shows a section of a hypothetical map of hinterlands associated with the influence pattern A. Figure C represents the analogous case for transport costs: equal production costs at cities A, B, and C, and equal transport costs from each city.*

distribution of hinterlands for a set of equal-sized cities with equal influence fields. In all cases, the divides are located at points equidistant between two cities.

Figure 1.11C represents an analogous case for transport costs. At point j, which falls inside the hinterland of city A, a consumer will be paying less (production costs plus transport costs) for goods produced at A and shipped to j than he will for goods produced at B and shipped to j. The hinterland in this case is defined as the zone within which the delivered price of goods from city A is less than that of similar goods from any other city (y to x on the diagram). Again the divides will be equidistant between any two cities, since production costs and the per-mile transportation costs are equal. A map formed by rotating these diagrams would look the same as Figure 1.11B.

Where cities are unequal in magnitude, the dividing lines are no longer equidistant between cities. As the size of a city increases relative to

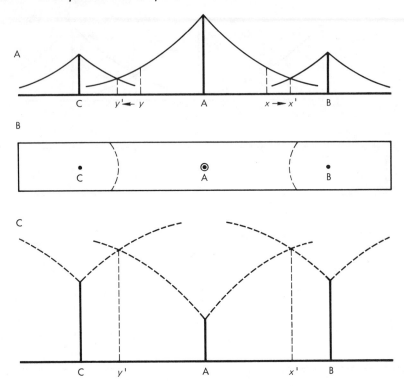

Fig. 1.12. Hinterlands for Cities of Unequal Magnitude. Figure A represents the effects of unequal magnitude. If city A is larger than B or C, the influence divides will move closer to the smaller cities—from x to x′ and from y to y′. Figure B shows the effects of unequal magnitude on a hinterland map. Figure C shows the analogous case for transport costs.

surrounding cities, its zone of dominance tends to expand at the expense of these cities. Thus in Figure 1.12A the influence divides move closer to the smaller cities (from x and y to $x′$ and $y′$) as city A increases in size relative to cities B and C. Figure 1.12B shows how much the hinterland structure would be altered simply by introducing a second size class for two cities. The analogy in the transport-cost diagram (Fig. 1.12C) would be in lowered production costs at city A, which would move the divides out from y and x to $y′$ and $x′$.

Still another variation is introduced in the rate at which influence declines with distance (Fig. 1.13). If the three cities are of equal size but the influence of city A declines less rapidly with distance, then A's zone of dominance will increase at the expense of the other two cities. This is analogous to a less rapid increase in city A's transport costs with distance.

Hinterland Studies

For many years geographers have carried on empirical studies of individual hinterlands, with particular reference to ports. Some of the

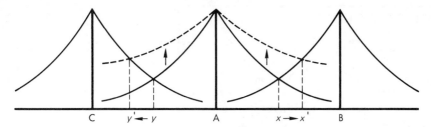

Fig. 1.13. Hinterlands for Cities with Unequal Influence Declines. If the influence field around city A declines less rapidly than that around the other cities, the influence divides will also be displaced away from city A toward the other cities.

studies dealt with such problems as the existence of different hinterlands for different commodities, the overlapping fields of influence of competing ports, and the effects of different political control on the reach of different ports.[7] A recent study of U.S. ports by Kenyon typifies some of these considerations.[8] Figure 1.14 shows the overlapping import fields of major U.S. ports. In Indiana, for example, imports come from New York, Chicago, and New Orleans. Ohio is within the import fields of New York, Philadelphia, Baltimore, and New Orleans. Figure 1.15 shows a set of hinterlands, defined by rates, for the major U.S. ports. Within each of the shaded areas the rates on general cargo to the indicated port are less than rates to any other port. In the areas among these hinterlands there is a tendency toward rate equalization, and rates to more than one port will be equal. It should be noted that the existence of a freight-rate hinterland for a port does not necessarily mean that all general cargo from that area will move to that port. One could, however, construct another set of hinterlands showing a port's traffic dominance simply by delimiting the zone within which that port's field of influence, as represented by traffic, was greater than that of any other port.

Individual and competitive hinterlands have also been studied for inland cities. Harris' pioneering study of Salt Lake City showed a relatively well-defined tributary area for a wide range of functions.[9] Variations in hinterland boundaries were traced to physical barriers and to lower population densities both to the east and the west. Sisco's study of Memphis (Fig. 1.16) shows the effect of nearby competitors in shaping retail-trade boundaries in a more densely populated and urbanized part of the country. Memphis's hinterland extends only a short distance north in the face of competition from St. Louis, but a relatively long distance against the competition of Jackson, Mississippi, a smaller center. This is an em-

[7] A classic work in the field is A. J. Sargent, *Seaports and Hinterlands* (London: A. & C. Black, 1939). A series of detailed African studies by William A. Hance and Irene Van Dongen provide empirical examples of the complex economic and non-economic forces affecting port hinterlands.

[8] James Kenyon, "Elements in Inter-Port Competition in the United States," *Economic Geography*, 46, No. 1 (January 1970), 1–24.

[9] Chauncy D. Harris, *Salt Lake City: A Regional Capital*, doctoral dissertation (Chicago: University of Chicago Libraries, 1941).

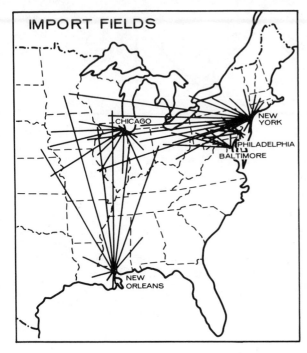

Fig. 1.14. Import Fields of U.S. Ports. Lines diverging from each major U.S. port represent imports shipped from the port to the indicated area. There is much overlap among these import fields, as is shown in the cases of Indiana and Ohio. From James Kenyon, "Elements in Inter-Port Competition in the United States," Economic Geography, 46, No. 1 (January 1970), 12.

Fig. 1.15. Rate Hinterlands of U.S. Ports. Shaded areas represent zones within which general cargo rates to the appropriate port are lower than rates to any other port. From James Kenyon, "Elements in Inter-Port Competition in the United States," Economic Geography, 46, No. 1 (January 1970), 9.

TRADE HINTERLAND: MEMPHIS

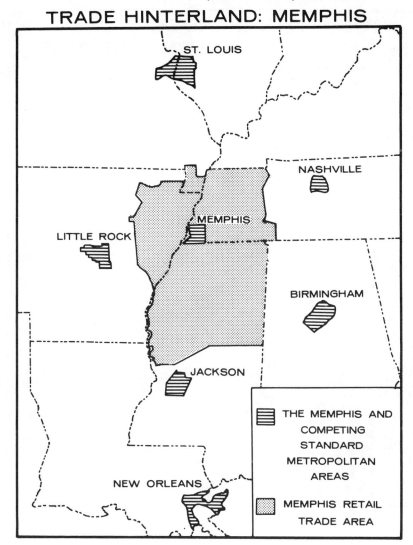

Fig. 1.16. Retail-Trade Hinterland of Memphis. Memphis's retail-trade hinterland shows the effects of unequal-sized centers. Since St. Louis is larger than Memphis, the northern divide is closer to Memphis; since Memphis is larger than Jackson, Mississippi, the southern divide is closer to Jackson. After Paul H. Sisco, The Retail Function of Memphis, University of Chicago, Department of Geography, Research Paper No. 37 (1954), 2.

pirical illustration of the tendency, noted previously in Figure 1.12A, of influence divides to be located near the smaller of any pair of centers.

The studies of hinterlands for inland centers led to investigations of the broader structural question of systems of hinterlands. An example of

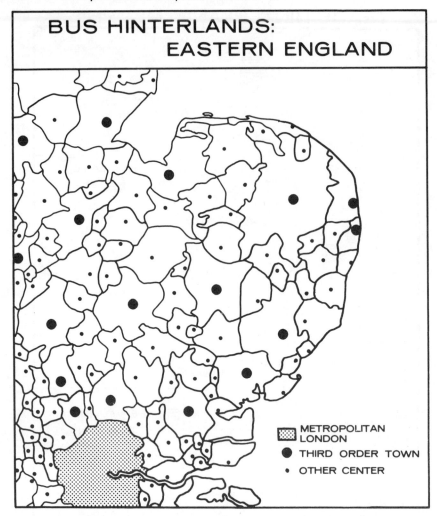

Fig. 1.17. Bus Hinterlands. The bus hinterlands on the map are based on the relative frequency of bus services to the different centers. Larger hinterlands may be noted in areas of lower population densities, and the effects of unequal-sized centers may also be noted. After F. H. W. Green, "Urban Hinterlands in England and Wales: An Analysis of Bus Services," The Geographical Journal, *116 (1950), 64–80. From John E. Brush and Howard L. Gauthier, Jr.,* Service Centers and Consumer Trips: Studies on the Philadelphia Metropolitan Fringe, University of Chicago Department of Geography Research Paper No. 113 (1968), 11.

the explicit use of transportation linkages to define the spatial organization of particular nodes is the bus-hinterland map of England and Wales by F. H. W. Green (Fig. 1.17). The hinterlands were delimited simply by examining bus schedules and noting points between two cities, A and B,

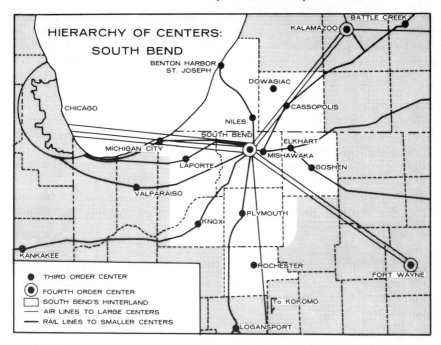

Fig. 1.18.   *Example of a Hierarchy of Centers. In this example of a hierarchy of centers, Chicago dominates cities such as South Bend, Kalamazoo, and Fort Wayne, which in turn dominate a group of smaller cities. South Bend dominates the cities classified by Philbrick as third-order cities. Note that the usual pattern is reversed in this classification, and third-order centers are smaller than fourth-order centers. After Allen K. Philbrick, "Principles of Areal Functional Organization in Regional Human Geography," Economic Geography, 33, No. 4 (October 1957), 338.*

where the schedules to A were greater than the schedules to B. The same procedure was carried on for other cities surrounding city A. A line connecting the resulting set of points defined a hinterland within which the bus schedules to city A were more frequent than those to any other city. Therefore, the fine mesh of bus hinterlands of Figure 1.17 represent a network of tributary areas for bus traffic which covers all of England and Wales. These hinterlands are by no means of uniform size or spacing. It is clear, for example, that population density has an effect on the size of hinterlands. The hinterlands close to London are smaller than those farther away. There is a general tendency for influence divides between any two cities to be at points equidistant from those cities, assuming that the cities are the same size.

Hierarchies

A further complication arises as we look at the ways in which linkages and nodes might be organized into systems of hinterlands. It is hard to visualize the United States divided neatly into a series of separate hinterlands. If we were to delimit an area within which highway traffic flows mainly to Chicago, we would be including areas with important subsidiary flows to such cities as South Bend, St. Joseph, and Kankakee. There tends to be a hierarchy of centers linked together, as shown in Figure 1.18. In this hypothetical example, the highway traffic of South Bend would be dominated by Chicago. The traffic of the small towns surrounding South Bend, however, would focus on South Bend rather than Chicago, and groups of still smaller villages would focus on the towns rather than South Bend. At the other end of the scale, Chicago is an important node in a national transport system, with strong trunk line linkages to New York and Los Angeles, as discussed earlier. This total pattern of hierarchical linkages, nodes, and hinterlands is further complicated by the effects of varying population densities and the varying size and location of major cities.

Figures 1.19, 1.20, and 1.21 represent a diagrammatic breakdown of a hierarchical pattern of linkages. Figure 1.19 shows both the gradually decreasing influence fields and the resultant hinterland structure associated with high-order activities, such as banking and art museums, found only in cities A and B. In the provision of these services, cities A and B dominate the entire region. A transportation example of high-order traffic might be air travel. Figure 1.20 represents middle-order activities, such as furniture shopping or intercity auto travel, with a somewhat steeper decline of influence with distance. For these activities, cities A and B now share the dominance of the region with cities C and D. Note that the hierarchical structure is accompanied in this case by a displacement of the influence

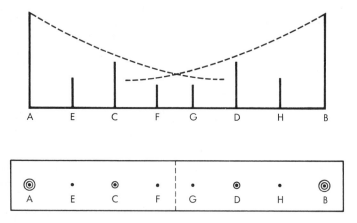

Fig. 1.19. Hierarchy Diagram: High-Order Activities. The upper diagram shows the gradually sloping influence fields associated with high-order functions found only at A and B. The lower diagram shows the hinterland structure in which E, C, and F are located within A's hinterland, and G, D, and H are within B's hinterland.

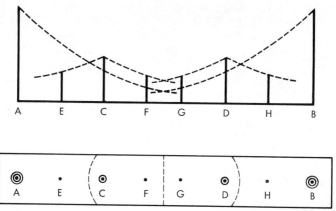

Fig. 1.20.   *Hierarchy Diagram: Middle-Order Activities. Influence fields and hinterland structure associated with middle-order activities, found at C and D, as well as at A and B.*

divides toward the smaller of any two centers. Figure 1.21 represents a low-order activity with a steeply sloping influence curve, as is true of grocery shopping or daily commuting. For these activities, small hinterlands exist around centers of both low and high levels. When these three levels are considered simultaneously, a complex hierarchical structure is formed, with the hinterland for each activity nesting within the hinterland for the next higher-order activity. An empirical example of a hierarchical hinterland structure in Estonia is shown in Figure 1.22.

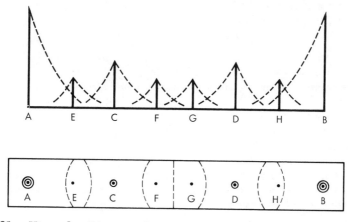

Fig. 1.21.   *Hierarchy Diagram: Low-Order Activities. Influence fields and hinterland structure associated with low-order activities, found at all eight centers.*

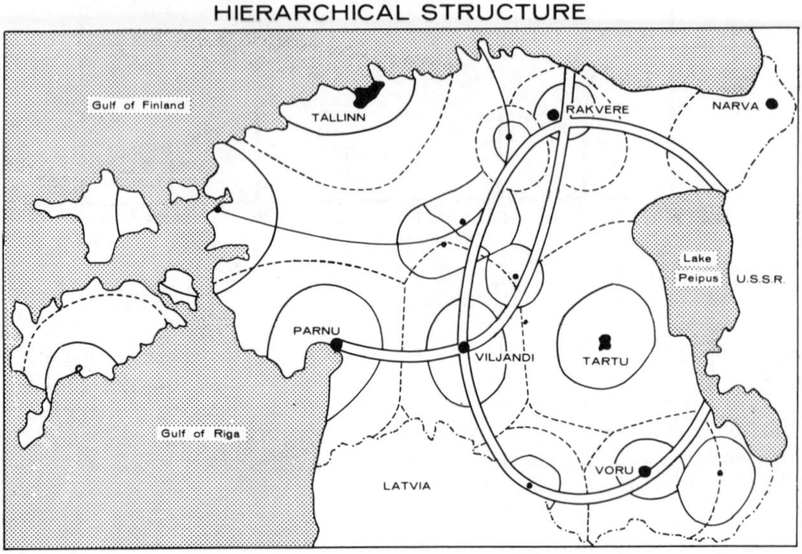

HIERARCHICAL STRUCTURE

Fig. 1.22.   A Hierarchical Hinterland Structure. This map shows an empirical example in Estonia of a hinterland structure resulting from the simultaneous consideration of three hierarchical levels. The thin lines enclose hinterlands for low-order activities. The dashed lines represent hinterlands for middle-order activities. The bands enclose hinterlands for the high-order activities found only at the large centers of Tartu and Tallinn. After Edgar Kant, "Umland Studies and Sector Analysis," in Studies in Rural-Urban Interaction, Lund Studies in Geography, Series B, Human Geography, No. 3 (Lund, Sweden: C. W. K. Gleerup, 1951), 3–14. From Geography, Report of the Geography Panel of the Behavioral and Social Science Survey, Edward J. Taaffe, ed. (Englewood Cliffs, N.J.: Prentice-Hall, Inc., 1970), 75.

There is a large and growing literature on the spatial systems of cities, but here we are primarily concerned with the hierarchies of cities as they relate to transportation.[10] A hierarchical structure may be noted at virtually all transport levels. Figures 1.23A and B show a profile of highway-traffic density of vehicles passing from one high-order center to another through centers of two lower orders. Figure 1.23A represents the cumulative flow of vehicles on the highway, with the lesser flows of lower-order centers (II and III) superimposed on the larger flows of the higher-order centers (I). Figure 1.23B presents the underlying hierarchical structure with progressively higher density of trip destinations associated with successively higher-order centers.

[10] For a discussion in this series of the literature on urban spatial systems in the context of central-place theory and its successors, see Brian J. L. Berry, *Geography of Market Centers and Retail Distribution* (Englewood Cliffs, N.J.: Prentice-Hall, 1967).

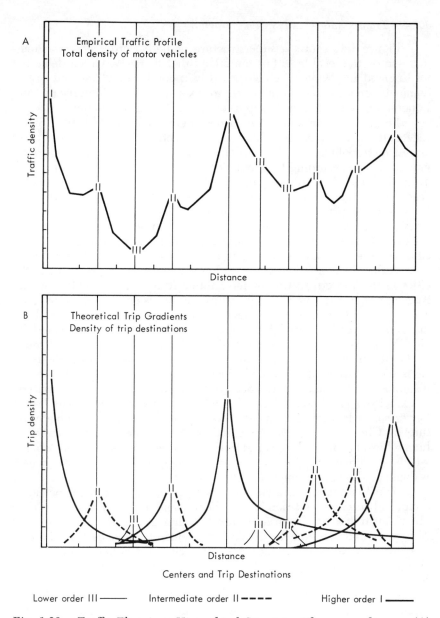

Fig. 1.23. *Traffic Flow in a Hierarchical Structure. The upper diagram (A) shows the cumulative flow of highway traffic, with the lesser flows that are associated with the smaller centers added to the greater flows associated with the larger centers. The lower diagram (B) breaks down the flow associated with the three levels of centers. From John E. Brush and Howard L. Gauthier, Jr.,* Service Centers and Consumer Trips: Studies on the Philadelphia Metropolitan Fringe, *University of Chicago Department of Geography Research Paper No. 113 (1968), 9.*

Figure 1.24 shows a superstructure of higher-order centers super-imposed on the local-level bus hinterland that F. H. W. Green delimited for England and Wales. Such cities as Liverpool, Birmingham, and Bristol dominate groupings of from three to six smaller bus hinterlands, and London dominates a large group of over twenty bus hinterlands.

Figure 1.25 shows how the air-passenger traffic of the United States reflects the hierarchical set of linkages connecting the one-hundred or so largest metropolitan areas. The circles representing cities on the map are graded in size according to population. If the city is dominated by New York, Chicago, Los Angeles, or San Francisco, the circles are shaded according to the dominant air-passenger generator. If they are dominated by some other city, they are left blank and the connection is indicated by arrows. The black shading at Chicago, for example, indicates that New York accounts for more of Chicago's air passengers than does any other city. All cities in the eastern section of the map are either dominated by New York or by a city that is in turn dominated by New York. Most of the cities in the western section of the United States are dominated by Los Angeles or San Francisco. A hierarchical pattern is evident in many cases. The cities with grey shading, such as Minneapolis, St. Louis, and In-dianapolis, are dominated by Chicago, which in turn is dominated by New York. Note also that these Chicago-dominated cities extend much farther to the west where the competition is less severe, as was true in the cases cited earlier of Memphis's retail hinterland (Fig. 1.17) and the diagram showing influence divides between centers of unequal magnitude (Fig. 1.13A). The dominance of Wichita by Kansas City leads into a longer set of hierarchical linkages because Kansas City is dominated in turn by Chicago, which is dominated by New York. Other examples of hierarchical linkages are the cluster of smaller centers focusing on Atlanta, which is dominated by New York, and the cities focusing on Seattle, which is dominated by San Francisco.

The Texas cities form an interesting pocket of what might be called reciprocal intraregional dominance. Dallas and Houston dominate each other's air traffic. As shown in Figure 1.25 they are far enough from both New York and Los Angeles so that the fields of influence from both of those great metropolitan centers fall, for each of them, below the fields of the other Texas city. The smaller Texas cities are, in turn, arranged in a hierarchy around Dallas and Houston.

The hierarchy of urban centers reflected by air-passenger flows rep-resents the highest level of the structure of linkages. As is obvious from the prominence of New York, Chicago, and Los Angeles, the linkages re-flected are those of the largest metropolitan areas, both with large metropolitan areas and with the smaller metropolitan areas that focus on them. However, each of the one-hundred cities on the map has a constellation of smaller nearby centers focused on it through highway linkages. A combined air-passenger and automobile-commuting map would show a hierarchical structure of spatial organization as it is traced out by certain transportation linkages and flows. The small urban centers

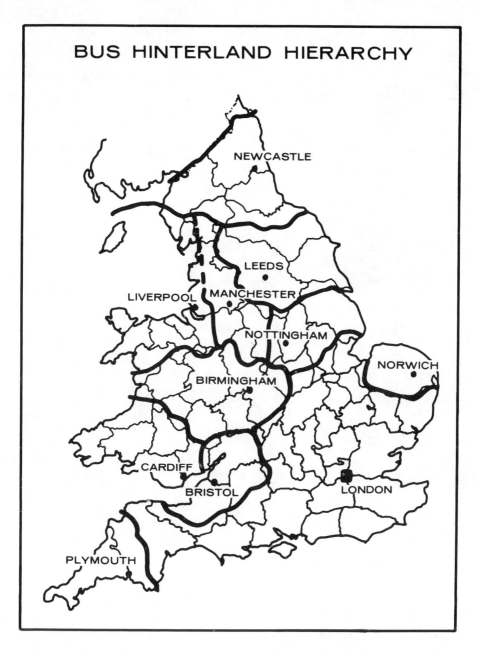

Fig. 1.24. Bus-Hinterland Hierarchy. The map shows a set of high-order hinterlands superimposed on a finer mesh of bus hinterlands. From F. H. W. Green, "Community of Interest Areas: Notes on the Hierarchy of Central Places and their Hinterlands," Economic Geography, 34, No. 3 (July 1958), 214.

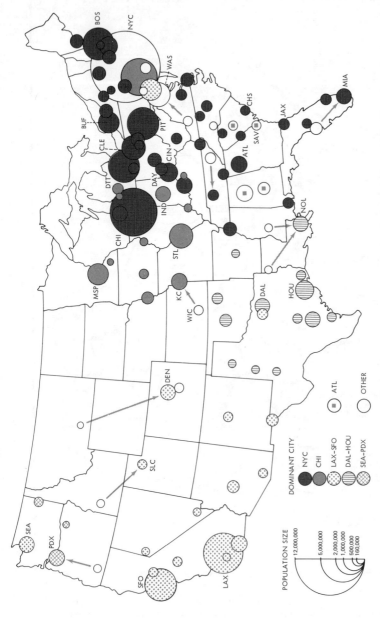

Fig. 1.25. *Air-Passenger Hierarchy. The United States is divided into three broad zones of air-passenger dominance. In the East is a zone within which the air-passenger traffic of all cities is dominated by New York, or in a hierarchical structure, by cities such as Chicago, Atlanta, and others that are in turn dominated by New York. The zone in the West encloses cities similarly dominated by Los Angeles, San Francisco, and Seattle. The hierarchy of dominance in the south-central zone focuses on Dallas, Houston, and New Orleans. After Edward J. Taaffe and Leslie J. King, "Networks of Cities" Guidelines, Unit 3 in Limited School Trials, High School Geography Project, Association of American Geographers (1966), 66.*

in the commuting areas around Wichita, for example, have their highway traffic focused on Wichita, which has its air traffic focused on Kansas City, which in turn has its traffic focused on Chicago in the hierarchical structure discussed above.

Summary

Certain features of the geographer's view of transportation have been identified and illustrated with examples in this chapter. The idea of the functional region was one of the first expressions of the geographer's view. The geographer looks to the transportation network in a particular region for evidence of the spatial structure of that region.

The structural elements in spatial organization are linkages and nodes. According to their function and their importance within the network, the linkages may serve as trunk lines, feeder lines, or bridge lines. The nodes vary in accessibility according to their position in a network, and some could be considered gateways, or significant entry-and-exit points, to the network. Linkages and nodes are organized into hinterlands, systems of hinterlands, and hierarchies. The hinterland of a node is the area in which that node's field of influence is stronger than the influence of adjoining nodes. Thus a system of hinterlands will reflect the position and relative importance of the major nodes in a network, with each node extending its influence farther toward weak competitors than toward strong competitors. The hinterlands of the smaller nodes are nested within those of larger nodes in a hierarchical pattern. A series of hinterlands of small centers will be contained within the hinterland of a medium-sized center; a series of hinterlands of medium-sized centers will be contained within the hinterland of a large center. Highway-transportation linkages and flows trace out the dominance patterns of the smaller and medium-sized centers. Air-passenger flows trace out the dominance patterns of the larger centers.

CHAPTER 2 transportation
and spatial processes

The spatial processes whereby linkages, nodes, hinterlands, and hierarchies evolve through time are complex and thoroughly intertwined with other processes of regional development. This chapter first treats the process of regional specialization that ties together the ideas of the functional and the uniform regions. Transportation cost structure and agglomeration economies are then discussed to emphasize certain important relations between transportation and regional specialization. A simple four-stage model is then presented to describe the typical evolutionary process of a transportation network. Finally, there is a brief historical survey of the development of transportation in the United States that is designed to provide one example of the interwoven processes of network development and regional specialization.

Regional Specialization

As a transport system evolves, it has a marked impact on the regional economy in the form of specialization. Changes in the web of transport linkages and flows bring about accompanying changes in the mosaic of land use.

Figure 2.1A provides a simplified view of the way in which transportation changes may affect regional specialization. In the initial stages of little or no transportation, cities X and Y are virtually isolated from each other and from all other cities. As shown in the diagram, a wide range of subsistence agricultural activities will be carried on around each city. The crops produced will depend upon the consumption needs of the individual cities, not upon the different resources of the surrounding areas. For example, the area surrounding X might have the best natural conditions in

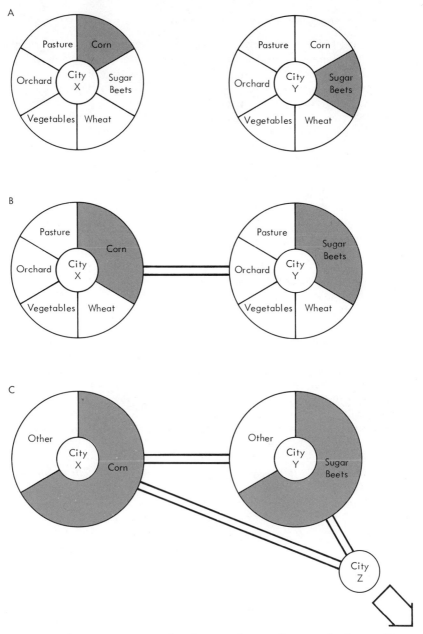

Fig. 2.1. Specialization Diagram. This diagram depicts the growth of speciali-zation between two regions as transport linkages improve. In A the agricultural regions around each isolated city are similarly diversified and are focused on the subsistence needs of the cities. In B the cities are linked by effective trans-port and X begins to specialize in corn, Y in sugar beets. In C the transport linkages are expanded to include national and world markets and the process of specialization is intensified.

35

the world for the production of corn, but the amount of land devoted to corn will depend upon the amount of corn consumed by the inhabitants of city X. Around city Y might be the best possible land for sugar beets, yet production will be limited by the sugar-beet needs of city Y itself. The first signs of regional specialization appear as transportation improves and the two cities are connected (Fig. 2.1B). Corn will expand around city X, sugar beets around city Y, and the two cities will ship their surpluses to each other. The two cities begin an interdependence, and their production patterns are now complementary. The area around city X produces corn more cheaply than the land around Y, so it is cheaper for Y to pay transport costs on X's corn than to raise corn itself. If we were to introduce a third city, Z, a port connecting both X and Y to cities in other parts of the world, the two areas could specialize still further, as shown in Figure 2.1C. The payment received by cities X and Y for their specialties would permit them to meet their other agricultural needs by importing from low-cost producers. Thus, changes in the linkages representing the functional organization of a region have brought about changes in the land-use mosaic representing its spatial uniformity, which illustrates the close relation between uniformity and functional linkages as parts of the region's overall spatial organization.

In addition to the usual economic mechanisms of supply, demand, and economies of scale that would of course influence the preceding oversimplified relationships, the role of transport costs would be critical to the resulting spatial pattern of agriculture. If, for example, the cost of corn production around city X were twenty cents a bushel, compared to twenty-five cents around city Y, no trade would take place unless transport costs were less than five cents per bushel. If transport costs were greater than five cents, it would not be profitable for Y, the inefficient producer, to abandon production and have corn shipped in from X.

Therefore it is possible to make an initial, simplified statement about the relation between transport costs and production cost differentials. For trade to take place between two points, i and j, the transport costs, C_{ij}, must be less than or equal to production cost or price differential between i and j, or $C_{ij} \leqq (P_j - P_i)$.

If transport costs are less than price differentials between any two points, trade may take place and regional specialization can begin. The development of U.S. transportation may be viewed as a progressive lowering of transport costs (or improvement of services) and a resultant increase in regional specialization that in turn became increasingly complex and intertwined with urbanization. Before considering this process more critically, however, it is necessary to note the relation between regional specialization and such things as the transport cost structure and economies of agglomeration.

Transportation Costs

The impact of any transportation system upon regional specialization is necessarily transmitted through a structure of transportation rates.

These transport rates are related to distance, as in the diagrams in Chapter 1. If the rates followed a strict distance principle, they would double when the distance was doubled, and the per-mile rate would be constant. However, transport rates are seldom based exclusively on an unmodified distance principle. Transport rates usually reflect such things as grouping, the cost characteristics of the different modes of transport, the existence of break-of-bulk points, and competition between producing areas.

GROUPING. The first departure from the distance principle is based on the need to group freight rates, both by types of commodities and by sets of origins and destinations. There is a long and complex history of the commodity-grouping of rail freight rates in the United States that is still reflected in the present structure, which is divided into class rates, covering large groups of commodities, and commodity rates, covering smaller, more specific groupings.[1]

Figures 2.2A and B show an example of first-class and commodity rates (coal) for shipments from Milwaukee. The greater generalization in the first-class rates is evident in their closer adherence to the distance principle. The grouping, of origins and destinations, further complicates the rate structure. Since rates do not increase in a consistent per-mile fashion, they are usually quoted between groups of origins and destinations. In general, such grouping is organized so that it benefits the larger centers and reinforces existing patterns. For interstate shipments in Wisconsin, for example, the state has been divided into 67 station group areas; for intrastate shipments, it has been divided into 180 station group areas. This results in a stepped structure (Fig. 2.3) with the most advantageous positions located at the far end of the group. Station B, for example, at the far end of its group, takes the same rate as Station A, even though A is closer to the shipping point. To ship even a short distance beyond B, on the other hand, results in an increased rate, as in the case of Station C. Certain cities, such as Chicago, St. Louis, and some Missouri and Ohio River crossings, have historically occupied strategic positions in rate groupings, thereby strengthening their positions as gateway cities.

TAPERING FARES. A second departure from the distance principle is the tendency for per-mile transport costs to taper, to decline with distance. To some extent this tapering structure depends on the ratio between terminal costs and line-haul costs for the different modes of transportation. Table 2.1 and Figure 2.4 show a hypothetical example in which the terminal cost for one hundred pounds of a particular commodity is thirty cents and the line-haul cost is one cent per mile. The

---

[1] For a description of the complex subject of freight rates, there are many works and trade publications providing exhaustive, often legalistic treatments. Some general transportation texts covering the subject are D. P. Locklin, *Economics of Transportation* (Homewood, Illinois: Richard D. Irwin, 1966); Marvin L. Fair and Ernest K. Williams, *Economics of Transportation* (New York: Harper and Brothers, 1960).

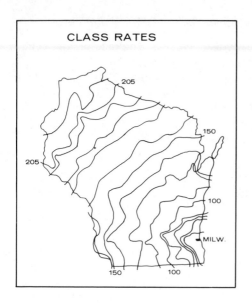

CLASS RATES

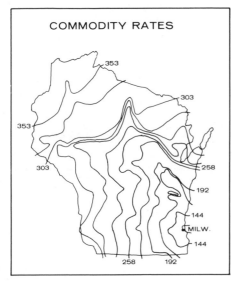

COMMODITY RATES

Fig. 2.2. Class and Commodity Rates. Figure A shows the first-class rates from Milwaukee to other cities in Wisconsin. B shows the rates for a particular commodity (coal) from Milwaukee to other Wisconsin cities. The class rates are more generalized and show a more regular increase with distance. After John W. Alexander, S. Earl Brown, and Richard E. Dahlberg, "Freight Rates: Selected Aspects of Uniform and Nodal Regions," Economic Geography, 34 (1958), 7, 15.

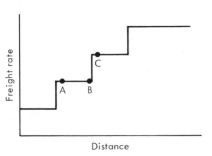

Fig. 2.3. Stepped Rate Structure. The grouping of rates is associated with a stepped rate structure as shown in the diagram. The most advantageous position in a rate structure is at the far end of a rate group or step, as in the case of B.

Table 2-1. Hypothetical Tapering Fare Structure

Distance (miles)	Terminal costs	Line-haul costs	Total costs	Per-mile costs
0	.30	0	.30	—
1	.30	.01	.31	.31
5	.30	.05	.35	.07
10	.30	.10	.40	.04
20	.30	.20	.50	.025
30	.30	.30	.60	.02
40	.30	.40	.70	.017
50	.30	.50	.80	.016
100	.30	1.00	1.30	.013
1000	.30	10.00	10.30	.010

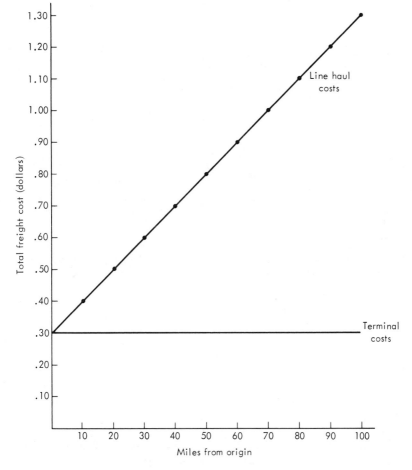

Fig. 2.4. Terminal and Line-Haul Transport Costs. The graph shows the terminal and line-haul costs listed in Table 2.1.

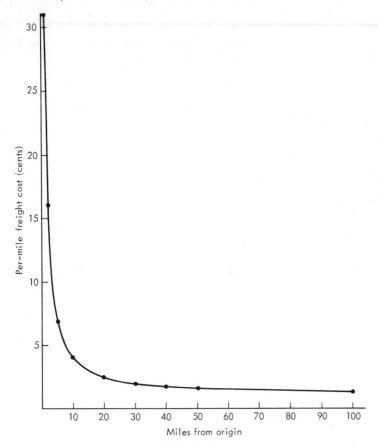

Fig. 2.5. *Per-Mile Transport Costs. When the total transport costs shown on Figure 2.5 are computed on a per-mile basis, there is a marked decline with distance, as shown on the graph and listed in Table 2.1.*

total per-mile cost will then decline with distance, as shown in Figure 2.5, since the thirty-cent terminal cost will be spread over a larger number of mile units. This tendency is intensified by the fact that many line-haul costs increase less than proportionately with distance, thus flattening out the top of the curve in Figure 2.4. In addition, price discrimination often works against the short-haul shipper. Low promotional rates were often placed on long-haul traffic by the railroads and compensated for by relatively high per-mile rates on short-haul traffic, causing actual per-mile rates to decline more rapidly than costs with distance.

Figure 2.6 shows a hypothetical example of the rate structures of the major modes: truck with relatively low fixed and terminal costs, and rail and waterway with higher costs in equipment and terminal operations. The distance at which rail becomes lower-cost than truck (*OB*)

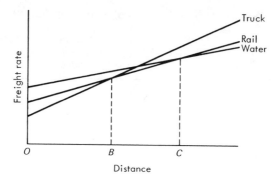

Fig. 2.6.   *Rate Structure of Major Modes. The diagram shows a hypothetical set of rate profiles for truck, rail, and waterway traffic. With low fixed costs relative to operating costs, truck transport is cheapest in the short haul (OB); water transport is cheapest in the long haul (beyond OC).*

and that waterway becomes lower-cost than rail (*OC*) depends on too great a variety of factors for any single numerical estimates. Some idea of these comparative distances is provided by Table 2.2, which gives estimates of the average line-haul distance for manufacturing commodities as shipped by different modes.

Although nearly all freight rates have a tapering structure, passenger fares usually do not. This results in the greater profitability of long-haul passenger traffic to the carriers. The airlines, for example, have offered more coach and tourist services on their long-haul flights than on their short-haul flights. In effect, this has resulted in a taper with distance in the average fare per mile.

LOCATION.   The effects of a tapering fare structure upon the location of economic activity are of some importance. In the simplest case of classical location theory—with one source of raw material at A, only one market at B, and equal transport rates that increase proportionately with

Table 2-2.

Mode	Average miles per ton shipped
Rail	515
Motor Carrier	253
Private Truck	113
Air	1,000
Water	844

Source: F. S. Pardee *et al., Measurement and Evaluation of Transportation System Effectiveness,* RM-5869-DOT. The Rand Corporation, September, 1969.

Table 2-3.   Locational Effects of Tapering Fare Structure

Distance from A	Rate per 10-mile block	Total transp. cost from A	Distance from B	Rate per 10-mile block	Total transp. cost from B	Total transp. cost
0	0	0	60	.05	.45	.45
10	.10	.10	50	.06	.40	.50
20	.09	.19	40	.07	.34	.53
30	.08	.27	30	.04	.27	.54
40	.07	.34	20	.09	.19	.53
50	.06	.40	10	.10	.10	.50
60	.05	.45	0	0	0	.45

distance—location at the raw material source, the market, or any inter-mediate point, would result in the same total transportation cost. With tapered fares, on the other hand, the two terminals become the low-cost locations and the intermediate points are disadvantaged (Table 2.3 and Fig. 2.7). For example, if the two points were sixty miles apart and the transport rate were a flat ten cents for each 10-mile block, an industry located at A would pay a total of 60 cents per unit in transport costs: noth-ing for raw materials, and 60 cents for shipping every unit of the goods produced to the sole market at B. An industry at B would pay a total of 60 cents per unit in transport costs, all of it for having raw materials shipped in from A, but none for shipping finished goods. An industry located at a point midway between A and B would also pay 60 cents per unit in transport costs: 30 cents for shipping raw materials and 30 cents for finished goods. Likewise, location at any other point between A and B would result in total transport costs of 60 cents per unit. Tapered fares, however, shift the advantages to the two terminals (Table 2.3 and Fig. 2.7). An industry locating at A, for example, still pays nothing for raw material and only 45 cents per unit for shipping its finished products. An industry locating between A and B saves less because of the taper. The transport cost for shipping raw materials 30 miles is 27 cents as is the cost for shipping finished products, so that the total transport cost is 54 cents, as shown in the table and the graph. As the situation becomes more complex and such things as multiple raw-material sources, weight-losing raw materials, and unequal rates for finished products and raw materials are introduced, locational advantages shift back and forth between market and raw-materials areas. The effect of the tapered structure itself, how-ever, consistently favors end-point rather than intermediate locations.

Intermediate locations are favored at a break-of-bulk point, as at a port, a rail-to-highway transfer point, or where rail lines of two different gauges meet. Since goods must be transferred at such a point, the addi-tional terminal costs could make it the location with the lowest transport costs, as shown in Figure 2.8 and Table 2.4. The ten cent transfer charge associated with a break of bulk increases the transport costs at both A and

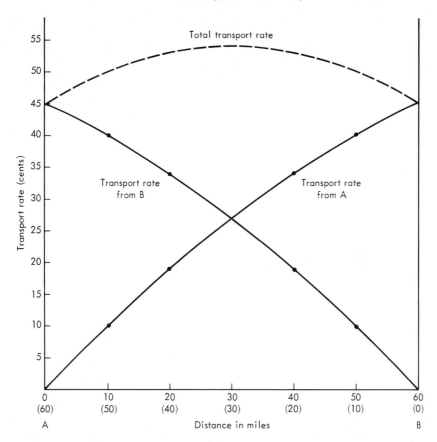

Fig. 2.7.   Locational Effects of Tapered Rates. This diagram shows the effects of tapered rates on the simplest case of classical location theory: one source of raw material, one market, and equal transport rates. A, B, and all intermediate locations would have the same total costs for procurement of raw materials and distribution to markets if the rates were not tapered. With tapered rates, the total transport costs for the terminal points, A or B, are less than for intermediate points, as shown in Table 2.3.

B by ten cents, from 45 cents to 55 cents. An industry located at the break-of-bulk point midway between A and B, does not have to pay the transfer charges. The total unit-transport cost, therefore, remains at 54 cents. Intermediate locations other than the break-of-bulk location do not share this savings and their total transport costs are increased by ten cents. The tapered fare thus maintains lower terminal than intermediate-point costs with the exception only of the break-of-bulk point.

COMPETITION.   Another factor complicating rate structures is com-petition among places and transportation systems. Transcontinental rates

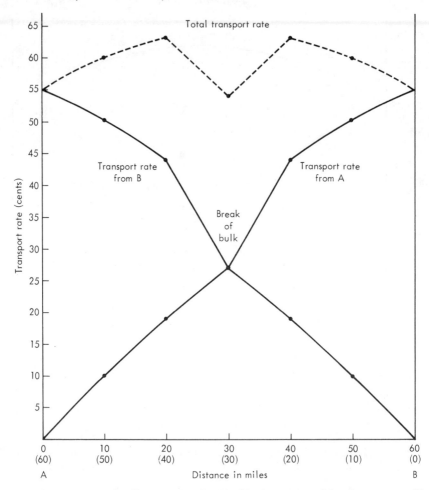

Fig. 2.8. *Locational Effects of Break-of-Bulk. An intermediate location could be the lowest cost location if a break-of-bulk is necessary and goods must be transferred either from one mode to another or between carriers of the same mode, as in the case of a break in rail gauge. This is illustrated in the graph, which is based on Table 2.4.*

on citrus fruit shipped from California are a good example. Rate groups become larger as the major market of the northeastern United States is approached, which in effect reduces the per-mile rate for cities in the groups in order to meet Florida's competition. A more extreme example of competition was the case of wine rates from California, when the whole eastern section of the country was blanketed to compete with the imported wine that usually entered the country through Eastern Seaboard ports. It cost no more to ship California wine to New York than it did to St. Louis.

Table 2-4. *Locational Effects of Break of Bulk*

Distance from A	Rate per 10-mile block	Total transp. cost from A	Break of bulk costs	Distance from B	Rate per 10-mile block	Total transp. cost from B	Total transp. costs
0	0	0		60	.05	.55	.55
10	.10	.10		50	.06	.50	.60
20	.09	.19		40	.07	.44	.63
30	.08	.27	.10	30	.08	.27	.54
40	.07	.44		20	.09	.19	.63
50	.06	.50		10	.10	.10	.60
60	.05	.55		0	0	0	.55

Agglomeration Economies

The impact of transportation upon regional specialization is also affected markedly by the existence of economies of agglomeration. To some extent, economies of agglomeration are similar to the economies of scale associated with lowered unit-costs as output increases. We are more interested in *external* economies of scale, however, than in those associated with the internal savings possible as a plant increases production. These agglomeration economies, or external economies of scale, are associated with the advantages experienced by firms that locate in large urban areas close to other firms. Some of the agglomeration economies are associated with the proximity of other firms in the same or similar industries.[2] Such an agglomeration tends to attract a corresponding group of suppliers for that particular industry. A large labor pool with skills needed by the industry is more likely to develop, and the process of intraindustry information exchange among firms will be accelerated. Agglomeration economies also occur when dissimilar firms are located in close proximity to one another. These firms may be linked in a series of interindustry transactions, acting partially as suppliers of each other's inputs and partially as consumers of each other's output. In addition, the grouping of firms itself accelerates the growth of large urban centers, and each firm is able to share in the full array of metropolitan advantages, such as specialized services, research facilities, and the large, diverse labor pool.

Agglomeration economies are also closely related to Gunnar Myrdal's principle of circular and cumulative causation. In Myrdal's words, ". . . a change does not call forth contradicting forces but, instead, supporting changes, which moves the system in the same direction but much further.

[2] Under the general heading of agglomeration economies Nourse makes a distinction between external economies of like firms and external economies of unlike firms. Hugh O. Nourse, *Regional Economics* (New York: McGraw-Hill, 1968). Isard makes a similar distinction, using the terms *localization economies* and *urbanization economies,* Walter Isard et al., *Methods of Regional Analysis: An Introduction to Regional Science* (The Technology Press of the Massachusetts Institute of Technology, and New York: John Wiley & Sons, 1960).

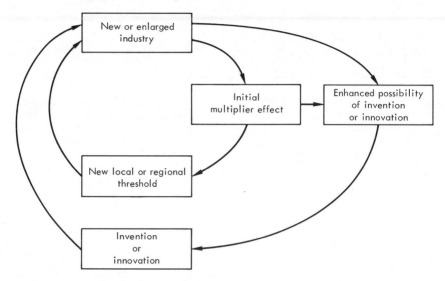

Fig. 2.9. Circular and Cumulative Causation. This diagram by Allan Pred applies Gunnar Myrdal's idea of circular and cumulative causation to urban and industrial growth. As each new firm locates in a city, it has an initial multiplier effect that permits the city to reach a new set of thresholds and to expand its local and regional markets, thereby increasing the probability of still other new firms. The process is reinforced by the effects of the intensified information on the probability of invention or innovation. From Allan R. Pred, The Spatial Dynamics of U.S. Urban-Industrial Growth, 1800–1914, *The Regional Science Studies Series (Cambridge: The M.I.T. Press, 1966), p. 25.*

Because of such circular causation, a social process tends to become cumulative and often to gather speed at an accelerated rate." [3]

Pred applies this idea to urban and industrial growth, as shown in Figure 2.9. As each new firm locates in a city, a series of new demands are created both by the firm and by its labor force. Production and employment tend to increase in local services, construction, and a wide range of associated activities. This increase will then cause a second, smaller round of increases in a new set of related activities, which in turn will cause a third round, and so on. This multiplier effect enables the city to attain a new set of thresholds—that is, its local markets will expand enough to call for additional firms in existing industries as well as industries that are new to the city. The entry of every new firm or industry sets the whole process in motion again. In addition, Pred points out that the increased intensity of information-flow associated with this process enhances the possibility of the development and adoption of innovations, which in turn reinforce the entire process of circular and cumulative causation.

[3] Gunnar Myrdal, *Rich Lands and Poor*, World Perspectives, 16 (New York: Harper Brothers, 1957), 13, as quoted in Allan R. Pred, *The Spatial Dynamics of U.S. Urban-Industrial Growth, 1800–1914*, The Regional Science Studies Series (Cambridge: The M.I.T. Press, 1966), 15.

The link between agglomeration economies and regional specialization becomes evident as markets continue to widen under the impact of improved transportation. Whereas the first evidences of regional specialization may have been in the form of a greater concentration of agricultural production, the later evidences may well be in the form of accelerated urbanization. The resultant economies of agglomeration for the larger urban centers permit them to lower their costs of production, thereby permitting an expansion of the hinterlands of these centers at the expense of smaller centers. This process of geographic concentration is further intensified by the freight-rate structure. The tapering nature of the rates favors major end-points or terminals. The effects of competition between carriers for the large traffic volumes generated by the largest centers has a tendency to further reduce the rates from raw material areas to these centers, as well as between the different centers themselves.

An Idealized Process of Transport Development

Although no consistent spatial model of transport development is available at present, certain regularities have been noted and can be expressed, as in Figure 2.10. Four phases in the process of transport network development are shown in the diagram.[4]

SCATTERED PORTS. The initial phase (A) of transport network development is marked by a number of small ports and trading centers scattered along the seacoast. Each port has an extremely limited hinterland and there are few connections among the ports. Scattered interior points are weakly connected to each other and to the ports. There is little specialization of production and each point is surrounded by diverse subsistence agriculture.

PENETRATION LINES. The second phase of development (B) is critical. Major lines of penetration develop from certain ports and connect with interior points. Markets then expand, both at the ports and at the interior centers, and regional specialization begins to appear. Feeder lines begin to develop, and agglomeration economies permit the major port to enlarge its hinterland by "pirating" the hinterlands of smaller, adjacent ports. As port concentration proceeds, the major ports become larger and develop coastal services among themselves, while the smaller ports grow less rapidly and decline or even disappear.

INTERCONNECTION. The third phase of the developmental pattern (C) is primarily one of interconnection. Small nodes develop along the penetration trunk line and feeder lines develop at the interior centers as well as at certain on-line nodes (N_1 and N_2 in the diagram). As the feeder networks continue to develop around the ports, interior centers, and the main, on-line nodes, some of the larger feeders begin to link up.

[4] This discussion of the idealized process is based on Edward J. Taaffe, Richard L. Morrill, and Peter R. Gould, "Transport Expansion in Underdeveloped Countries: A Comparative Analysis," *Geographical Review*, 53 (1963), 503–29.

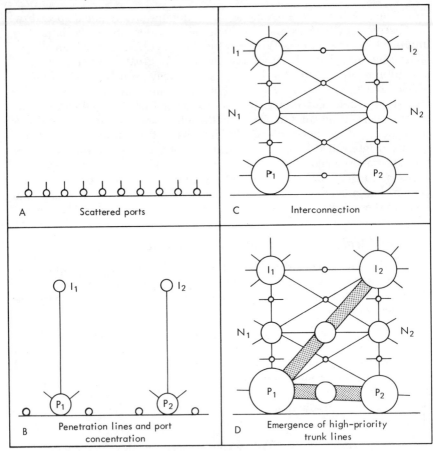

Fig. 2.10. *Idealized Process of Transport Development. The diagram shows four phases in the typical development of a transport network. An initial phase of scattered ports is followed by the development of a few penetration lines and the beginnings of concentration on a few ports. The next phase is one of interconnection of the penetration lines, followed by the emergence of certain high-priority trunk lines. After Edward J. Taaffe, Richard L. Morrill, and Peter R. Gould, "Transport Expansion in Underdeveloped Countries: A Comparative Analysis," Geographical Review, 53 (1963), 504.*

As this interconnection continues, there is a tendency toward increased specialization and toward an expansion of markets for urban centers. The result is an intensified competition between cities. The cities most successful in competing over this network experience further agglomeration economies and generate, in turn, demands for improved transportation to each other.

HIGH-PRIORITY LINKAGES. The fourth phase (D) is the development of trunk lines and high-priority linkages between the largest centers. These linkages will be the outcome largely of the spatial competition that developed during the interconnection stage. Those linkages will have the best roads, the heaviest traffic, and the most frequent common-carrier schedules. In some cases the emerging trunk line will confirm the primacy of the initial penetration lines that gave the advantageous early start to the cities along their routes. In other cases, as in the diagram, the trunk lines are newer connections that reflect the heavy interaction among the largest urban centers, I_2 to P_1, which may or may not be aligned along a former penetration route.

SOME EMPIRICAL EXAMPLES. Empirical evidence for the first two phases of transport network development is not lacking. Figure 2.11 shows an example by Peter Rimmer of the process of port concentration in New Zealand. Rimmer also noted that coastal linkages by sea are a typical concomitant of the scattered-port stage. The development and importance of penetration lines that accompany port concentration is also evident in most parts of the world. The emergence of the first major penetration line from the seacoast to the interior is perhaps the most important single phase in the transportation history of an underdeveloped country. Later development typically evolves around the penetration lines, which serve as trunk lines around which the interconnected networks develop. The initial motivations for penetration lines have been both political and economic. In the case of Ghana, the political-military motive was strong. Ghana needed a short rail line to an interior administrative center, and later a longer highway extension, the Great North Road, to a town that had been selected earlier as the capital of the Northern Territory. Sometimes penetration lines became conspicuous loci of settlement, as in the case of Kenya, where the "White Highlands" development around the interior center, Nairobi, became a more critical node of development than the original development around the major port of Mombasa.

The lateral interconnection phase is not as well-defined and there is correspondingly less evidence. Figure 2.12 shows the developmental process at work in Ghana from 1922 to 1958. The shaded areas, representing road densities, expand from a pattern dominated by penetration lines in 1922 to one dominated by lateral interconnection in 1958. There is also less evidence for the fourth phase in which, it is postulated, high-priority trunk lines develop. The lack of evidence is partially due to the fact that many countries have not yet reached the fourth stage. It is also due to the relative difficulty of identifying such trunk line linkages merely from the examination of transportation facilities. Detection of such linkages requires that the traffic flow, the types of schedule and equipment, and other factors be mapped.

The four phases illustrated in the diagram do not exist as a distinct sequence of separate stages. The evolution of a transport network is a relatively continuous process and evidence of all four phases can usually be found at any time in any given network. Some development of high-priority linkages among large centers is usually occurring at the same time as interconnection between both large and medium-sized centers.

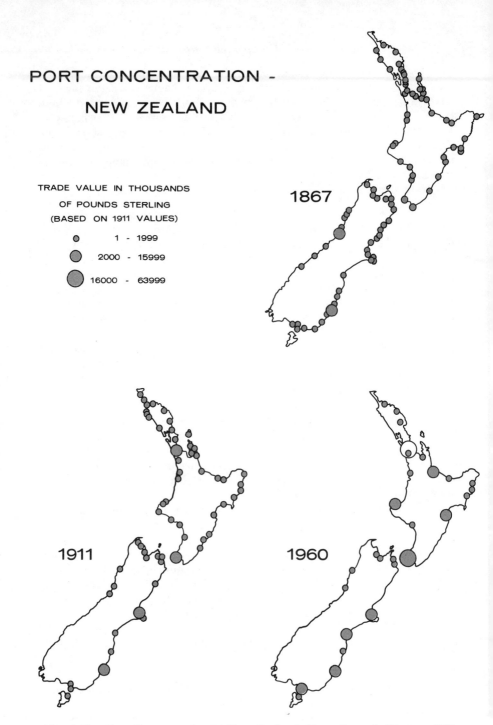

Fig. 2.11. Port Concentration in New Zealand. From Peter J. Rimmer, "The Changing Status of New Zealand Seaports, 1853–1960," Annals, The Association of American Geographers, 57, No. 1 (March 1967), 91, 94, 97.

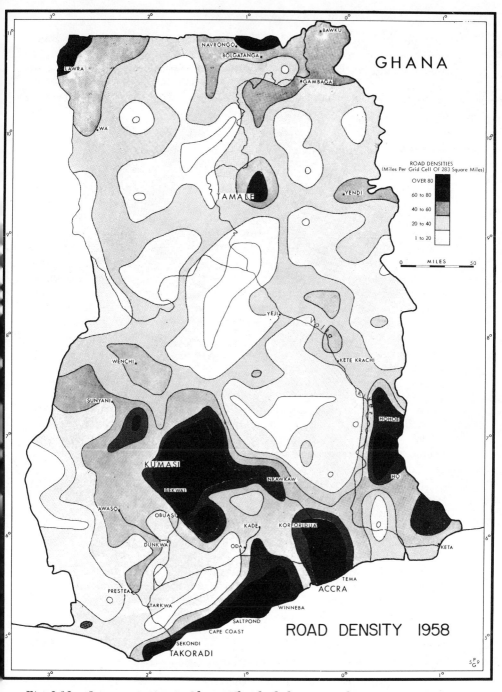

Fig. 2.12. *Interconnection in Ghana. The shaded areas on the map, represent-ing road densities, expand from a highway network dominated by penetration lines to one dominated by interconnection. From Edward J. Taaffe, Richard L. Morrill, and Peter R. Gould, "Transport Expansion in Underdeveloped Coun-tries: A Comparative Analysis,"* Geographical Review, 53, (1963), 512.

New penetration lines often develop from outlying nodes in frontier zones at the edges of moderately built-up networks, as in Brazil. The four-phase model should be thought of only as a convenient and preliminary way of describing a complex and overlapping process. For a better understanding of this process it will be necessary to provide more precise definitions of the component parts and their interrelationships.

The Development of U.S. Transportation as a Spatial Process

The development of U.S. transportation has been marked not only by the lowering of transport costs, but also by the evolution of shifting networks of linkages and nodes, together with accompanying sets of hinterlands and hierarchies. As the networks for the different modes of transportation developed from scattered ports through penetration lines to a strongly interconnected system with a superstructure of high-priority trunk lines, a concomitant pattern of regional specialization and urbanization developed. The remainder of this chapter consists of a condensed survey of the evolution of U.S. transportation as an example of the complex and intertwined nature of these spatial processes. For purposes of this discussion, transportation development has been arbitrarily divided into four eras: Local Transport, Trans-Appalachian, Railroad Dominance, and the present Era of Competition.[5]

LOCAL TRANSPORT.   The Era of Local Transport that preceded the completion of the Erie Canal and the Trans-Appalachian railroads was marked by conditions similar to those in the initial phase of the four-phase model. There were many small ports, inland centers were poorly connected with each other, port hinterlands were restricted, and regional specialization was minimal.

A network of small canals east of the Appalachians provided a few weak interconnections among certain Eastern Seaboard cities. The agriculture that developed around those canals was diversified usually and focused on the needs of the nearby cities. Agriculture was carried on in areas such as New England despite poor soil and poor climatic conditions. Specialization was similarly restricted on the other side of the Appalachians, even though there was much agricultural land suitable for effective grain farming. Prices were low in the Ohio country and there was no incentive to shift from subsistence- to cash-farming since the farmer could not dispose of his grain surplus.

There were some connections between the Eastern Seaboard and the interior before the Erie Canal, but these connections were quite costly. A circuitous water route involved shipping grain from the Ohio country

---

[5] This discussion is drawn largely from Edward J. Taaffe, "The Transportation Network and the Changing American Landscape," in *Problems and Trends in American Geography,* ed. Saul B. Cohen (New York: Basic Books, 1967), 15–30.

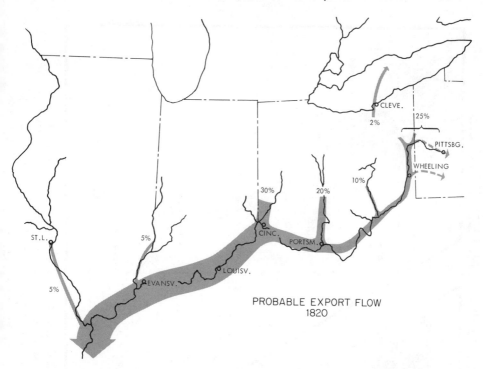

Fig. 2.13. Probable Export Flow in Midwest: 1820. The Ohio River was the trunk line of the Midwest before the Erie Canal. Grain was shipped downstream on the Ohio and its tributaries to New Orleans, where it was transshipped on sailing vessels to Eastern Seaboard ports. After Arnold Isaacs, "Traffic Patterns in the Old Northwest, 1815–1860," Northwestern University Department of Geography honors paper (April 1957), Figure 3.

downstream on the Ohio River to the Mississippi, then to New Orleans, and then transshipping it on a sailing vessel to the Eastern Seaboard ports. Figure 2.13 shows a probable traffic flow in 1820 before the opening of the Erie Canal. The role of the Ohio River as the region's trunk line was clear and virtually unchallenged. A direct connection, the National Road from Baltimore, reached Wheeling, West Virgina on the Ohio River in 1818. Although it might be considered the first penetration line, its high costs precluded a sizable flow of goods. Transport costs clearly exceeded the price differentials for most agricultural goods, and the main trade between East and West was in higher-value goods—including grain in the form of whiskey—where price differentials presumably exceeded transportation costs.

TRANS-APPALACHIAN TRANSPORT. There was an interesting eco-nomic competition among the large Eastern Seaboard cities as they at-

PORT CONCENTRATION - UNITED STATES

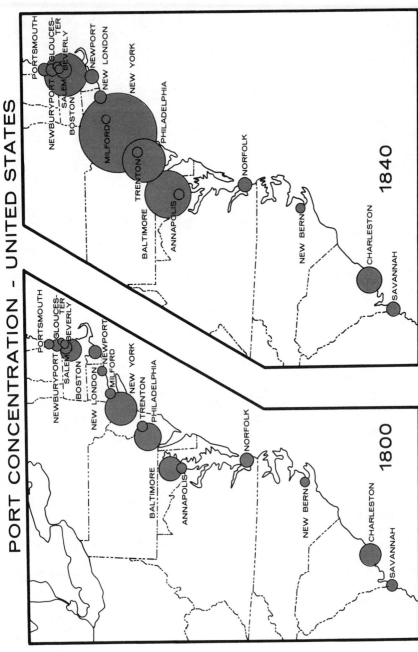

Fig. 2.14. Eastern Seaboard Ports: 1800 and 1840. The circles for New York, Philadelphia, Baltimore, and Boston show how the process of port concentration proceeded from 1800(A) to 1840(B). From Allan R. Pred, The Spatial Dynamics of U.S. Urban-Industrial Growth, 1800–1914, The Regional Science Studies Series (Cambridge: The M.I.T. Press, 1966), p. 188.

54

tempted to penetrate the Appalachian Barrier and reach the Ohio country. Although Baltimore was the first to breach the Barrier with the National Road, New York quickly gained the most efficient, low-cost access to the interior with the completion of the Erie Canal in 1825. Estimated cost was one cent per ton-mile on the Erie Canal, compared to thirteen cents on the National Road.[6] Despite Washington's abortive Chesapeake and Ohio Canal and Philadelphia's cumbersome Pennsylvania Public Works (1834), which was a costly combination of canals and short rail portages, the Erie Canal developed into a strong trunk line and helped New York establish its supremacy while the process of port concentration went on among the Eastern Seaboard ports (Fig. 2.14).

With transport costs now lower than agricultural price differentials, it became profitable for Ohio farmers to ship grain to Eastern markets. This tended to raise grain prices in the Ohio country, which attracted more farmers away from subsistence to cash-crop agriculture, thereby increasing specialization on grain in that area. In a high-cost grain-producing area such as New England the prices were being driven down by the Western competition. Farmers were either shifting toward more profitable forms of agriculture less vulnerable to Western competition, or forsaking agriculture entirely and moving into the cities, where industry was growing rapidly. As transport costs decreased, markets for Eastern manufactured goods also began to widen. Eastern manufacturing goods began driving out many of the local handicraft industries west of the Appalachians, thereby increasing the Eastern movement from agriculture to manufacturing and intensifying the developing complementarity of production between the two areas. The economies of agglomeration associated with the increased industrialization of the cities further accelerated the growth of the Eastern Seaboard cities.

After the Erie Canal was opened, a certain amount of waterway interconnection began to take place between Lake Erie and the Ohio River. Canals were built from Cleveland to the Pittsburgh area, and across Ohio to such river cities as Marietta, Portsmouth, and Cincinnati (Fig. 2.15). This expansion continued until the 1850s, when the first set of rail penetration lines broke through the Appalachian Barrier. The Erie, the Baltimore and Ohio, and the Pennsylvania railroads came through the Appalachians between 1851 and 1854, and by 1862 the New York Central had linked up enough of its components to provide a through route along the Hudson and Mohawk Valleys. Thus a major change in spatial organization had become evident before the Civil War. Figure 2.16 shows the pattern of grain traffic, which stands in marked contrast to the earlier pattern.

---

[6] Truman C. Bigham and Merrill J. Roberts, *Transportation, Principles and Practice* (New York: McGraw-Hill, 1962), 53–57.

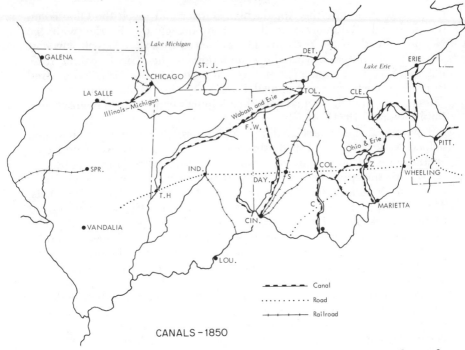

CANALS – 1850

Fig. 2.15. Canal Interconnection in the Midwest: 1850. The map shows the network of canals as it had developed in the Midwest in the 1850s, a few years before the railroads had broken through the Appalachian Barrier. The Ohio and Erie and the network of short canals in the East connected Lake Erie with the Ohio River system. The abortive Wabash and Erie Canal and the Illinois–Michigan Canal also were designed to connect the Great Lakes with the Ohio–Mississippi System. After Arnold Isaacs, "Traffic Patterns in the Old Northwest, 1815–1860," Northwestern University Department of Geography honors paper (April 1957), Figure 1.

RAILROAD DOMINANCE. The period roughly from the Civil War to World War I may be characterized as the Era of Railroad Dominance. Although canal traffic continued to increase, the railroads established their supremacy soon after the first penetration lines, and interconnection was proceeding rapidly even before the Civil War. Figure 2.17 shows the extent of railway interconnection in 1860. The canals were losing their primacy and soon became absorbed into the system as feeders to rail trunk lines. The Civil War helped confirm the emerging east-west flow of traffic by turning the Midwest away from its river-based ties with the South and strengthening Midwestern linkages with the industrial East. The expansion and interconnection of the rail network after the war was given further impetus in the Midwest by competitive overbuilding associated with postwar speculation and industrial expansion. Well-interconnected subsystems began emerging in groups bounded by the variety of rail

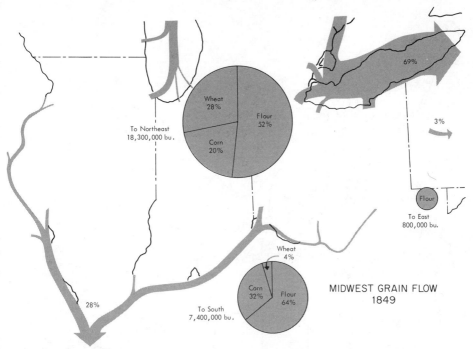

Fig. 2.16. *Midwest Grain Flow: 1849. By 1849 there was a marked change in the spatial organization of the Midwest as shown by this map, contrasted to Figure 2.13. The shift of emphasis to the north is evident both in Lake Erie and Lake Michigan. After Arnold Isaacs, "Traffic Patterns in the Old Northwest, 1815–1860," Northwestern University Department of Geography unpublished honors paper (April 1957), Figure 9.*

gauges existing at that time. Before 1880 it was necessary to transfer cargo because of the break in gauge at such cities as Chicago, Pittsburgh, Cincinnati, and Louisville.

At the same time that interconnection was taking place, new rail penetration lines were being extended toward the West. The first transcontinental link was completed in 1869, followed by three other connections in the 1880s (Fig. 2.18). High-priority linkages were also becoming evident as gauges became standardized and through rail travel between larger cities became possible. Electrification around the turn of the century strengthened the railroad's ability to provide good intercity and intracity passenger services. The skeletal beginnings of a network of electric interurban services between large and medium-sized cities were evident before the 1920s.

The impact of improved transportation on regional specialization and urbanization during the Era of Railroad Dominance was marked, and a host of examples could be cited. One example was the tendency for certain patterns of specialization to develop in areas far from Eastern

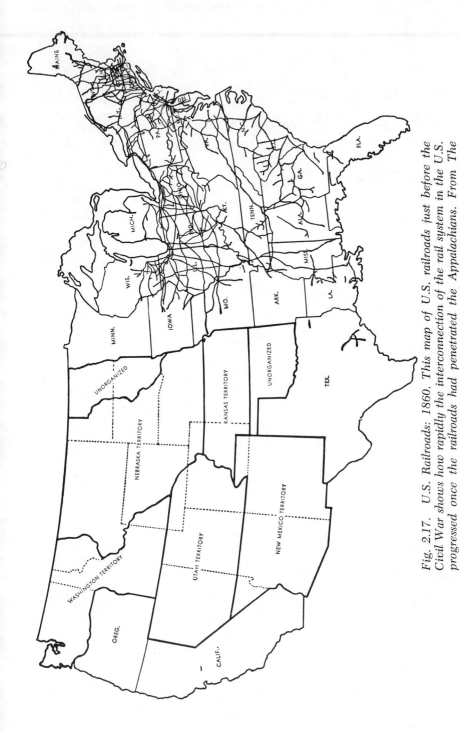

Fig. 2.17. U.S. Railroads: 1860. This map of U.S. railroads just before the Civil War shows how rapidly the interconnection of the rail system in the U.S. progressed once the railroads had penetrated the Appalachians. From The Association of American Railroads, Railroads of America (Washington: 1966), p. 8.

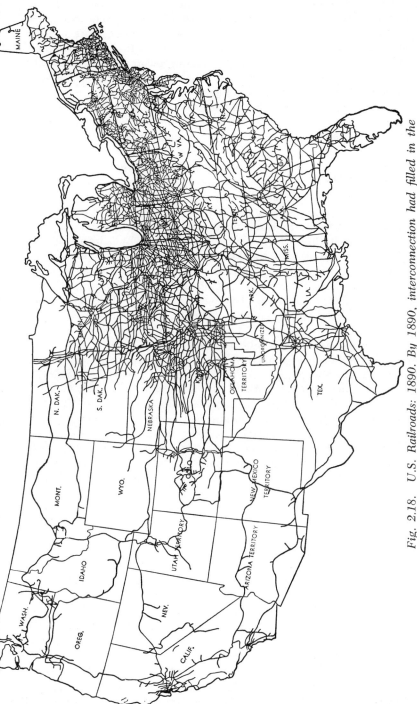

Fig. 2.18. U.S. Railroads: 1890. By 1890, interconnection had filled in the Eastern, and to some extent, the Southern patterns. In addition, interconnected networks had developed west of the Mississippi, and the three major transcontinental penetration lines were evident. From The Association of American Railroads, Railroads of America (Washington: 1970).

markets. This development was aided not only by the railroad's tapering fare structure, but by a policy of setting even lower promotional rates on some long-haul commodities. This gave agriculture a start in new Western areas by keeping transport costs low enough to permit competition in Eastern markets. Low promotional rates accompanied the rise of citrus-growing in California. The low rates made California oranges competitive in Eastern markets with Florida oranges and as a substitute for other fruit products. With the entire country as a potential market, California farmers could expand their scale of production and make effective use of their natural resources. Agriculture in California still epitomizes the far-flung patterns of regional specialization associated with low-cost, long-haul U.S. transportation. Many nationally consumed fruit, vegetable, and nut specialties have more than eighty percent of their production concentrated in California.

Regional specialization was also evident in the urbanization and the rapid growth of industry that accompanied the interconnection process during the Era of Railroad Dominance. The break-of-bulk principle was exemplified in the growth of cities located at break-of-gauge points such as Cincinnati and Pittsburgh. The tendency to base freight rates on these cities, as well as on such gateways as Chicago and St. Louis, confirmed the transport advantages of these cities even after the 1880s, when gauges had been standardized and an effective national rail system existed. Interdependence and complementarity in manufacturing increased as cities developed manufacturing specialties and sold them in other cities. Agglomeration economies reinforced this process and demands for more effective transport between the largest cities were increased. High-priority linkages grew along such emerging trunk lines as the New York–Chicago route. Another trunk line along the Eastern Seaboard connected Boston, New York, Philadelphia, Baltimore, and Washington, a grouping later to be known as Megalopolis. These primary alignments together with several lesser clusters and alignments formed a large and powerful group of cities known as the American Manufacturing Belt, which typified the growing dominance of the United States by metropolitan areas during the Era of Railroad Dominance.

The Era of Competition.   The Era of Competition from World War I to the present can be characterized as one of continuing competition among the different modes of transportation. Before World War I the railroad was virtually unchallenged for nearly all kinds of traffic: long-haul and short-haul, passenger and freight, low-value bulky goods and high-priced manufactured goods. The rapid advance of technology, however, had ramifications beyond the railroads, and other forms of transportation became competitive. Truck transport took away short-haul manufactured goods; inland waterways took certain long-haul and bulky goods; private auto took the short-haul passengers; and the airlines took the long and medium-haul passengers.

First came the highway. The rate structure of the railroad, which had promoted long hauls and thereby penalized short hauls, provided a protective umbrella for truck competition, which had its initial impact on the short haul of manufactured goods. In the 1920s the private auto took over most of the short-haul passenger traffic, all but wiping out the short-haul electric interurban trains. In the 1930s truck and auto transportation were further strengthened by the expansion of the country's highway system. State control of highway building had the effect of emphasizing rural roads, and the highways first expanded as feeder-line connections to rail trunk lines. Federal grant-in-aid programs favored certain major interstate routes, however, and soon the highways were competing with rail trunk lines, as well as forming a major portion of the dense network of transportation interconnections between these trunk lines. Nonetheless, a superstructure of high-priority highway linkages was slow to emerge. The toll roads, which began with the Pennsylvania Turnpike before World War II, were the first of these high-priority highway linkages. Their divided lanes and limited access assured a fast and steady flow of traffic. It was not until the early 1950s, however, that the Pennsylvania, Ohio, and Indiana Turnpikes linked up to provide through traffic over the country's major New York–Chicago trunk line. The New Jersey Turnpike connected the cities of Megalopolis, but the New York State Thruway had not as yet linked up with the Ohio system. Elsewhere in the United States there were only a few scattered segments of high-capacity, limited-access highways. The toll-road movement faded in 1956 with the initiation of a massive federal program for an Interstate Highway System. When completed, the Interstate System (Fig. 2.19) will be a nationwide network of high-speed, high-capacity expressways that will function as a set of high-priority linkages between the country's large metropolitan areas.

Inland waterways also provided intensified competition to the railroads, although in a less spectacular and comprehensive fashion. From the 1930s through the postwar period many waterways were deepened and improved by Federal projects and became effective low-rate carriers of bulky commodities between points that were on or readily accessible to the waterways. Figures 2.20 and 2.21 illustrate two conspicuous features of the role of waterways in the U.S. transportation network. The flow map (Fig. 2.20) shows how inland waterway traffic is heavily concentrated only on relatively few of the country's many navigable waterways. The heaviest traffic is on the Monongahela, the Ohio, the Mississippi, and the Illinois Waterways, which link areas producing industrial raw materials such as coal and petroleum with major industrial complexes in the American Manufacturing Belt. Figure 2.21 emphasizes the dependence of all water traffic on a relatively few bulky commodities. Overseas, coastal, Great Lakes, and inland waterway traffic are all represented on the map, which is dominated by the symbols for petroleum, petroleum products, coal, iron ore, sand, and gravel. Inland waterway transportation shows little evidence of interconnection; rather, it seems to function as a superstructure of specialized linkages focused on the movement of bulky commodities between relatively few areas. In Western Europe, on the other hand, waterway interconnection is well-developed, particularly in the area of intensive economic activity in Belgium, the Netherlands, and adjacent sections of France and Germany.

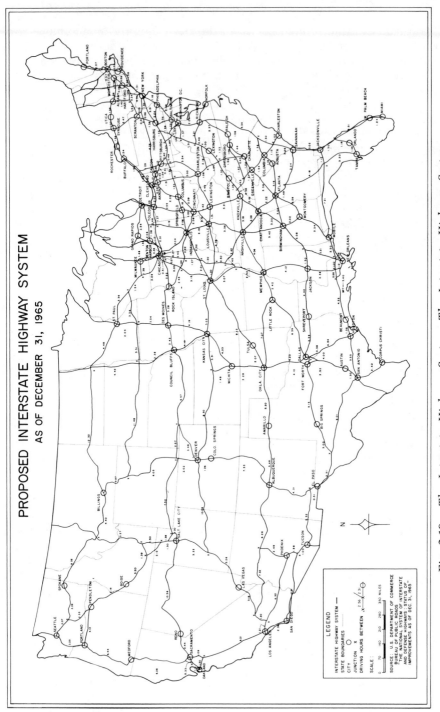

Fig. 2.19. *The Interstate Highway System. The Interstate Highway System has replaced the toll-road system, and when fully completed it will provide a network of high-priority linkages between major metropolitan areas.*

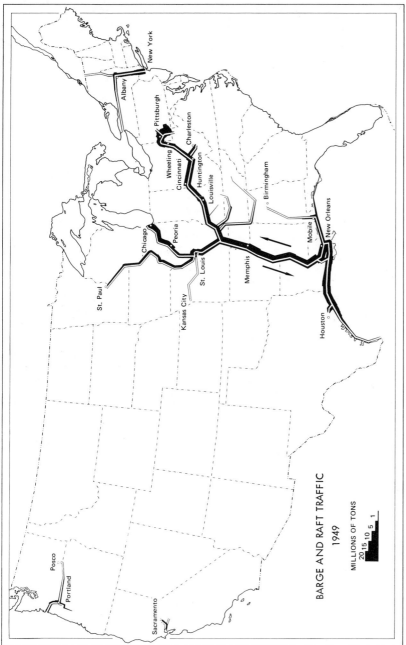

Fig. 2.20. *Traffic Flow on U.S. Inland Waterways. This map shows the concentration of traffic on a relatively few waterways. The flow of traffic is dominated by petroleum and coal moving over the waterways of the Ohio and Mississippi system. From Donald Patton, "The Traffic Pattern of American Inland Waterways," Economic Geography, 32, No. 11 (January 1956), 30.*

BARGE AND RAFT TRAFFIC
1949

MILLIONS OF TONS
20 15 10 5 1

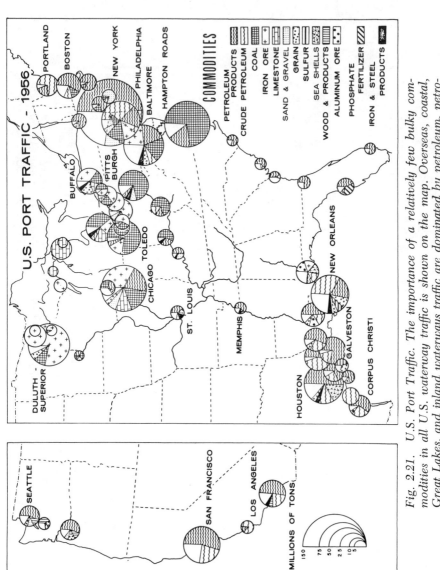

Fig. 2.21. U.S. Port Traffic. The importance of a relatively few bulky commodities in all U.S. waterway traffic is shown on the map. Overseas, coastal, Great Lakes, and inland waterways traffic are dominated by petroleum, petroleum products, coal, iron ore, and sand and gravel. From Richard E. Carter, "A Comparative Analysis of United States Ports and Their Traffic Characteristics," Economic Geography, 38 (1962), 168.

Table 2.5.   *Typical Average Rates of Transport Modes*

(per ton-mile)

Water	0.22
Pipeline	0.27
Railroad	1.27
Truck	6.70
Air	19.89

Source: F. S. Pardee *et al.*, *Measurement and Evaluation of Transportation System Effectiveness*, RM-5869-DOT. The Rand Corporation, September, 1969.

The airlines were the last to provide effective competition to the railroad. Although there were a number of isolated penetration lines, including a multiple-stop transcontinental link before World War II, a well-interconnected system did not develop until the postwar period. Interconnection and the development of high-priority linkages proceeded together during the rapid expansion and improvement of air transportation. Such high-priority services as low-fare coach travel developed and were first put into operation in such high-density travel markets as New York–Chicago and New York–Los Angeles. The same was true of jet services as they expanded through the network in the late fifties and early sixties. Interconnection has been represented first by the growth of the regional carriers, such as Braniff, Western, and Delta, and then by the development of local-service carriers, each focused on certain nodes.

The railroads also shared in the great surge of technological improvements in transportation, particularly the changes in automated freight handling and shipping procedures. The railroads continued to provide fast, low-cost transportation for medium- and long-haul freight, although much of the passenger and short-haul freight was gone. By the 1970s the lines were also blurring between the different modes of transportation as containerization became more common, permitting easy transfers between rail, truck, and water transportation. Table 2.5 lists some comparative figures for 1967. Rail transportation was still quite a bit cheaper than truck transportation in 1967, although it continued to be more expensive than water or pipeline. Figure 2.22 shows some comparative freight-traffic data for the major transport modes. From 1945 to 1966 the railroads' ton-mile share of total traffic had declined from two-thirds to less than one-half. The motor-vehicle share, including both for-hire carriers and private carriers, had increased from approximately 6 percent to 22 percent during the same period, and both pipelines and inland waterways had also increased. The residual importance of the railroad in freight traffic should be noted, however, since it still accounted for 40 percent of the total ton-miles, approximately five times as much as for-hire motor carriers and twice as much as private carriers. In intercity passenger traffic, however, the railroad played a negligible role. Figure 2.23 shows the overwhelming dominance of the private automobile, which accounted for 88 percent of the total intercity passenger traffic in 1966. The railroads

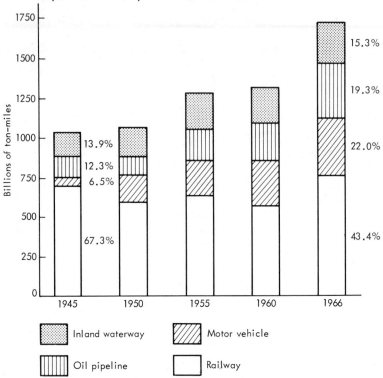

Fig. 2.22. Intercity Freight Traffic, 1945–1966. The diagram shows the decline in the railroad's share of total traffic from two-thirds in 1945 to less than one-half in 1966. From Norman S. Fieleke, "Toward a More Efficient Railroad System," New England Economic Review, *Federal Reserve Bank of Boston (March/April 1969), 2–20.*

had just about changed places with the airlines from 1945 to 1966, declining from 6.5 percent to 1.8 percent, while the airlines increased from 2 percent to 7.3 percent. More recent developments in passenger traffic include some efforts on the part of both the railroads and government to reassess the potential role of rail passenger traffic. In 1971 a new form of high-priority rail linkage appeared in the Amtrak program, whereby a selected set of routes that focused on New York and Chicago were designated for government support (Fig. 2.24).

The net result of the explosion of transport technology and the rise of competition during the last fifty years has been the overall lowering of transport costs and the broadening of areas of high accessibility to national and regional markets, which in turn has increased the opportunities for regional specialization and the resultant interdependence of cities and regions in different parts of the country. Truck farmers around large Eastern cities face increased competition as early vegetables from the

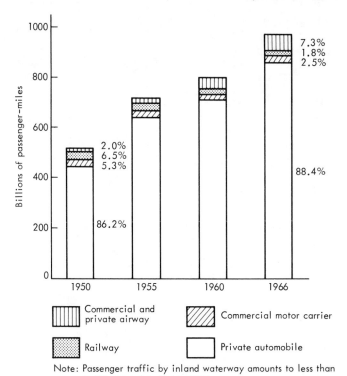

Fig. 2.23. Intercity Passenger Traffic, 1950–1966. The diagram shows the overwhelming dominance of the private automobile in intercity passenger travel and the increased importance of airline relative to rail travel from 1950 to 1966. From Norman S. Fieleke, "Toward a More Efficient Railroad System," New England Economic Review, *Federal Reserve Bank of Boston (March/April 1969), 2–20.*

South and Southwest have become easier to transport and threaten to wipe out the rings of vegetable production surrounding these cities; manufacturers, wholesalers, and retailers in widely separated areas have become more dependent upon each other for the quick supply of materials and distribution of a diversity of products; milksheds around big cities have expanded and become more overlapping and competitive.

Much of the impact of improved transportation on regional specialization has been transmitted through the effect of transportation upon economies of agglomeration. The more effective linkages between cities have accelerated the growth of the largest cities by expanding their markets. This tendency has been evident at local, regional, and national scales. In the constellation of villages, towns, and cities surrounding a large metropolitan center, there is a continual tendency for the large center to reach out and usurp small city and town functions as travel into

INTERCITY RAILROAD PASSENGER ROUTES

NATIONAL RAILROAD PASSENGER CORPORATION

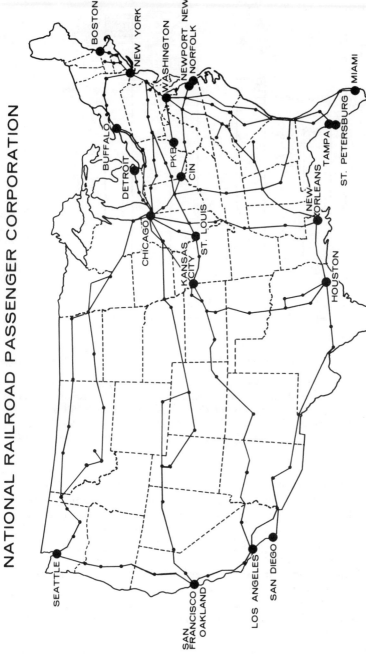

Fig. 2.24. Amtrak Rail Passenger Routes. The map shows the set of rail passenger services selected in 1971 by the U. S. Government for support in the Amtrak program. Included are regular Amtrak Routes, experimental Amtrak Routes and certain connecting non-Amtrak passenger services. After Amtrak timetable, effective January 16, 1972.

the metropolis becomes easier.[7] The small cities, in turn, reach out and take over functions of towns and villages. The virtual disappearance of the hamlet at the lowest end of the urban hierarchy is clearly related to the improvements in highway transportation.

On a national scale at the other end of the hierarchy, a similar process of increased concentration on the largest centers may be noted. Figures 2.25 and 2.26 show the air-passenger dominance patterns in 1940 and 1962. A comparison of these maps shows the marked increase in the prominence of the larger centers such as New York, Chicago, and Los Angeles. An examination of the percentage of New York, Chicago, and Los Angeles traffic of the total traffic for one hundred cities for a period of approximately ten years shows a small but remafkably consistent tendency for these percentages to increase for these three cities at the expense of nearby centers.

Transportation dvelopments in the early 1970s seem likely to further accentuate the process of concentration on the largest centers. The large Boeing 747 will improve services between the more widely separated large centers. Amtrak will benefit only a limited number of large centers, and the completion of the Interstate Highway System, although it will reduce cost to a wider set of centers, may also permit the largest cities to use their economies of agglomeration to extend their influence over even wider areas.

Summary

In this chapter we have noted some characteristic features of the processes whereby transport networks evolve and how they affect the development of their region. Transport improvements between two points lead to increasing regional specialization by reducing transport costs below price differentials. The tapered freight-rate structure broadens the area within which specialization takes place and intensifies its impact at the terminals. Agglomeration economies at the large cities serve to accelerate their growth, widen their markets, and increase their dominance of the transportation system. Both functional and uniform regions are therefore closely related facets of a broader pattern of spatial organization. A change in one brings about a change in the other through the mechanisms of regional specialization and agglomeration economies.

The historical development of a transportation system may be summarized in four idealized phases: a beginning phase of scattered ports, followed by penetration lines, interconnection, and the growth of high-priority linkages.

A brief survey of the development of U.S. transportation shows the complex intertwining of ideas of regional specializations, economies of agglomeration, and the processes whereby a transport structure evolves. There is not at present a clear and consistent theory of transport structure

[7] Brian J. L. Berry, *Geography of Market Centers and Retail Distribution* (Englewood Cliffs, N.J.: Prentice-Hall, 1967), 116–17.

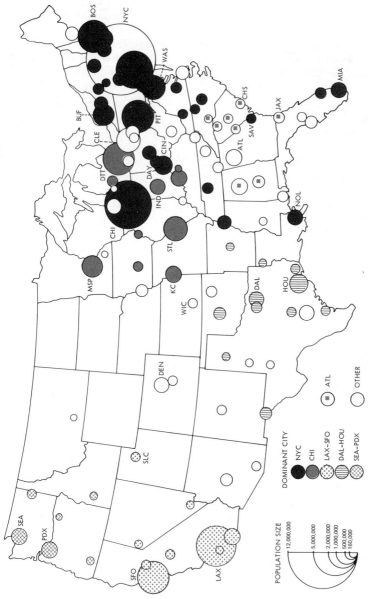

Fig. 2.25. *Air-Passenger Dominance: 1940. The air-passenger dominance pattern in 1940 shows New York's area of dominance largely restricted to the eastern half of the Manufacturing Belt. Atlanta dominates the Southeast and is dominated by Birmingham. Edward J. Taaffe and Leslie J. King, "Networks of Cities," Guidelines, Unit 3 in Limited School Trials, High School Geography Project, Association of American Geographers (1966), p. 78.*

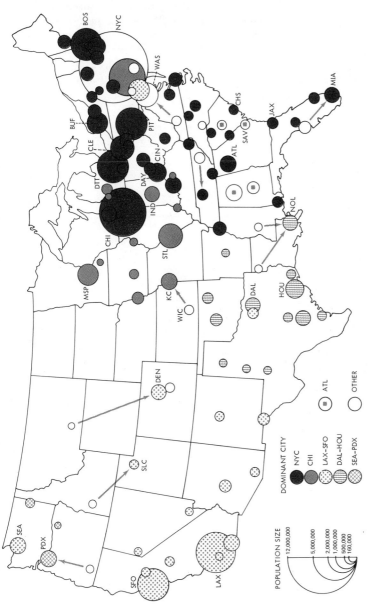

Fig. 2.26. Air-Passenger Dominance: 1962. New York's dominance area has expanded through the entire northern tier of Manufacturing Belt cities and into the Southeast to dominate Atlanta. Los Angeles and San Francisco have extended their areas of dominance west to Denver and Albuquerque and north to Seattle. In general, there has been a clear increase in dominance by the larger centers. After Edward J. Taaffe and Leslie J. King, "Networks of Cities," Guidelines, Unit 3 in Limited School Trials, High School Geography Project, Association of American Geographers (1966), p. 66.

and development. What we have are a few puzzling and often contradictory glimpses of a system of spatial structures and processes that seem to be related to each other in something more than a random fashion. We can provide a broadly generalized overview of this system in a preliminary and tentative way, but presently we cannot provide clear or precise specifications of either the components of the system or the relationships between components. The next four chapters will consider three separate models that represent different approaches to a partial understanding of the complex system briefly surveyed in Chapters 1 and 2. Each of these models deals with some of the questions already raised.

the gravity model

As the geographer looks at a pattern of transportation linkages and flows, one of his first concerns is to understand the forces underlying the patterns. Why does the transport network show strong linkages and flows between some centers, weak linkages and flows between other centers? What are the characteristics of the centers and their spatial arrangements that tend to increase or decrease flows? The gravity model and its many variations have been applied in attempts to answer those questions in cases involving intercity travel, commodity flow, identification of hinterlands and hinterland systems, and the general concept of accessibility. In this chapter, we first identify the basic gravity model. Next we discuss the application of the gravity model and certain variations to traffic analysis, hinterland study, and the construction of potential maps as a means of evaluating accessibility. Finally the concepts of complementarity and intervening opportunity are discussed in relation to further variations in the gravity model.

The Basic Gravity Model

The gravity model, one of the earliest models to be applied in the social sciences, is a simple attempt to treat two basic factors affecting the amount of flow, or interaction, between any two points: population and distance. The greater the population of the two centers, the greater the interaction; the greater the distance, the less the interaction. Figure 3.1 illustrates this statement. If we were to compare the linkages between A and B with those between A and C in terms of expected interaction, it is clear that in the absence of other information, more interaction would be expected between A and B. Both B and C are 500 miles from A, but B has a population of 1 million and C has a population of 500,000. If we assume

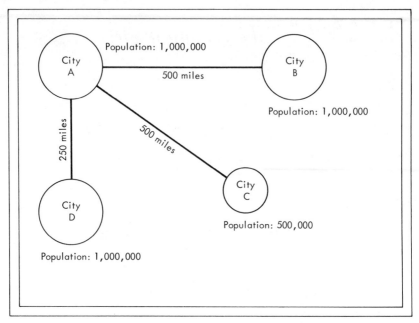

Fig. 3.1.   Gravity-Model Diagram. This diagram represents in simple form the basic effects of population and distance upon expected interaction. One would expect more interaction between A and B than between A and C, although the distance is the same, because the population of C is less than that of B. The expected interaction between A and D could, in turn, be greater than that between A and B, even though D and B are equal in population, because the distance between A and D is less than that between A and B. From Edward J. Taaffe and Leslie J. King, "Networks of Cities," Guidelines, Unit 3 in Limited School Trials, High School Geography Project, Association of American Geographers (1966), p. 61.

that the probability of interaction between any pair of individuals in the two cities is equal, then the population of City A multiplied by the population of city B would give a figure that would be helpful in ascertaining the probability of total interaction between these two cities. In this example, the figure for expected interaction between A and B ($P_A P_B$) would probably be twice as great as that for expected interactions between A and C ($P_A P_C$). This interaction might take the form of phone calls, the movement of freight, air passengers, auto trips, and so on.

The effect of distance may be illustrated by comparing the expected interaction between A and B with that between A and C. Both C and B have the same population, but since D is closer than B we would expect the link between A and D to have the greater interaction. All other things being equal, we would expect the probability of interaction between any two points to decline as distance increases.

We may now generalize and say that the expected interaction between any two cities i and j will increase as the product of the populations of the two cities (P_iP_j) increases, and it will decrease as the distance between i and j (d_{ij}) increases. This may be expressed as a ratio $I_{ij} = P_iP_j/d_{ij}$. In the above example, this would lead us to expect twice as much interaction between A and D $(P_AP_D/d_{AD} = 10^{12}/250)$ as between A and B $(10^{12}/500)$. This fraction is referred to as the gravity model because of its similarity to Newton's law of gravity.[1]

The gravity model should not be regarded as a magic formula whereby one may compute the P_iP_j/d_{ij} figure for any pair of cities and automatically produce a number close to the actual number of phone calls or air passengers between the two cities. It is necessary first to adjust the P_iP_j/d_{ij} figure by a constant so that the orders of magnitudes of the two sets of numbers will be comparable. For example, the gravity-model figures for a series of city pairs might average in the millions, as in the example above. This does not mean that we expect millions of air passengers. If the annual air-passenger totals averaged in the thousands, we would simply adjust the gravity-model estimate by a constant with a value in the thousands. Thus, a constant $k = 1/1000$ should be added to the basic model as follows:

$$I_{ij} = k \frac{P_iP_j}{d_{ij}}$$

The constant would seldom be an even multiple of ten and would vary for different sorts of interaction. If gravity-model estimates averaged four times greater than telephone calls, for example, an appropriate constant would be $k = 1/4$. Whether modified by a constant or not, however, the gravity-model figure should show a consistent tendency to increase as phone calls or air traffic increases, and to decrease as these evidences of interaction decrease.

The Gravity Model and Traffic

INTERCITY PASSENGER TRAFFIC. One extensive use of the gravity model has been as a predictor of intercity passenger traffic.[2] Empirical tests indicate that roughly 50 percent of the variation in air traffic tends to be associated with population and distance expressed as an unmodified gravity model.

Table 3.1 lists in the first column the actual air traffic in 1960 between Salt Lake City and 25 large cities. In the second column, gravity-model

---

[1] The distance term in the law of gravity is squared of course, but we defer until later in this chapter a discussion of the appropriate power to which distance should be raised in order to describe different sorts of traffic.

[2] In this section and for the remainder of the chapter it is assumed that the reader is familiar with simple regression and correlation. Those who are not familiar with these techniques should refer at this point to Appendix A for a brief and simplified discussion.

Table 3.1.   Salt Lake City Air Traffic

To	Actual (10% sample) air passengers (1960)	$\dfrac{(P_iP_j)}{D}(10^{-8})$	Distance
1. New York	1,949	28.73	1.968
2. Chicago	1,423	20.70	1,257
3. Los Angeles	5,907	44.60	579
4. San Francisco	5,979	17.83	597
5. Washington	736	4.16	1,843
6. Miami	126	1.72	2,087
7. Boston	260	4.74	2,094
8. Detroit	239	10.13	1,488
9. Philadelphia	368	8.66	1,921
10. Cleveland	198	4.40	1,564
11. Pittsburgh	187	5.54	1,664
12. Dallas	279	4.16	998
13. St. Louis	196	6.81	1,159
14. Minn.–St. P.	559	5.76	958
15. Seattle	154	7.82	700
16. Denver	4,381	9.62	370
17. Kansas City	266	4.32	922
18. Houston	134	3.97	1,199
19. Cincinnati	82	2.83	1,449
20. New Orleans	73	2.32	1,433
21. Phoenix	1,388	5.04	504
22. Indianapolis	100	1.98	1,353
23. Portland, Ore.	952	4.96	635
24. San Diego	387	6.31	627
25. Las Vegas	1,268	1.34	362

Source: David A. Smith, Department of Geography, State University of New York at Buffalo.

expectations that use a simple (P_iP_j/d_{ij}) formulation are listed. Since the gravity-model figures are so large, they have been expressed in one-hundred millions (10^8). Thus the gravity-model figure of 28.73 for New York is really 2,873,000,000. The relation between these two is shown graphically by Figure 3.2, a scatter diagram with the gravity-model expectations on the X-axis, actual traffic on the Y-axis.[3] Thus, Salt Lake City's New York traffic (Y) and gravity-model estimate (X) are represented by a single point located at $Y = 1,949$ and $X = 28.73$ (times 10^8). Similar points represent Salt Lake City's air traffic and gravity-model estimates for 24 other major cities. The resulting scatter of points provides a visual summary of the relation between the two variables. This relation is summarized by the addition of a regression line, drawn to minimize the (squared) deviations of each point from the lines. Since it is a straight line, its equation is of the form $(Y) = a + b\ (X)$—in this case, $(Y) = 56.2 + 126.2\ (X)$. A correlation coefficient r may then be computed as an

[3] The notation used in this chapter is based on that used in Gerald A. P. Carrothers, "An Historical Review of the Gravity and Potential Concepts of Human Interaction," *Journal of the American Institute of Planners*, 22, No. 2 (1956), 94–102.

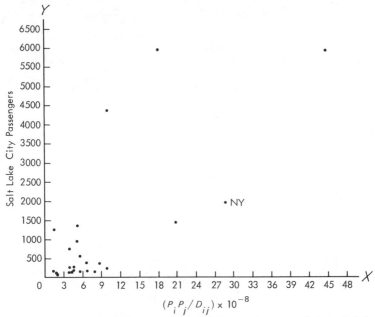

Fig. 3.2. Scatter Diagram: Gravity-Model Expectations and Actual Salt Lake City Air Traffic. On this scatter diagram, gravity-model expectations for Salt Lake City air traffic (P_iP_j/d_{ij}) *are shown on the X-axis, while actual Salt Lake City air traffic is shown on the Y-axis.*

index of the closeness of fit between the regression line and the scatter of points. The square of the correlation coefficient r^2, when multiplied by 100, indicates the percentage of variation in the dependent variable (Y) accounted for by the independent variable (X). In this case, an r^2 of .677 indicates that a little more than two-thirds of the variation in Salt Lake City's air traffic in 1960 was related to the population and proximity of other cities as expressed in the equation: (Expected Air Passengers) = 56.2 + 126.2 (P_iP_j/d_{ij}).

Visual inspection of Figure 3.3, however, does not suggest such a close relationship, and the correlation may be overstated since it is strongly influenced by extreme values. It is difficult to fit a meaningful line to a scatter diagram with a cluster of points concentrated in the low-value end of both scales and only a few widely separated high values. This difficulty suggests that a simple arithmetic relationship between air traffic and the gravity model is unlikely. The relationship may be more geometric than arithmetic, which suggests the use of logarithms. If air passengers per capita are plotted against distance for Salt Lake City traffic, the decline with distance approximates a straight line when the logarithms of the values are plotted (Fig. 3.4). Other studies have demonstrated a similar relationship, which indicates that traffic tends to decline with distance raised to a power rather than with distance multiplied by some constant. Thus, a second modification of the basic model is to insert a distance ex-

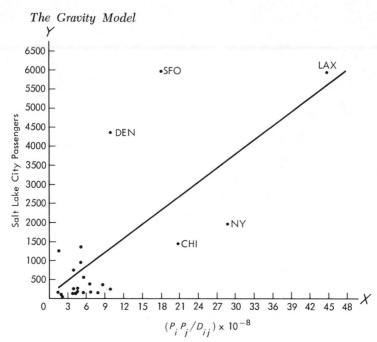

Fig. 3.3. *Regression Line and Scatter Diagram: Salt Lake City Air Traffic. The regression line fitted to the scatter diagram in Figure 3.2 does not provide a very close correspondence to the points representing gravity-model expectations and actual Salt Lake City air traffic. Too many points are clustered in the lower left-hand corner, and the placing of the regression line is unduly influenced by a relatively few high values.*

ponent $\propto$, as follows:

$$I_{ij} = k \frac{P_i P_j}{d^{\propto}_{ij}}.$$

Figure 3.5 shows the relation between Salt Lake's air passengers and the gravity-model formulation when both are expressed in logarithms. The relationship is closer ($r^2 = .978$) and it is easier to fit a line to the dots. The log transformation is equivalent to raising the entire gravity-model expression to a power $(P_i P_j/d_{ij})^b$. The equation for the regression line on Figure 3.5 is: $\log (Y) = 1.88 + 1.05 \log (X)$. This indicates that the best fit will be obtained by raising the gravity model to the power of 1.05: $(P_i P_j/d_{ij})^{1.05}$. Those routes over which Salt Lake City's traffic is greater or less than would be expected from the average relation between air traffic, on the one hand, and population and distance, on the other may now be identified. The recreational function of Las Vegas is evident in its extremely high positive residual. City function is also evident in the high air-passenger figures for Washington, D.C. and Miami. Positive residuals for such Western cities as San Francisco, Denver, Seattle, and Phoenix indicate the position of Salt Lake City as a regional center.

Since raising the entire gravity model to a power does not permit the

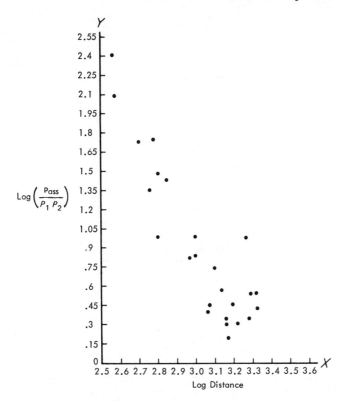

Fig. 3.4. *Relation Between Distance and Air Traffic. In this diagram Salt Lake City air passengers per capita of population product, P_1P_2 (on the Y-axis) are plotted against distance (on the X-axis) logarithmically. The resultant scatter of points for 25 cities may be reasonably well approximated by a straight line. This indicates that the tendency for per-capita air traffic from a given city to decline is better approximated by distance raised to a power rather than by distance multiplied by some constant.*

isolation of a distance exponent, a common procedure in empirical studies of traffic between cities has been to use multiple regression models with data expressed in logarithms. A regression equation in the form $\log (Y) = a + b_1 \log (P_iP_j) - b_2 \log (d_{ij})$ when taken out of logarithms is equivalent to a gravity model with empirically derived exponents:

$$Y = A \frac{(P_iP_j)^{b_1}}{(d_{ij})^{b_2}}.$$

Thus the regression equation value of b_2 is equivalent to the distance exponent $\propto$. This equation generally provides a better approximation of the actual traffic, and since the effect of population and distance may be treated separately, it also provides a single measure of the best exponent of distance for any particular set of traffic flows. In the example of the

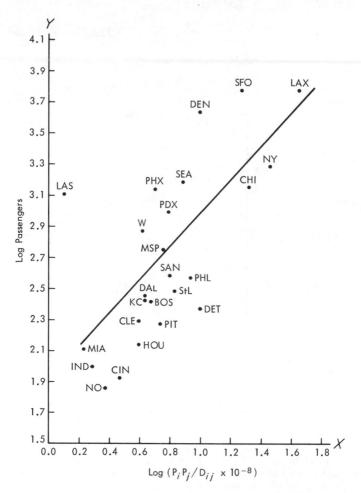

Fig. 3.5. *Scatter Diagram and Regression Line: Logarithmic Model. This diagram uses the same values as Figure 3.3 but the logs of the values are plotted. Gravity-model expectations* $[\log(P_iP_j/D_{ij})]$ *are plotted on the X-axis; actual Salt Lake City air traffic (in logs) is plotted on the Y-axis. It is clear that a regression line provides a considerably better approximation of the relationship than it did in Figure 3.3.*

traffic between Salt Lake City and a larger number of cities, the equation resulted in an R^2 of .85 and indicated that a distance exponent of 2.69 would result in the best description of Salt Lake City's air traffic to the 100 largest centers during the period studied.[4]

In a study by David A. Smith the R^2 and distance exponent figures for the 1960 traffic among the 100 largest centers were calculated.[5] Table 3.2 lists the results for the first 49 cities. In most instances the R^2 values

[4] The R^2 of .85 and the distance exponents of 2.69 for the larger sample are more realistic measures of the relationship than the deceptively high figure of .978 for the 25 cities chosen in a biased fashion for illustrative purposes.

[5] These figures were obtained from studies made by David A. Smith, Department of Geography, State University of New York at Buffalo.

Table 3.2 Relation Between Air-Passenger Traffic and Gravity Model (1960)

$$\log (PASS) = a + b_1 (\log P_i P_j) - b_2 (\log d_{ij}) \text{ or } P = A \frac{(P_i P_j)^{b_1}}{(d_{ij})^{b_2}}$$

City	R^2	(Distance) Exponent b_2
1. New York	.75	.42
2. Chicago	.72	.53
3. Los Angeles	.86	1.70
4. San Francisco	.82	1.40
5. Washington, D.C.	.76	.40
6. Miami	.88	1.40
7. Boston	.79	.43
8. Detroit	.77	.53
9. Philadelphia	.69	.31
10. Cleveland	.75	.51
11. Pittsburgh	.78	.66
12. Dallas	.57	1.35
13. St. Louis	.78	1.02
14. Atlanta	.78	1.72
15. Minneapolis	.68	1.32
16. Seattle	.88	2.13
17. Denver	.83	2.73
18. Kansas City, Mo.	.72	1.46
19. Houston	.81	2.22
20. Buffalo	.83	.78
21. Tampa	.78	1.41
22. Cincinnati	.80	.75
23. New Orleans	.78	1.92
24. Phoenix	.86	1.99
25. Indianapolis	.78	.74
26. Portland	.86	2.41
27. Milwaukee	.71	.83
28. San Diego	.83	1.55
29. Las Vegas	.85	2.29
30. Columbus	.82	.72
31. Baltimore	.61	.03
32. Louisville	.81	1.10
33. Dayton	.80	.42
34. Hartford	.76	.50
35. Syracuse	.84	.69
36. San Antonio	.68	1.33
37. Memphis	.72	1.65
38. Jacksonville	.86	1.93
39. Rochester	.82	.75
40. Salt Lake City	.85	2.69
41. Omaha	.70	1.50
42. Charlotte, N.C.	.78	1.40
43. Nashville	.72	1.34
44. Oklahoma City	.71	1.80
45. Tulsa	.69	1.78
46. Albany	.78	.84
47. Birmingham	.73	1.62
48. Norfolk	.82	1.00
49. Providence	.75	.48

Source: David A. Smith, Department of Geography, State University of New York at Buffalo.

indicate that the gravity model accounted for more than three-quarters of the variation in air traffic. The distance exponents for all 100 cities were mapped by Smith and showed a concentration of low exponents in the American Manufacturing Belt. Exponents with absolute values of .42 and .53 for New York and Chicago, for example, indicate that air traffic to other cities declines only with the square root of the distance. Exponents with absolute values greater than 2 for traffic from such Western cities as Denver, Seattle, Houston, and Salt Lake City indicate that traffic declines more rapidly than the square of the distance. Further studies have indicated a tendency of the distance effects to decline through time, relative to the population-product effects, as larger and faster aircraft have been introduced.

The distance exponent in a gravity-model formulation will vary of course with the mode of transportation. Since auto transportation to and from a given city declines more rapidly with distance than does air transportation, one would expect absolute value of the distance exponent to be highest in the case of auto transportation, lowest in the case of air transportation. Alcaly's study of traffic within the state of California confirms some of these expectations.[6] The distance exponent for auto traffic in this case is approximately 2.6, a considerably higher figure than the figures recorded for rail (1.2), bus (1.3), and air (0.3). The R^2 figures in all cases are somewhat higher than the air-traffic figures, which took the 100 major cities into account.

As empirical studies of traffic between pairs of cities have progressed, additional factors have been taken into account and the multiple regressions have become more complex. The attractive force (P_iP_j) and impedance force (d_{ij}) in the basic gravity model have evolved into more extended and specific travel-demand, or abstract mode, equations. The attractive forces include such things as per-capita income and percentage of city income derived from hotels and motels. Instead of simple distance, the impedance factors include travel-time, travel-cost, schedule frequency, and a series of ratios comparing each of these to the time, cost, or frequency of other modes.

The following demand equation was derived from an analysis of air travel from Cleveland to 30 other large cities in 1960.[7]

$$T_{ij} = 0.6\ (P_jP_i)^{.8}\ (S_iS_j)^{.7}\ (C^r_{ij})^{-.1}\ (H^r_{ij})^{-.3}\ (F^r_{ij})^{.2}\ (C_{ij}/Y_{ij})^{-.47}$$

where

P_iP_j = population product.

S_iS_j = product of percentage of receipts from selected service industries.

C^r_{ij} = air trip-cost relative to the least expensive common carrier cost.

H^r_{ij} = air trip-time relative to the next fastest mode of common carrier service.

[6] Roger E. Alcaly, "Aggregation and Gravity Models: Some Empirical Evidence," *Journal of Regional Science*, 7 (1967), 61–73.

[7] E. P. Howrey, "On the Choice of Forecasting Models for Air Travel," *Journal of Regional Science*, 9, No. 2 (1969), 215–24; also see Richard E. Quandt and Kan Hua Young, "Cross-Sectional Travel Demand Models: Estimates and Tests," *Journal of Regional Science*, 9, No. 2 (1969), 201–14.

Fr_{ij} = frequency of flight departure relative to the most frequent commercial service available.

C_{ij}/Y_{ij} = cost of travel relative to the income of the two centers.

The results of the analysis indicated that population product was still the most important index to air travel but that the service component of economic activity was also important, as was the ratio between air travel-time and that of the next fastest mode. The term $(C_{ij}/Y_{ij})^{-.47}$ is simply one way to represent the effects of costs of travel relative to the income of the two centers.[8] If the travel costs between centers is high relative to their income, the net effect will be to decrease expected travel. This equation resulted in an R^2 of .76 as compared to .65 for a gravity model (with travel-time substituted for distance). In 1965 the results were .86 for the demand equation as compared to .77 for the gravity model.

COMMODITY FLOW. The gravity model and its variations have also been applied to the study of commodity movements both within and between countries.

An example of a commodity-flow study within a country is Robert H. T. Smith's analysis of interstate rail shipments of agricultural products to the New England states (Fig. 3.6).[9] In this case the major modification of the gravity model was in the numerator, since the population of the state shipping agricultural products to New England could not be considered an attractive force. Shipments to New England could be expected to vary with the size of the agricultural surplus of that state, however. To some extent this surplus may be represented by total rail shipments out of that state. The attractive force was therefore the size of the rail surplus from the originating state multiplied by the New England population. Smith also weighted the rail surplus figures according to their percentages of New England's actual imports, and he used a simple linear distance figure with an exponent of 1. The result was a high R^2 of .92, even though the model consistently overestimated the shipments from nearby states, presumably because the agricultural flow data did not include truck shipments. William R. Black, using a formula similar to Smith's, obtained strong correlation for a variety of commodity groups (R^2 greater than .90).[10] Using a trial-and-error (iterative) method for obtaining the distance exponent that provided the best fit, he obtained very high exponents for stone, clay, and glass products (5.3), canned and frozen foods (2.8), and meat and dairy products; low exponents for industrial machinery (.25), petroleum and coal products (.27), electrical products (.37), and

[8] The term in the study was actually $e^{-.47}$ (Cij/Yij)

[9] Robert H. T. Smith, "Toward a Measure of Complementarity," *Economic Geography*, 40 (1964), 1–8. A more comprehensive survey, including methods discussed in later chapters, is Robert H. T. Smith, "Concepts and Methods in Commodity Flow Analysis," *Economic Geography*, 46, No. 2 (1970), supplement.

[10] William R. Black, "The Utility of the Gravity Model and Estimates of its Parameters in Commodity Flow Studies," *Proceedings* of the Association of American Geographers, 3 (1971), 28–32. The model used was a variation on the gravity model similar to that used by Huff and described below, p. 193. The data included truck as well as rail traffic for commodities moving between major regions.

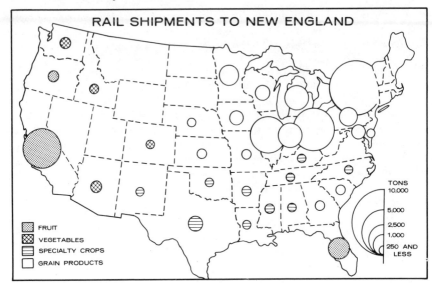

Fig. 3.6.   Rail Shipments to New England. The map shows agricultural commodity shipments by rail to New England in 1959. The general decline in circle-size with distance indicates that a distance effect exists. The somewhat larger circles in certain important agricultural states (fruit in Florida and California, grain in Illinois) indicate that agricultural production has some effect on traffic. From Robert H. T. Smith, "Toward a Measure of Complementarity," Economic Geography, 40 (1964), 1–8.

communication products (.42). From these results it seemed that the expected inverse relation between the distance exponent and value per unit of weight did obtain. Commodities for which distance had a weak effect usually had a high value per unit of weight. Closer examination of results for a number of commodities led Black to conclude, however, that patterns of regional specialization have a greater effect on distance exponents than value does. The production of a highly specialized commodity was usually concentrated in relatively few regions and registered low exponents, indicating that distance had little effect on the volume of shipment. Other relatively widespread commodities had high exponents of distance.

In studies of international trade, demand equations of the gravity type have been used by geographers and economists to describe total movements of goods between countries. For such aggregative flows, gross national product and distance gave the best estimates (R^2 approximately .60).[11] Examination of residuals indicated that trade preference group-

[11] James E. McConnell, "An Analysis of International Trade Networks: The Examples of EFTA and LAFTA" (Ph.D. diss., Ohio State University, 1969). Studies by economists include Hans Linnemann, *An Econometric Study of International Trade Flows*, Contributions to Economic Analysis, No. 42 (Amsterdam: North Holland Publishing Co., 1966); Jan Tinbergen, *Shaping the World Economy* (New York: The Twentieth Century Fund, 1962).

ings, such as the European Economic Community and the European Free Trade Association, also had a significant effect on the overall magnitude of trade between nations.

CONSUMER MOVEMENT. Gravity-model variations have long been applied to general intraurban traffic flow as well as to such specific components of flow as the journey to work and consumer travel. In the case of consumer travel, efforts have been made to place the gravity model into a more probabilistic context. Gauthier and Brush estimated shopping trips for a particular good or service (k) to a given destination area (j) by assuming that the probability of such a trip from a given origin area (i) was directly proportional to the number of establishments in j offering that good or service (e_{jk}) and inversely proportional to the distance between origin and destination (d_{ij}).[12] The probability of a trip from i to j for good k could thus be expressed: $P_{ijk} = e_{jk}/d_{ij}$. The expected number of trips from i to j for good k (T_{ijk}) could then be obtained by prorating the total trips to all destination areas ($j = 1 \ldots m$) for good k ($\sum_{j=1}^{m} T_{jk}$) by the probability function, or

$$T_{ijk} = P_{ijk} \left(\sum_{j=1}^{m} T_{jk} \right)$$

An application of this to suburban Philadelphia showed a close resemblance between expected and actual trips, except in those cases involving less frequently purchased goods where competing supply areas presumably existed outside the study region.

Another sort of probabilistic formulation was suggested by Huff in which he expresses the probability of a consumer going from origin i to destination j as follows:[13]

$$P(C_{ij}) = \frac{S_j/d^{\alpha}_{ij}}{\sum_{j=1}^{m} (S_j/d^{\alpha}_{ij})}$$

S_j in this case represents the size of the shopping center (floor space devoted to retail sales). This formulation simply expresses the interaction expected between i and j (I_{ij}) as a portion of the total expected interaction ($\sum I_{ij}$) between i and all m destination areas j, or ($I_{ij}/\sum_{j=1}^{m} I_{ij}$). This proportion may be expressed as a set of contours decreasing regularly in value with distance from an individual shopping center.

[12] John E. Brush and Howard L. Gauthier, Jr., *Service Centers and Consumer Trips: Studies on the Philadelphia Metropolitan Fringe,* University of Chicago Department of Geography Research Paper No. 113 (1968), 115–72.

[13] David L. Huff, "A Probabilistic Analysis of Shopping Center Trade Areas," *Land Economics,* 39, No. 1 (February 1963), 80–90.

Fig. 3.7.   *Phone-Call Hinterland of Chicago. The line encloses the area of posi-tive residuals from a regression equation that related actual Chicago telephone calls to gravity-model expectations. Within this area there were more Chicago phone calls than would be expected from the average relationship between phone calls, on the one hand, and population and distance on the other. After Walter Schroeder, unpublished master's thesis, "The Telephone Hinterland of Metropolitan Chicago," University of Chicago, 1958.*

The Gravity Model and Hinterland Analysis

The gravity model and its variations have been used to delimit some of the types of hinterlands, hinterland systems, and hierarchies discussed in Chapter 1. Figure 3.7 is one example of a study of the hinterland of a single city without reference to the competitive hinterlands of other cities. The map shows the residuals from a regression equation that related actual Chicago telephone calls to gravity-model expectations. The high concentration of positive residuals immediately west of the city indicates more phone calls than would be expected from population and distance. This is in contrast to the zone immediately east of the city, where there are fewer phone calls than expected.

One of the most common uses of the gravity model has been to delimit expected influence divides between two competing centers. This would call for a different form of the basic equation. In the equation $P_i/d_{xi}^2 = P_j/d_{xj}^2$, the point x would be on the dividing line, the line of equal influence from P_i and P_j. The expected distance of the divide be-tween the two centers may be expressed as

$$d_{xj} = \frac{d_{ij}}{1 + \sqrt{P_i/P_j}}.$$

This equation, developed many years ago by W. J. Reilly, has been widely applied and modified in marketing studies.[14] The term Reilly's Law has been used to describe gravity models in general, but particularly when they have been used to delimit trade areas of cities and towns or of shopping centers within cities. Diagrams of the idea of influence divides were shown in connection with the development of a set of hinterland systems in Chapter 1. The rate at which influence falls off with distance may now be seen to be analogous to the exponent of distance. With a high exponent of distance, the friction of distance is great and the line falls off more rapidly, resulting in a relatively large number of small hinterlands.

Figure 3.8 represents a set of hinterlands constructed by applying a modified gravity model to expected interaction between 100 large U.S. metropolitan areas. A distance exponent of 2 was used, and the model was modified by including a traffic shadow effect, whereby cities within 120 miles of a major center are excluded from that center's theoretical hinterland. For each city (i) the $P_i P_j / (d_{ij})^2$ figure was calculated for each of the other j cities on the map, and city i was assigned to ("dominated by") that city j with which it had the highest gravity-model figure—unless that city j was within 120 miles of city i. If we were to consider Figure 3.9 a map of expected air-passenger dominance and if we compared it with Figure 3.9, the actual air-traffic dominance in 1962, there is a rough, general correspondence between the two. New York and Los Angeles–San Francisco have large dominance areas on both maps, with other areas dominated by Chicago, Dallas–Houston, and Seattle–Portland. There are many significant differences, however, indicating instances in which a simplistic gravity-formulation fails to provide an accurate description of the hinterland structure formed by air-passenger flows among major U.S. cities. For example, it understates the importance of New York to the cities of the American Manufacturing Belt. According to expectations, New York's hinterland would extend only to Pittsburgh. Chicago's hinterland would include Dayton and Cincinnati, and between Chicago and New York would be a zone dominated by Detroit and Cleveland. In actual air passenger dominance (Fig. 3.9), New York's attraction wipes out the intermediate Detroit–Cleveland zone and extends into Chicago's expected zone to dominate Cincinnati. Thus the model has overestimated the effect of distance. Between New York and certain Southern cities the effects of distance are underestimated. Charleston, Savannah, and Jacksonville are dominated by Atlanta and are not dominated directly by New York as might be expected simply from their population and their distance from New York. Thus the historical ties that have created strong linkages between New York and the other large cities of the Manufacturing Belt, but weak linkages between New York and many Southern cities, are too complex to be completely described by the model. It is clear, however, that the overall pattern of air-passenger

[14] W. J. Reilly, *Methods for the Study of Retail Relationships*, University of Texas Bulletin, No. 2944 (November 1929), as quoted in David L. Huff, "A Probabilistic Analysis of Shopping Center Trade Areas," *Land Economics*, 39, No. 1 (February 1963), 82.

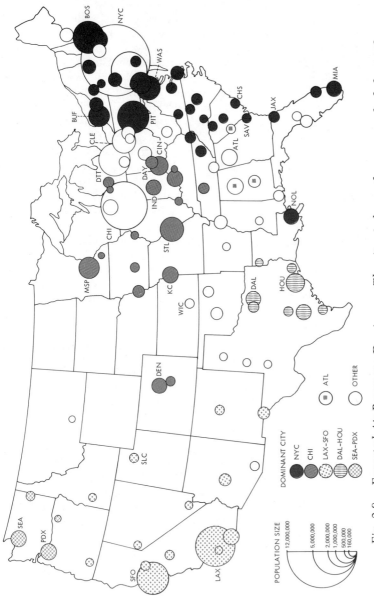

Fig. 3.8. Expected Air-Passenger Dominance. The city circles on the map are shaded according to the city that should be dominant using a modified gravity model in which a distance exponent 2 was used and all cities within 120 miles of each other were excluded from the calculations. After Edward J. Taaffe, "The Urban Hierarchy: An Air-Passenger Definition," Economic Geography, 38, (1962), 5, or Edward J. Taaffe and Leslie J. King, "Networks of Cities," Unit 3 in Limited School Trials, High School Geography Project, Association of American Geographers (1966), p. 77.

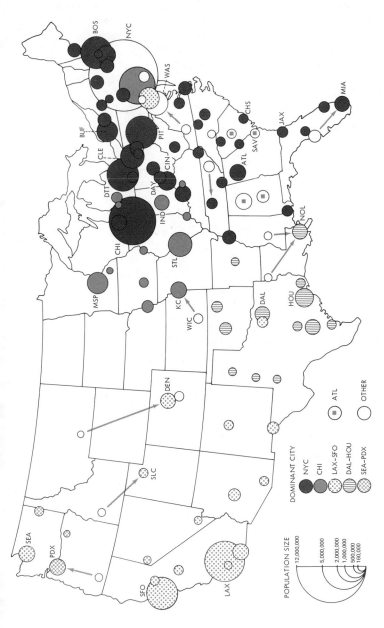

Fig. 3.9. *Air-Passenger Dominance: 1962. This map of actual air passengers shows a general similarity to the gravity-model map. There are also several important differences, however. New York is considerably more dominant in the Manufacturing Belt than one would anticipate from the gravity model. In the South, New York is considerably less dominant than expected.*

flows between major metropolitan areas is set in a general context of population and proximity.

When applied to more general hinterland systems involving large and small cities, sensitivity to the distance exponent seems to be less and the relation between actual and expected hinterland systems seem closer. Sven Illeris constructed a series of hypothetical hinterlands for Danish cities using gravity-model formulations with distance exponents ranging from 3.0 to 1.5.[15] Although some smaller centers did decline in importance with a lowering of the distance exponent, the overall hinterland systems were not strikingly different. In addition, the correspondence with an actual map based on travel, phone calls, and shopping, was reasonably close. A large percentage of the cities fell within the same hinterlands on both the theoretical and actual maps.

Huff's probability contours for consumer travel are particularly well-adapted to hinterland delimitation.[16] When overlapping probability contours from competing shopping centers are mapped, any household may be assigned to the center with the highest probability figure. The Huff contours could also be used as a basis for prorating trips from a given residential area to different centers, according to the relative strength of their probability fields in that area.

The Gravity Model and Potential Maps

Another widely used form of the gravity model is in the construction of potential maps. This consists of summing for center i all the possible gravity-model interactions to n other j centers. The potential $(_iV)$ from i to n other centers may be written as:

$$_iV = \sum_{j=1}^{n} \frac{P_iP_j}{d_{ij}}.$$

Each center on the map is treated in turn as center i, and the sum of all possible gravity-model interactions is computed for that center. Cities located close to other large cities will tend to have large sums of all potential interactions; cities far from large cities will have small potential figures. When sums are recorded for every city, a potential map may be constructed by drawing a series of contour lines of equal potential.

Figure 3.10 shows a market potential map of the U.S. constructed by Harris and based on a modified gravity model.[17] Harris used retail

[15] Sven Illeris, "Functionelle Regionen in Danmark, Omkring, 1960," *Geografisk Tijdskrift*, 66 (1967), 225–51.

[16] David L. Huff, "A Probabilistic Analysis of Shopping Center Trade Areas," *Land Economics*, 39, No. 1 (February 1963), 80–90.

[17] Some of the initial works on potential maps are Chauncy D. Harris, "The Market as a Factor in the Localization of Industry in the U.S.," *Annals*, The Association of American Geographers, 44, No. 4 (December 1954), 315–48; John Q. Stewart and William Warntz, "Macrogeography and Social Science," *Geographical Review*, 48, No. 2 (April 1958), 167–84. William Warntz has developed a number of models that are interesting and complex variations on this basic theme.

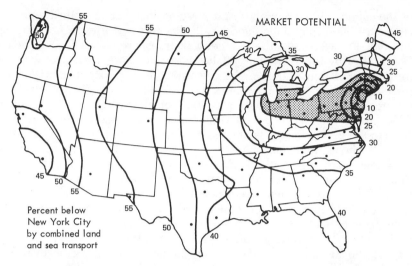

Fig. 3.10. Market Potential. The contours on this map represent lines of equal market potential. County retail sales are used as an attractive force and distance is expressed in the form of a generalized estimate of transport rates. The highest market potential is at New York City, and contour lines are based on percentages less than New York City. The shaded area is less than 20 per cent below New York in market potential. From Chauncy D. Harris, "The Market as a Factor in the Localization of Industry in the U.S.," Annals of the Association of American Geographers, 44, No. 4 (December 1954), 315–48.

sales by county as his attractive force (M) and a generalized estimate of transport rates by different modes of transport as his impeding force (d). For each city on the map he simply calculated the (M/d) figure for reaching every county in the U.S. and recorded this $\Sigma(M/d)$ as the market potential for that city. The resultant map showed New York City to have the highest market potential, and contour lines were drawn on the basis of the percentage below New York City. The resulting market-potential maps provide one type of measure of accessibility. Each city is evaluated in terms of its proximity to the *total* market of the United States as represented by retail sales. For example, we might have two counties with exactly the same retail sales. If one county were located in a rural part of Idaho, however, and the other in a rural part of Ohio, the Ohio county would have a higher market potential, reflecting its more advantageous location with respect to the entire national market. The market potential map would be a better guide to such things as land values and density of transportation network within the counties than would the retail sales map, all other things being equal.

Figure 3.10 shows that the American Manufacturing Belt, particularly the Eastern Seaboard cities, represents the most accessible part of the country according to Harris' formulation. Accessibility declines both to the west and the south of the shaded zone. The least accessible part of the country is the mountain states region, because of both the greater concentration of population and retail sales in such cities as Los Angeles and San Francisco and the reduction in transport costs afforded Pacific Coast cities by the availability of low-cost sea transport. Harris went on to apply similar methods to the construction of market potential maps for different types of commodities and for different regions. Cleveland, for example, had the highest potential for the manufacturing market; Chicago had the highest potential for the Midwest market. Further variations in the gravity model as the basis for any sort of potential map could of course be as numerous as the examples cited in the transport demand equations. Variations could be in the form of different measures of attraction (mass) and in different measures of impedance, whether in the form of distance exponents, transport costs, or specific barriers.

It should also be noted that the potential map may be used as an optimizing type of model. If someone wishes to maximize his accessibility to the U.S. market and is willing to accept retail trade and Harris' formulation of the distance effect as the key factors determining accessibility, Figure 3.11 shows him the areas in which such accessibility is greatest. He could use the same values to minimize transport costs, as Harris did in his study. Here the map is based on total retail sales in each county multiplied by the transport cost to that county. Thus the contour lines represented total transport costs of reaching the entire national market from city i if one assumes that total sales from city i in each county are directly proportional to the retail sales. In this instance the Eastern Seaboard cities were the minimum transport-cost locations and the mountain states were the maximum cost locations.

Ullman's Triad

An important step in the development of the geographic study of transportation came in the 1950s when Edward Ullman summarized some of the work on the gravity model and its variations into three useful concepts, each addressed to the question of why linkages and flows between some centers are stronger than those between other centers. The concepts are transferability, complementarity, and intervening opportunity.[18]

Transferability may be considered a more generalized way of expressing the gravity model. The greater the mass, be it population or income, the greater the flow; the greater the distance, the smaller the flow. All of the discussion thus far in this chapter may be considered as related to the basic attracting and impeding forces that affect the transferability of goods and people.

The idea of complementarity is closely related to the process of regional specialization in Chapter 2. As one region moves toward a greater

---

[18] Edward L. Ullman, "The Role of Transportation and the Bases for Interaction," *Man's Role in Changing the Face of the Earth,* ed. William L. Thomas, Jr. et al. (Chicago: The University of Chicago Press, 1956), 867–71.

concentration on corn and a lesser concentration on sugar beets, and the other region moves in an opposite fashion, they develop complementary patterns of production. Thus interaction between any two centers with a high degree of complementarity would be greater than ordinary gravity-model expectations. If we were simply to express complementarity as a coefficient (β), the gravity-model statement would be:

$$I_{ij} = k\beta \, \frac{P_i P_j}{d_{ij}{}^\propto}$$

The effect of intervening opportunity, on the other hand, is to reduce the interaction between any two centers below the gravity-model expectations. A gravity model based on population and distance will give the same predicted interaction between city i and city j whether or not there is a city k between them. City k, however, represents an opportunity for interaction from both city i and city j. Therefore, the presence of city k is an intervening opportunity and should reduce the probability of interaction between i and j. If we assume that this relationship is similar to the distance relationship and if we express intervening opportunity as O_{ij}, the Ullman version of the gravity model might therefore be expressed as

$$I_{ij} = k\beta \, \frac{P_i P_j}{O_{ij} \, (d_{ij}) \propto}$$

Complementarity

The idea of complementarity, although of obvious importance as a determinant of commodity flows between centers, has been a difficult one to express precisely. One attempt at developing a measure for complementarity within the context of the gravity model was made by Robert H. T. Smith in the study of the flow of agricultural commodities by rail to the six New England states referred to earlier.[19] The expected flow values based on the regression equation were compared with actual traffic. The discrepancies were interpreted as high or low complementarity (Fig. 3.11). The shading in the states is based on this type of residual analysis. The dark shading represents high complementarity. Illinois and California, for example, both ship approximately ten times the expected tonnage of agricultural goods, so their production patterns may be interpreted as strongly complementary to those of New England.

The concept of complementarity is an elusive one, however. For example, the low values associated with New York and Pennsylvania in Figure 3.11 may be associated just as much with the absence of informa-

[19] Robert H. T. Smith, "Toward a Measure of Complementarity," *Economic Geography*, 40 (1964), 1–8.

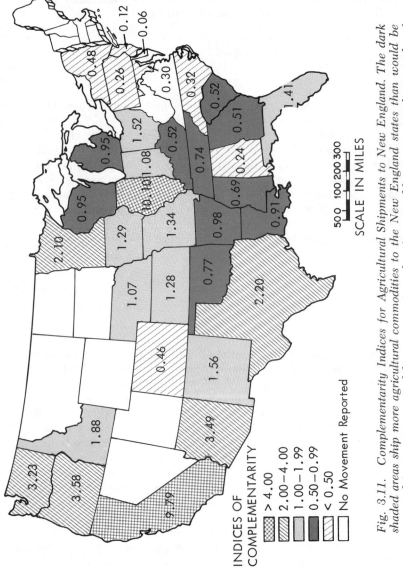

Fig. 3.11. Complementarity Indices for Agricultural Shipments to New England. The dark shaded areas ship more agricultural commodities to the New England states than would be expected from a gravity-model regression. It is therefore possible to interpret the agricultural production patterns of such states as Illinois and California as complementary to that of the New England states. From Robert H. T. Smith, "Toward a Measure of Complementarity," Economic Geography 40 (1964), 1–8.

INDICES OF
COMPLEMENTARITY

> 4.00
2.00–4.00
1.00–1.99
0.50–0.99
< 0.50
No Movement Reported

50 0   100 200 300
SCALE IN MILES

tion on truck shipments as with low complementarity of production. The level of aggregation of commodity groups represents another problem. Empirical studies of international trade flows by geographers and economists have indicated that trade between raw-material counties and industrial countries is usually less intensive than that between industrial countries themselves. As the trade between these industrial countries is disaggregated and examined more closely, however, it is evident that there are consistent differences in the types of manufactured goods exported by the countries broadly classified as industrial, again suggesting the importance of complementarity. It is still quite difficult to determine the level of commodity aggregation at which complementarity becomes evident. In some cases, for example, a trade-generating complementarity might exist between automobile production in one country and the manufacturing of electrical machinery in another. In other cases both countries may specialize in electrical machinery but still have a high degree of complementarity and carry on intensive trade if one is more efficient in electronic instruments and the other in heavy electrical equipment.

A further complication lies in the relationship of the complementarity of production between any two areas to the different supply-demand relationships between the two areas, which gives rise to price differentials in excess of transport costs. In an empirical investigation this would call for the inclusion of price ratios as independent variables. In a time-series study of international trade, for example, changes through time in imports were seen to be related to changes in the ratio between import price indexes and domestic wholesale price indexes.[20] The farther prices of imported goods fall below domestic wholesale prices, the greater the tendency for imports to increase, and conversely. Complementarity is still far from being a precise and operationally definable concept, however. Problems of commodity aggregation remain, as do problems of gathering enough comparable data to warrant comparative studies of different countries through time in order to detect sensitivity to changing price ratios.

Intervening Opportunity

Intervening opportunity is another difficult concept to express precisely. It was first formulated by Stouffer in connection with intraurban migration.[21] Stouffer reasoned that the number of migrants from any point within the city to a zone at the periphery of the city was directly related to the number of opportunities or vacancies in that zone and inversely related to the number of opportunities between the originating point within the city and the zone at the periphery.

One approach to the study of intervening opportunity is represented in a study by Herman Porter in which he postulated several definitions

[20] H. S. Houthakker and Stephen P. Magee, "Income and Price Elasticities in World Trade," *Review of Economics and Statistics,* 51 (May 1969), 111–25.

[21] Samuel A. Stouffer, "Intervening Opportunities: A Theory Relating Mobility to Distances," *American Sociological Review,* 5 (1940), 845–07.

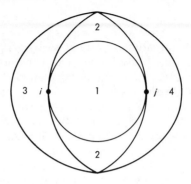

*Fig. 3.12.   Intervening Opportunity Fields. This diagram represents some varia-
tions on the basic theme of intervening opportunity. Field 1, between the origin
center* (i) *and the destination city* (j), *is an area of intervening opportunity.
Population in fields 2 and 3, however, diverts some interaction from* i *which
otherwise would have gone to* j. *From Herman Porter, Application of Intercity,
Intervening Opportunity Models to Telephone, Migration and Highway Traffic
Data, Northwestern University Department of Geography Ph.D. dissertation
(1964).*

of the concept and subjected them to a series of empirical tests.[22] Porter
first attempted to define the areas in which intervening opportunity or
something analogous to it might exist. Figure 3.12 shows some of the areas
considered. Field 1, a circle drawn with d_{ij} as its diameter, intuitively
seems to be the most likely area in which the existence of cities would
reduce the expected interaction from i to j. Porter also postulated that the
other areas in the diagram could affect interaction. The denser the
population in field 3, for example, the more likely it is that possible
interaction from i would be diverted from j to some of the centers in
field 3. In cases of commodity flow or migration from i to j, field 4 could
be regarded as an area of competing supply or competing migration to
center j, which would reduce the opportunities at j for commodity shipment or migration from i.

Phone calls between a group of Nebraska cities were used to test the
effects of the population in each of the four types of fields on phone-call
interaction. Using a multiple regression with variables transformed into
logarithms, he found that the populations of fields 1, 2, and 3 all had a
significant negative effect on phone calls between two centers. The effect
of field 1 was consistently stronger than the others. When the population
of these three areas was grouped and included as a single variable, the
r^2 from a gravity-model formulation improved from 83 to 92 percent.
Although the overall improvement in correlation over the gravity model

[22] Herman Porter, "Application of Intercity, Intervening Opportunity Models to
Telephone, Migration and Highway Traffic Data," Northwestern University Department of Geography Ph.D. dissertation (1964).

was not striking, the changes in the residuals map were quite revealing. The negative residuals from a gravity-model regression were all concentrated in the eastern part of the state near Omaha, while the positive residuals were in the west. Since the gravity-model regression considers only the population of cities i and j, it takes no account of the presence of Omaha, even though Omaha could be expected to divert phone calls for the cities in the eastern part of the state. The intervening-opportunity model accounts for Omaha, which falls into field 3 for many of the city pairs. The residuals from the regression, including an intervening-opportunity variable, showed no consistent concentration in either the eastern or western part of the state.

Intervening opportunity also remains a puzzling concept. When Porter attempted to apply the model to Nebraska highway flow, the results were quite different. Contrary to expectations, field 1, the zone between the two cities, proved to be insignificant. Instead, the significant intervening opportunities are to be found in a "hollow ellipse" surrounding cities i and j (fields 2, 3, and 4). When the population of field 1 was redefined to include only those cities with a population greater than P_j, however, the intervening opportunities in field 1 did exert a significant negative influence on highway traffic, indicating that only the presence of *large* cities between i and j reduces interactions. In all the formulations, however, some confusion existed about the degree to which field 1 was simply another way of transmitting the effects of d_{ij}. The greater the distance between i and j, the greater the population of field 1.

Weaknesses of the Gravity Model

In its relatively literal form, the weaknesses of the gravity model are abundant.[23] These weaknesses are largely related to its failure to provide plausible explanations for spatial behavior, although empirical tests often show that the model has a surprisingly close fit to actual flow patterns. The meaning of these fits is by no means clear, however. As discussed earlier, the population product does seem to bear a logical relationship to the probabilities of expected interaction between any two points. But even the meaning of this term becomes less clear when it is raised to some empirically derived power, as in the case of the log-transformed

[23] Some of these weaknesses are discussed in Walter Isard et al., *Methods of Regional Analysis: An Introduction to Regional Science*, The Technology Press of the Massachusetts Institute of Technology, and (New York: John Wiley & Sons, 1960), in Chapter 11, "Gravity Potential, and Spatial Interaction Models," 493–568. Other critical discussions include Gunnar Olsson, *Distance and Human Interaction, A Review and Bibliography*, Regional Science Research Institute, Bibliography Series No. 2 (Philadelphia: 1965); Gunnar Olsson, "Explanation, Prediction and Meaning Variance: An Assessment of Distance Interaction Models," *Economic Geography*, 46. No. 2, Supplement, Proceedings International Geographical Union Commission on Quantitative Methods (June 1970); I. G. Heggie, "Are Gravity and Interactance Models a Valid Technique for Planning Regional Transport Facilities?," *Operational Research Quarterly*, 20, No. 1 (1969), 93–110.

regressions. The meaning of the distance term is even more puzzling. There is usually no theoretical basis for saying that one should divide by distance or that it should have an exponent of 1 or 2. In the cases of empirically derived "best-fit" exponents, the meaning of a particular value for a distance exponent is not always clear, nor is it always possible to make meaningful comparisons of distance exponents for flow patterns of differing magnitudes. There are also cases where a discontinuous distance function provides a better description of distance effects.

When gravity types of formulations are broadened and conceived of as formulations that relate interaction between two centers as a set of positive attractive forces and a set of negative impedance forces (including distance in some form), they do have descriptive value. Gravity models in the form of such expanded demand equations can be fitted with appropriate weights to most traffic flows. Such equations, although useful in identifying forces affecting traffic, do not by any means constitute a consistent theory of traffic flow, since there is seldom a clear behavioral basis for the weights used or the functions fitted. Also, the equations are usually cross-sectional in nature (based on data for a single point in time), and are therefore of limited predictive utility.[24] A change in transport costs (a reduction in the friction of distance) will not necessarily have the impact on traffic that one would expect from a given equation since the equation was based on cross-sectional comparisons among linkages between cities of different sizes and distances apart. Equations based on previous effects of changes in the friction of distance on traffic over the same route through time would provide a better predictive base, but they would introduce difficulties in separating distance effects from nationwide trends in traffic. For example, a nationwide increase in traffic over the same time period might cause traffic to increase over a single route, which could then be erroneously attributed to the effects of lowered transport costs over that route.

Since the earlier formulations, a number of more efficient methods have evolved for study of some of the questions treated initially with gravity-model variations. The next few chapters, for example, discuss more versatile measures than a potential map both for study of accessibility in a network and for identifying minimum transport costs.

Summary

The gravity model provides a simplified initial description of the patterns of flows and the linkages between. The basic model

$$I_{ij} = k \frac{P_i P_j}{d_{ij}{}^\alpha}$$

assumes that flow between centers i and j is directly proportional to the product of their populations and inversely proportional to the distance

[24] Heggie, "Gravity and Interactance Models," 93–110.

between them (d_{ij}^{∞}). Variations on this model have been applied to inter-city travel and commodity flow, to the identification of influence divides, hinterlands, and systems of hinterlands, and to the measurement of certain types of accessibility in the form of potential.

The addition of ideas of complementarity (β) and intervening opportunity (O_{ij}) to the basic model could be approximately expressed as

$$I_{ij} = k\,\mathring{\beta}\,\frac{P_i P_j}{O_{ij}\,(d_{ij})^{\infty}}$$

Further empirical work expanded the model into sets of demand equations that were based on more complex attractive forces as well as impedance forces. Although these equations, and even simpler versions of the gravity model, have descriptive utility and are widely used in predicting traffic, their theoretical meaning is not clear.

4

structural analysis of transport networks: aggregate measures

In the preceding chapters we have seen that the description and analysis of network structure has been a traditional concern of geographers. Among the methods employed in the description of networks have been the preparation of maps and tables listing distances, capacities, flows, and such indices as network densities and isochrones. During the past several years a more consistent set of summarizing measures of network characteristics has been developed in order to provide a better basis for the comparison and evaluation of networks. These efforts have drawn heavily on the concepts of graph theory to describe the topological structure of networks.

The Network as a Graph

A major difficulty in describing and analyzing the properties of a network is the complexity of the task. In reality, networks are highly complex spatial systems. Only by a substantial simplification of their reality are we able to study some of their characteristics. In order to apply graph theory to the analysis of a transportation network it is necessary to idealize the network into the form of a graph. This requires that some information about the network be deliberately discarded. Transportation linkages are identifiable in terms of such characteristics as capacity, type of use, and cost of construction, but some of these characteristics which are important in the analysis of a transportation network, do not lend themselves readily to analysis by graph theory. For this reason it is important that a word of caution precede any attempt to describe a network in graph-theoretic terms. In idealizing any network as a graph, we are treating only the topological properties of the transportation system, not the whole range of properties that are identifiable with any given network.

As a branch of topology, graph theory deals with abstract configurations consisting of points and lines. As such, it makes no direct reference to the real world; nevertheless, graph theory has a potential usefulness in empirical analysis. It can provide some measures of the structural properties of a real-world system if that system is idealized as a set of points (vertices) connected by a set of line segments (edges).

At the highest level of abstraction, transportation networks can be represented by a series of vertices (representing nodes on a network) and a set of edges (representing network linkages), together with a relationship of incidence that associates each edge with two vertices.[1] When so defined, the network is a minimal one in terms of its information content—we know only the presence or absence of connections between nodes. Measures of the spatial properties of such a network are structural and deal with the geometrical pattern of the network. Two types of measurements can be constructed: (1) a single number describing the aggregate geometrical pattern of the network, or (2) a vector of numbers that measures the relationship of the individual elements (vertices or edges) of the network to the entire network.[2] Only the first, the aggregate type of measurement, will be considered in this chapter. Measures of the accessibility of individual nodes to the network will be considered in Chapter 5.

Connectivity

When a network is abstracted as a set of edges (linkages) that are related to a set of vertices (nodes), a fundamental question is the degree to which all pairs of vertices are interconnected. The degree of connection between all vertices is defined as the connectivity of the network. It is probably the most important structural property of the network.

Although we may measure the degree of connection between the vertices of a given network at a given point in time, the concept of connectivity is most meaningful when a given network is either (1) compared with other networks or (2) its growth is viewed through time. Since the expansion or intensification of transport linkages between nodes is directly related to increases in demand for transportation facilities to move goods and people, the degree of connectivity of a transport network is indicative of the complexity of the spatial order that it imposes on the region it serves.

Let us consider the two networks in Figure 4.1. In both cases our information about the networks is minimal. Each has a set of thirteen nodes, and each of the nodes in the set is connected to at least one other node. Because there are no nodes isolated from the network, both networks can be defined as connected graphs.

[1] Technically the terms *vertices* and *edges* are used to refer to abstract networks, whereas the terms *node* and *linkage* refer to a real-world network before it is abstracted. This distinction is difficult to follow in practice. *Vertices* and *nodes*, and *edges* and *linkages*, will be used interchangeably in this chapter.

[2] For an excellent introduction to graph theory, see R. Busacher and T. Saaty, *Finite Graphs and Networks* (New York: McGraw-Hill, 1965). For a general review of the applications of graph theory to network problems in geography, see R. Chorley and P. Haggett, eds., *Models in Geography* (London: Methuen and Co., 1967), Chapter 15.

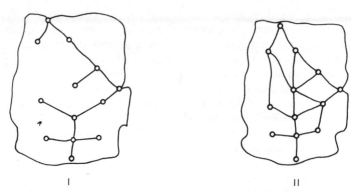

Fig. 4.1.   Networks as Graphs. Two hypothetical networks are abstracted as graphs. The amount of information known is minimal. Given only the node-linkage associations of both networks, several primitive measures of connectivity can be derived.

In the first network the twelve edges are incident to the thirteen nodes in such a fashion that there is one, and only one, sequence of edges between any two pairs of nodes. The network is minimally connected. In a minimally connected network the number of edges will always be one less than the number of vertices, or nodes: $e_{min} = (v - 1) = (13 - 1) = 12$. The removal of any edge from the graph will divide the network into two disconnected parts.

The second network has eighteen edges incident to the set of thirteen nodes in such a fashion that most of the nodes are connected to more than one other node. Obviously this network is more structurally complex than the first; it is more than minimally connected. Between most pairs of nodes there exists more than one sequence of edges. When this condition exists, the removal of one edge will not disconnect the network.

To compare the structural complexity of two or more networks, we need measurements that permit us to describe the degree of network connectivity. Graph theory provides a number of such simple, yet discriminating, measures. Two of the most commonly employed graph-theoretic measurements of connectivity are the gamma and alpha indices.

THE GAMMA INDEX.   The gamma index is simply the ratio of the number of edges in a network to the maximum number possible in that network:

$$\gamma = \frac{\text{actual edges}}{\text{maximum edges}} = \frac{e}{e \text{ max}}$$

The actual edges or linkages in Figure 4.1 may be readily ascertained by counting. There are twelve edges in the first network (A) and eighteen edges in the second network (B). The maximum number of edges possible (e_{max}) may be computed from the number of vertices or nodes in the

Vertices	Maximum Number of Edges	Diagramatic Representation
3	3	
4	6	
5	9	
6	12	
7	15	

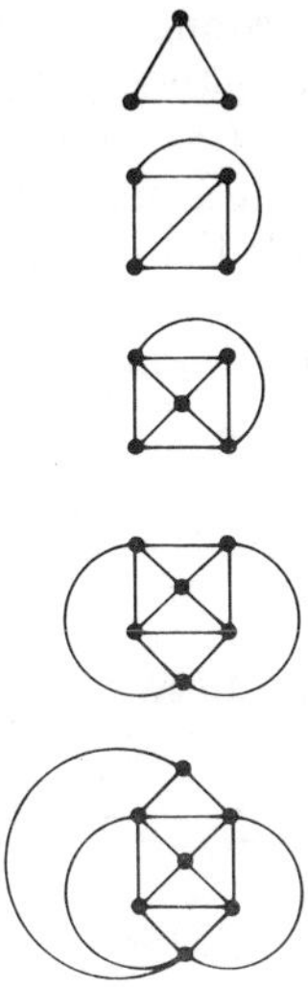

Fig. 4.2. Maximal Connectivity. The relationship between the number of nodes (v) *and the maximum number of linkages* (e) *in a planar graph is always* e = 3(v − 2). *The inclusion of one additional node to a network of more than 2 nodes increases the number of possible linkages by a value of 3. There is no intersection of linkages except at a node.*

system. Assuming a network is abstracted as a planar graph, the addition of each vertex to the system increases the maximum number of edges by three.[3] This progression is true for any planar network of more than two vertices, as shown in Figure 4.2. As the number of vertices is increased from three to four, the maximum number of edges possible increases from six to nine. Since the graph is planar, the new edges cannot intersect without creating a new vertex—as would be true of a highway system, for example. Thus it is possible to express e_{max} as $3(v − 2)$, and the equation for the gamma index becomes:

$$\gamma = \frac{e}{e_{max}} = \frac{e}{3(v − 2)}$$

[3] By definition, a planar graph is one in which no edges (arcs) intersect except at vertices (nodes). A planar graph configuration is typical of the networks of surface modes of transport. The distinction between planar and nonplanar representations is critical in determining aggregate measures of structure. For a nonplanar graph, the gamma index is $\gamma = \dfrac{e}{v(v − 1)}$ and the alpha index is $\propto = \dfrac{e − v + 1}{v(v − 1) − (v − 1)}$.

Network connectivity as measured by the gamma index is expressed in terms of a graph-theoretic range that varies from a set of nodes having no interconnections at one extreme to a set of nodes in which every node has an edge connecting it to every other node in the graph. The connectivity of the network is evaluated in terms of the degree to which the network deviates from an unconnected graph and approximates a maximally connected one. The numerical range for the gamma index is between 0 and 1. For convenience in interpretation, the numerical value may be expressed as a percentage of connectivity.

For the minimally connected network (A) in our example, the gamma index is

$$\gamma = \frac{e}{3(v-2)} = \frac{12}{33} = .36$$

In the second network (B), the ratio is

$$\gamma = \frac{e}{3(v-2)} = \frac{18}{33} = .55$$

In terms of maximal connectivity, the first network is 36 percent connected, whereas the second is 55 percent connected.

THE ALPHA INDEX.   We have defined a minimally connected network as one in which there are no isolated nodes and the number of connecting linkages is one less than the number of nodes. If one linkage is removed, the network is divided into two completely separate parts. On the other hand, if one or more linkages is *added* to the network, the connectivity is increased beyond the minimal configuration in which only a single and unique path can be identified between all pairs of nodes. Additional linkages in a network create circuitry. A *circuit* is defined as a finite, closed path in which the initial node of the linkage sequence coincides with the terminal node. In practical terms, the existence of circuitry means the establishment of additional or alternative paths between nodes in the network. The number of alternative paths is determined by the number of linkages added to a minimally connected network.

Given a finite connected network in which the number of linkages is e and the number of nodes is v, the number of linkages is equal to one less than the number of nodes ($e = v - 1$) only when the network is minimally connected. When circuits exist in the network, the number of linkages is greater than ($v - 1$), or: $e > v - 1$. The number of circuits in the network may be obtained simply by subtracting the number of linkages needed for a minimally connected network ($v - 1$) from the actual number of linkages (e). This may be expressed as: $e - (v - 1) = e - v + 1$. It is a measure of the number of independent circuits in the network.

The maximum number of independent circuits in a network is also a function of the number of nodes in the network and the number of linkages necessary for minimal connection between nodes. For a planar network, the maximum number of edges is $3(v - 2)$, thus the maximum number of circuits would be: $3(v - 2) - (v - 1) = 2v - 5$. The alpha index is a ratio measure of the number of actual circuits, given by $(e - v + 1)$, to the maximum number possible in a given network $(2v - 5)$:

$$\propto \: = \: \frac{\text{actual circuits}}{\text{maximum circuits}} = \frac{e - v + 1}{2v - 5}$$

The range of the index is from a value of 0 for a minimally connected network to a value of 1 for a maximally connected one. For convenience, the numerical value may be expressed as a percentage of circuitry in a network.

For the networks in Figure 4.1 the alpha values are

$$\propto \: = \: \frac{e - v + 1}{2v - 5} = \frac{0}{16} = 0$$

and

$$\propto \: = \: \frac{e - v + 1}{2v - 5} = \frac{6}{16} = .29$$

As expected, the simple structure of the first network has no circuitry. Because of the greater number of edges relative to those necessary for minimal connectivity in the second network, there are 6 circuits. The maximum possible is 16, so this network circuitry is 29 percent of the maximum.

Another example of an application of the simple gamma and alpha indices is provided by Figure 4.3, showing the proposed Interstate Highway System and the existing U.S. highway network as they connect large cities in Ohio. Both indices are higher for the more extensive U.S. highway network. The gamma index of the U.S. network shows it is 67 percent connected while the Interstate System is only 51 percent connected. The alpha index of the U.S. network shows that circuitry is 48 percent compared to only 24 percent on the Interstate. The greater difference in alpha indices is to be expected, since the Interstate Highway System was not designed to provide a number of alternate connections to cities within the state.

Stages in Network Growth

In addition to their usefulness in the static comparison of the structure of two or more networks, graph-theoretic indices of connectivity are useful in identifying network changes through time. For illustrative purposes, let us consider the two networks in Figure 4.1 as representing two stages in an idealized sequence of transport development similar to the

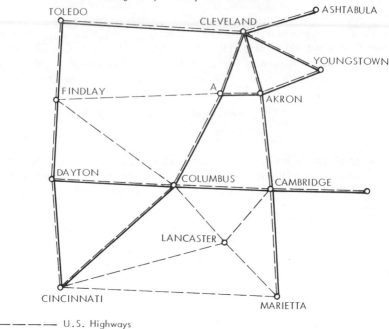

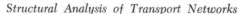

— — — — — U.S. Highways

——————— Interstate Highways

Fig. 4.3. Ohio Highways. The major U.S. highways and the Interstate Highway System in Ohio are represented as graphs. The more extensive network of U.S. highways is reflected in higher gamma and alpha indices.

ideal, typical pattern discussed in Chapter 2 (pp. 47–52). In addition to these two familiar networks, let us add a stage prior to the minimal connectivity of the first network and a stage subsequent to the second network (Fig. 4.4). Consider the following interpretation of the four-stage sequence. In stage A there are a few penetration lines leading from three ports, or gateways, to a limited number of interior centers. The penetration lines are not interconnected, and as a result many interior centers are not included on the network. As growth in the region continues, as evident in stage B, the network expands through the interconnection of the initial penetration lines and includes all of the nodes in the region. The process of nodal interconnection continues in stages C and D with an increasing intensification of feeder-line construction.

Because the number of nodes has remained constant while the number of transportation linkages has increased, the connectivity of the network has changed. To what degree has it changed? How can we identify the changing spatial structure of the network? The alpha and gamma indices can be used in seeking answers to these questions (Table 4.1). For example, applying the gamma index to the network sequence in Figure 4.3, the range in network connectivity is from a value of .15 in stage A to a value of .79 in stage D. Obviously the index

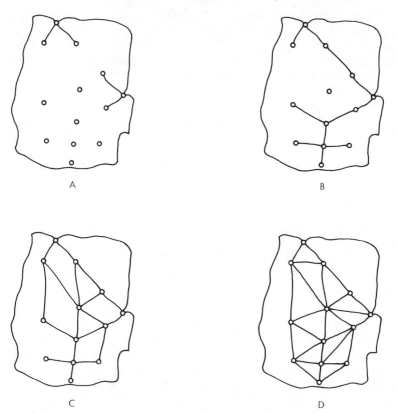

Fig. 4.4. *Stages of Transport Development. A four-stage idealized sequence of transport development is represented as a series of changing planar graphs. Aggregate measure of connectivity can be computed for each stage. The resulting values are meaningful only when considered in terms of the limit of network connectivity, as shown on pages 110–11.*

increases as the network becomes more structurally complex. The same is true of the alpha index, which ranges from 0 in stage B to .67 in stage D.

Table 4.1 **Structural Indices for an Idealized Four-State Sequence of Transportation Development**

	γ	α
Stage A	.15	–
Stage B	.36	0
Stage C	.55	.29
Stage D	.79	.67

THE THREE BASIC NETWORK CONFIGURATIONS. In examining stages of network development, it is useful to relate the numerical values of the gamma and alpha indices as shown in Table 4.1 to more specific network characteristics. A classification used by engineers consists of three basic network configurations: spinal, grid, and delta.

The spinal pattern is characteristic of a minimally connected network. Every node is connected to at least one other node on the network, and it is possible for flow to occur between any two nodes in the network, but only by a single path. Each path is unique because there exists one, and only one, sequence of linkages between any pair of nodes. As discussed earlier, the number of edges necessary for a minimally connected network is always $(v - 1)$, one less than the number of vertices in the network. Thus the gamma index $\dfrac{e}{3(v - 2)}$ will always be $\dfrac{v - 1}{3(v - 2)}$ for a minimally connected network. The alpha index $\dfrac{e - v + 1}{2v - 5}$ is zero since there are no circuits in a minimally connected network:

$$\frac{(v - 1) - v + 1}{2v - 5} = \frac{0}{2v - 5}.$$

The antithesis of the spinal network with only enough linkages for minimal connectivity is the delta network, which is characterized by a high density of linkages relative to the number of nodes. The delta configuration approximates a state of maximal connectivity, with several paths, or sequences of linkages, between pairs of nodes. As shown in Figure 4.5, the dominant geometric pattern in a delta network is triangular for each set of three nodes. Each time a node is added to a network of more than three nodes, two new linkages are required. The relationship between nodes and linkages thus will always be $2v - 3$.

Since the number of edges (e) in the delta network configuration will always be $2v - 3$, the gamma index will be

$$\gamma = \frac{e}{3(v - 2)} = \frac{2v - 3}{3(v - 2)}.$$

The alpha index $\dfrac{e - v + 1}{2v - 5}$ will always be

$$\propto = \frac{(2v - 3) - v + 1}{2v - 5} = \frac{v - 2}{2v - 5}.$$

The third type of network configuration, the grid, is simply transitional between the minimally connected spinal and the maximally connected delta types.

In order to permit classification of a given transport network into a spinal, grid, or delta configuration, precise cutoff values are required. These are provided by establishing limiting values of the gamma and alpha indices for each of the three network configurations.

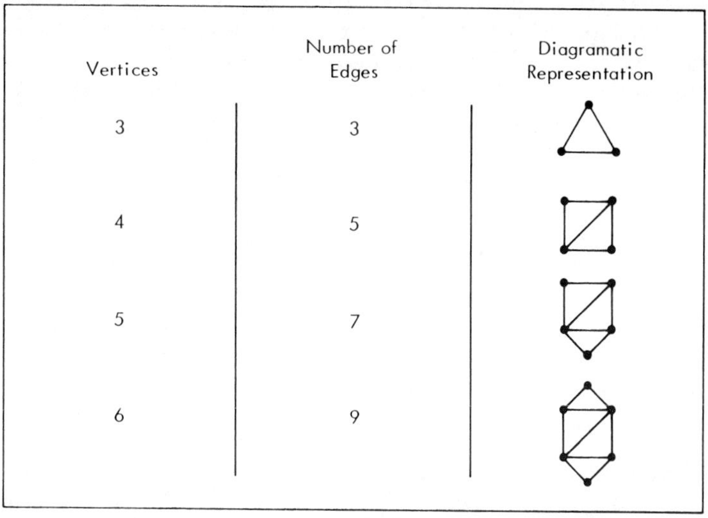

Vertices	Number of Edges	Diagramatic Representation
3	3	
4	5	
5	7	
6	9	

Fig. 4.5. Connectivity in a Delta Network. The relationship between the number of nodes (v) and the number of linkages (e) for a delta pattern of network connectivity is e = 2v − 3, when v ≥ 3. To maintain the delta pattern on the number of nodes on the network increases, two new linkages are required for each nodal addition.

INDEX LIMITS AND NETWORK CONFIGURATIONS. In identifying the spinal network, we look for the largest and smallest possible values of the gamma index for such a network. The gamma index for a spinal network configuration is

$$\gamma = \frac{v-1}{3(v-2)}.$$

This may also be expressed as

$$\gamma = \left(\frac{1}{3}\right)\left(\frac{v-1}{v-2}\right) \quad \text{or} \quad \frac{1}{3}\left[\left(\frac{v}{v-2}\right) - \left(\frac{1}{v-2}\right)\right].$$

For networks with an infinitely large number of vertices, $\frac{v}{v-2}$ will approach 1 and $\frac{1}{v-2}$ will approach zero. Therefore, the limit of the entire expression will approach 1/3 of (1 − 0), or 1/3. This may be expressed as

$$\lim_{v \to \infty} \left(\frac{1}{3}\right)\left(\frac{v-1}{v-2}\right) \quad \text{or} \quad \frac{1}{3}\left[\lim_{v \to \infty}\frac{v}{v-2} - \lim_{v \to \infty}\frac{1}{v-2}\right] = \frac{1}{3}.$$

At the lower end of the range, if the number of nodes is four, the value for the gamma index will be 1/2. For networks with a spinal configuration, the gamma index will have, therefore, a range of values between 1/3 and 1/2, i.e., $1/3 \leqslant \gamma \leqslant 1/2$.

A similar procedure may be used to establish a range for the delta network configuration, which approaches maximal connectivity. The gamma index for the delta configuration is

$$\gamma = \frac{2v - 3}{3(v - 2)} \quad \text{or} \quad \left(\frac{1}{3}\right)\left(\frac{2v - 3}{v - 2}\right).$$

For networks with an infinitely large number of vertices,

$$\frac{1}{3}\left[\lim_{v \to \infty}\frac{2v}{v - 2} - \frac{3}{v - 2}\right] = \frac{1}{3}\,(2 - 0) = \frac{2}{3}.$$

For smaller networks, when the number of nodes is three, the gamma index will be unity (1.0). The connectivity for networks having a delta configuration will range between values of $2/3$ and 1.0, i.e., $2/3 \leqslant \gamma \leqslant 1.0$.

In determining the range of values for the spinal and delta patterns of network connectivity, we have established the values for the grid configuration. Theoretically, the grid configuration is a transitional structure between the minimal connectivity of the spinal pattern and the dense linkage pattern of the delta configuration. Thus the range of values for the three classical network patterns are

Spinal:	$1/3 \leqslant \gamma \leqslant 1/2$	where	$v \geqslant 4$
Grid:	$1/2 < \gamma < 2/3$		$v \geqslant 4$
Delta:	$2/3 \leqslant \gamma \leqslant 1.0$		$v \geqslant 3$

Let us consider the example of the network series in Figure 4.4. Theoretically the range in values of the gamma index is between 0 for a set of completely isolated nodes and 1 for a completely connected network. In stage A, the network connectivity is .15 (Table 4.1). This lower level is to be expected, given the many nodes that are isolated from the penetration lines leading from the three ports. Given the fact the lowest value associated with minimal connectivity is .33, it is obvious that values below this limit will always be associated with partially connected networks such as we have in stage A.

In stage B the gamma value is .36 (Table 4.1). The network is connected, but only to a minimal degree. This is the spinal pattern of network structure—between any two nodes there exists one, and only one, path. In stage C, network connectivity has increased to .55 (Table 4.1). The addition of linkages has created alternative paths between many of the nodal pairs in the networks. However, linkage saturation has not yet been achieved. This is the transitional stage of network growth, identifiable as the grid pattern. In stage D the continued intensification of linkage construction has increased the gamma value to .79 (Table 4.1). The resulting geometrical pattern of node-linkage associations is the delta configuration.

Like the gamma index, the alpha index may be used to discriminate between the three basic configurations of network structure. By definition the spinal configuration characterizes a minimally connected network in which there are no circuits. The absence of circuits means the value of the alpha index will always be zero. The addition of linkages to the spinal network results in the creation of either the grid or delta configuration, depending on how many circuits are created. By determining the limits of the alpha index it is possible to discriminate between them. For the delta configuration, the alpha index is

$$\alpha = \frac{(2v - 3) - v + 1}{2v - 5} = \frac{v - 2}{2v - 5}.$$

For infinitely large networks,

$$\lim_{v \to \infty} \frac{v - 2}{2v - 5} = \left[\lim_{v \to \infty} \frac{v}{2v - 5} - \lim_{v \to \infty} \frac{2}{2v - 5} \right] = \frac{1}{2}.$$

For smaller networks, if the number of nodes is three, the value of the alpha index will be unity (1.0). As the grid configuration is transitional from the spinal to the delta, the alpha index ranges for the three basic configurations are

$$
\begin{array}{llll}
\text{Spinal:} & \alpha = 0 & \text{where} & v = e + 1 \\
\text{Grid:} & 0 < \alpha < .50 & & v \geqslant 3 \\
\text{Delta:} & .50 \leqslant \alpha \leqslant 1 & & v \geqslant 3
\end{array}
$$

When compared with the gamma values for these three configurations, it is apparent that the alpha offers a complementary measurement. In response to the increasingly complex spatial structure of a network, the relative increases for both indices will be the same.

The association of the two indices is evident in the network sequence of Figure 4.4. According to the gamma index, the second stage (B) of network development corresponds to the spinal configuration. This is supported by an alpha value of 0 (Table 4.1). The third stage (C) of development has been related to the transitional phase of the grid configuration. An alpha value of .29 supports this identification (Table 4.1). Finally, the fourth stage (D) is one in which network structure is characterized by the existence of multiple paths between most nodes. We would expect this delta configuration to have a high degree of circuitry resulting from increasing connectivity, and the alpha value of .67 supports this expectation (Table 4.1). By measuring network connectivity and circuitry respectively, the gamma and alpha indices together provide a description of the state of network development.

Network Structure and the Region

Two simple graph-theoretic measurements have been presented in the previous sections as succinct, though perhaps unfamiliar, ways to describe the structural complexity of transportation networks. We have focused on their utility in the static comparison of the structure of two or more networks, and in the identification of specific configurations in network growth. We might also ask if these measurements can be related to the features of the areas within which the networks are located. Are the graph-theoretic measurements useful in investigating the relationship between network structure and levels of national development?

In their efforts to establish criteria for evaluating the future requirements of regional transportation systems, Garrison and Marble provide some answers to this question.[4] Utilizing regression analysis, they considered a number of graph-theoretic indices as a set of dependent variables and selected as a set of independent variables several of the physical, economic, and social characteristics of the regions analyzed. The rationale underlying their study is that transportation structure is dependent upon the characteristics of the area containing the network.

INDEPENDENT VARIABLES. ·For measuring levels of national development there are a variety of statistics dealing with such features of the economy as Gross National Product, per-capita income, value of industrial production, value of foreign trade, value of imports, and development of energy resources, to mention only a few. To determine suitable development variables for their analysis, Garrison and Marble drew heavily on the work done by Brian Berry on the statistical measurement of levels of development.[5] Berry recognized that a set of national statistics contains many measures that are redundant. His contribution was synthesizing the statistics in a way that revealed the basic factors underlying variations in the measurements. By means of a direct factor analysis on the rankings of ninety-five countries on forty-three statistical measures, Berry extracted four basic factors underlying variations in the measures of development. Nearly all of the variability in the forty-three statistical measures was attributable to two factors: a "technological" factor and a "demographic" factor. The technological factor incorporates measurements of the degree of urbanization, industrialization, transportation, trade, and income. The demographic factor reflects birth and death rates, population densities, population per unit of cultivated land, and similar measures.

By using Berry's measurements of technological and demographic factors, Garrison and Marble were able to incorporate national development in their analysis and avoid the problem of having to treat a large number of redundant statistical measures as independent variables. Also, recognizing that the structural complexity of a transportation network might depend on the physical properties of the area it serves, they included as additional independent variables three measures of size, shape, and relief for each area. Values for these five independent variables were computed for twenty-five nations.

[4] W. Garrison and D. Marble, *The Structure of Transportation Networks* (Washington, D.C.: U.S. Department of Commerce, Office of Technical Services, 1961).

[5] Brian Berry, "An Inductive Approach to the Regionalization of Economic Development," University of Chicago, Department of Geography Research Paper No. 62, *Essays on Geography and Economic Development*, ed. N. S. Ginsburg (Chicago: University of Chicago Press, 1960).

Table 4.2. **Summary of the Coefficients of Determination (R²)**
of the Regression Analysis

	Technological level	Demographic level	Size	Shape	Relief
1. Vertices	.73	.73	.76	.77	.77
2. Edges	.73	.73	.75	.76	.77
3. Alpha Index	.42	.44	.46	.54	.57
4. Gamma Index	.37	.40	.41	.52	.56
5. Cyclomatic Number	.54	.56	.59	.62	.62
6. Diameter	.62	.62	.67	.75	.80
7. Eta Index (Highway)	.45	.46	.66	.67	.67
8. Eta Index (Rail)	.43	.51	.63	.65	.77

Source: W. L. Garrison and D. F. Marble, *The Structure of Transportation Networks* (Washington, D.C.: U.S. Department of Commerce, Office of Technical Services, 1961), p. 62.

DEPENDENT VARIABLES.   Six measures of a graph-theoretic type were made on the transportation networks for each of the twenty-five nations selected for study. These were (1) the number of nodes (vertices), (2) the number of linkages (edges), (3) alpha index, (4) gamma index, (5) number of circuits, and (6) diameter.

The first five measures are discussed in the preceding sections. The diameter is a measure of the span of a transportation network. It is defined as the *minimum* number of linkages required to connect the two nodes that are the greatest distance apart on the network. Topologically, distance is measured by the number of linkages in a path between a pair of nodes.

To the six graph-theoretical measures of the transportation network Garrison and Marble added a ratio measure (eta index) for both railways and highways in order to introduce scale into the measurement of network structure. Because graph-theoretic indices measure only topological properties, they treat all linkages in a network as being equal. To introduce scale into their analysis, Garrison and Marble used a ratio of the total mileage of the network to the observed number of linkages. The resultant value is a measure of the average length of edges in the network.[6]

RESULTS.   The strength of the relationship between the eight dependent variables and the five independent variables is shown in Table 4.2. The coefficient of determination may be interpreted as the percent of variability in the dependent variable that is associated with variation in the independent variables. The first entry in Table 4.2 indicates that 73

[6] For a similar type of analysis that involves more structural indices and a larger sample of nations, see K. Kansky, "Structure of Transportation Networks," University of Chicago, Department of Geography Research Paper No. 84 (1963).

percent of the variation in the number of vertices in the transportation networks of the twenty-five nations may be associated with the factor of technological development. As the coefficients are expressed as cumulative values, the last entry in the first row states that 77 percent of the variability among the twenty-five nations in the number of vertices is associated with all five independent variables.

Using the information in Table 4.2, Garrison and Marble were able to make some general interpretations of the relationships between structure of transportation networks and the features of the areas in which they are located. Of all the variables, the factor of technological development is the major determinant of network structure. No other independent variable approaches its explanatory power. The high R^2 values under technological development in Table 4.2 indicate that in all cases most of the variability in the measures of network structure is associated with the national level of development. In contrast, the demographic factor is of little significance in explaining the structural complexity of transportation networks. Furthermore, the physical characteristics of an area are considerably less significant in explaining network structure than the level of development in the area. The physical variables show close relations to only a few of the structural variables. Size is of importance only in relation to the average length of railroad and highway. Relief has its greatest effect on the average length of railroad.

Summary

In this chapter, some elementary concepts of graph theory have been introduced to describe some basic structural properties of networks. Because of the highly complex spatial nature of any transport network, it is necessary to idealize and simplify a network in order to study its structural characteristics. When applying graph theory to the analysis of a network, we idealize and simplify the network as a graph. Only the most minimal information about the topological properties of the network is retained in this idealization. By treating only the topological properties of a network we are able to describe its structure in relatively simple fashion. A number of aggregate measures may be derived for this purpose. To describe the important property of connectivity, two structural indices are suggested: the gamma and alpha indices. By establishing the limits for these indices, it is possible to consider changes in the structural complexity of a given network in terms of three basic network configurations: spinal, grid, and delta. The utility of these measures is not limited to the static comparison of the structure of two or more networks, or to the identification of limits in the stages of network growth. As studies by Garrison and Marble and by Kansky have demonstrated, these aggregate measures can also be used to investigate the relationship between network structure and levels of national development.

A principal drawback to the use of these primitive measures of network structure is their limitation to the topological properties of the network. Usually we are interested in analyzing transport systems in terms of such real-world characteristics as capacity, type of use, and cost of construction. Also, the same measure may apply to networks of different internal spatial organization. Unfortunately, most of these properties, which are important in the analysis of a transport system, do not lend themselves readily to an analysis by aggregate measures of graph theory. Nevertheless, the utility of these measures in providing a consistent and comparable set of network characteristics cannot be overlooked. The next chapter will consider some ways in which transport geographers have endeavored to introduce greater reality into the abstraction of a network as a graph—specifically, by treating more than the topological properties of a network and by more explicit treatment of the internal relationships of nodes within a network.

CHAPTER 5   *structural analysis of transportation networks: measures of nodal accessibility*

When examining a transportation network for evidence of the spatial organization of an area, a geographer is not limited to considering only the aggregate characteristics of the network. His emphasis may be placed on the identification of the spatial structure of the component node-linkage associations of the transport network. He may examine linkages and flows between centers, or he may look at the nodes themselves in terms of their function and accessibility to the rest of the network. In the latter case, the concern is with spatial dominance and competition among the nodes. For example, as the structure of a network changes in response to the addition of new linkages or the improvement of existing linkages, it is probable that the accessibility, or relative position, of individual nodes in the network will be affected. Certain centers will be advantaged by the change in spatial structure while others will be disadvantaged. These changes are reflected in changes in nodal accessibility. Graph theory provides a convenient means of measuring and recording changes in nodal accessibility.

The Network as a Matrix

Any network, or an abstraction of a network such as a graph, may be represented as a matrix (Fig. 5.1). By convention, the horizontal rows of a matrix are identified as a set of origin nodes and the vertical columns of the matrix are defined as a set of destination nodes. The number of rows and columns in the matrix will each correspond to the total number of nodes in the network. Each cell entry in the matrix may be used to record some information on the relationship between a pair of nodes. A familiar example of a network represented by a matrix is a

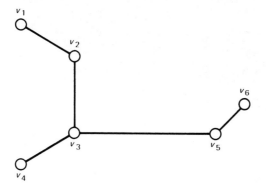

Fig. 5.1. *Network as a Matrix. A simple network is abstracted as a graph and represented in a matrix format. The number of rows and columns in the matrix are each equal to the total number of nodes in the network. Cell entries record either the presence or absence of linkages between nodal pairs.*

highway mileage table in which the mileage between a given pair of nodes is recorded in individual cells.

Depending on the information recorded in the cells, the matrices may represent network structure, or network flow. If the matrix represents network structure, the cell entries will be quantitative measures of the linkages between the origin and destination nodes. At the simplest level the cell entries may merely record the presence or absence of a linkage between a pair of nodes in the network. At a more complex level of analysis, interregional commodity shipments may be represented by a commodity-flow matrix, in which case each cell entry records the amount of a commodity being shipped from one node to another.

To illustrate a matrix representation of a network, let us consider the transport system in Figure 5.1. The network has been abstracted as a graph, and this graph can be represented in a 6 × 6 matrix in which the cell entries record the presence or absence of a linkage between every pair of nodes on the network. If a linkage exists between any given pair

DIRECT AIRLINE CONNECTIONS

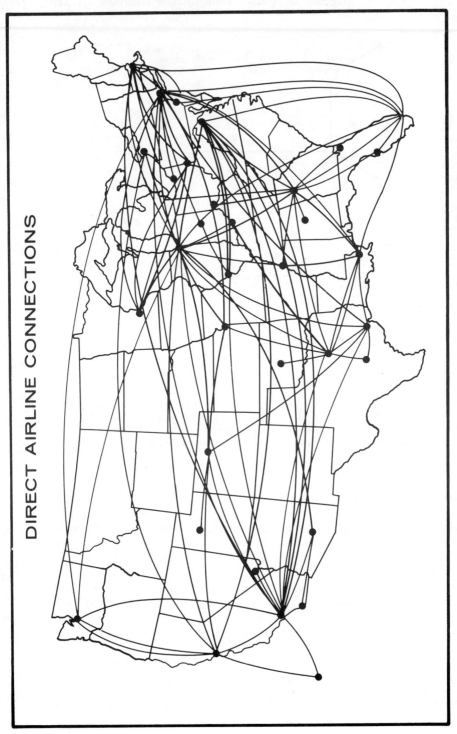

Fig. 5.2. Direct Airline Connections. The map provides a familiar and generalized format for presenting information on the existence of direct jet flights between the forty largest cities in the United States. After Adams, "Airline Connectivity Matrix: Growth and Disequilibrium."

of nodes, a value of 1 is entered in the appropriate cell. If no direct linkage exists between a pair of nodes, then a value of zero is recorded. Because the connection of a node to itself is meaningless in this example, the value of zero is also recorded in the cells comprising the main diagonal of the matrix. Thus the entries for $v_1 \to v_1, \ldots, v_6 \to v_6$ will all be zero.

In this matrix we have recorded only the minimal information about the network, which is the presence or absence of connectivity. Therefore it is called a connectivity matrix. However, we are looking at connectivity on a nodal-pair basis rather than the aggregate basis of Chapter 4. In addition to recording the simple structure of the network, it is possible to derive from this matrix some measures of centrality or accessibility.

Nodal Accessibility

DEGREE OF A NODE. The most primitive measurement of accessibility is obtained directly from the connectivity matrix. A summation of the individual rows of the matrix produces a column, or vector, of values. Each row sum equals the total number of direct linkages from a given center to the set of all other centers in the network and is defined as the degree of a node. The higher the value of an individual node, the greater is its accessibility to all other centers. For illustrative purposes, consider a map of direct jet connections between forty large cities in the United States (Fig. 5.2).[1] These direct connections may be considered linkages between nodes, and the network may be abstracted as a graph and represented in a matrix format (Fig. 5.3). Summing across the rows of the matrix gives a vector, each element of which represents the total number of direct linkages from a given city to the other thirty-nine cities in the network. For example, New York and Chicago are both connected by direct flights to all of the other thirty-nine cities in the network, whereas Birmingham has direct connections to only seventeen of the other cities. By ranking cities in terms of the magnitude of direct airline connections, it is possible to establish a hierarchy for these forty centers (Table 5.1).

The degree of a node has serious limitations as a measure of accessibility. For surface modes of transport, accessibility involves more than the direct connections between nodal pairs. We are frequently interested in knowing the accessibility between nodes that takes into account indirect connections—that is, a linkage between a pair of nodes which passes through one or more intermediate centers. For example, Indianapolis has the largest number of direct Interstate Highway linkages (seven) to other major cities in the American Manufacturing Belt. This does not mean, however, that Indianapolis is the most accessible city in the network, because most of the major cities are connected by a series of

---

[1] Data on air-passenger traffic is from Russell B. Adams, "Airline Connectivity Matrix: Growth and Disequilibrium," a paper presented at the annual meeting of the Mid-Continental Division of the Regional Science Association, Winnipeg, Manitoba (June 1971).

	Atlanta	Birmingham	Boston	Buffalo	Chicago	Cincinnati	Cleveland	Columbus	Dallas	Denver	Detroit	Honolulu	Houston	Indianapolis	Jacksonville	Kansas City	Las Vegas	Los Angeles	Louisville	Memphis	Miami	Minn.-St. Paul	New Orleans	New York	Oklahoma City	Omaha	Philadelphia	Phoenix	Pittsburgh	Portland	Providence	Rochester	St. Louis	Salt Lake City	San Antonio	San Diego	San Francisco	Seattle	Tampa	Wash.-Baltimore	
Atlanta	X	1	1	1	1	1	1	1	1	1	1	1	1	1	1	1	1	1	1	1	1	1	1	1	0	0	1	0	1	0	1	1	1	1	0	1	1	1	1	1	35
Birmingham	1	X	1	0	1	1	1	0	1	0	1	0	1	1	0	1	0	0	0	1	1	0	1	1	0	0	1	0	1	0	0	0	1	0	0	0	0	0	0	1	18
Boston	1	1	X	1	1	1	1	1	1	1	1	1	1	1	1	1	1	1	1	1	1	1	1	1	1	1	1	0	1	1	1	1	1	1	1	0	1	1	1	1	37
Buffalo	1	0	1	X	1	1	1	1	0	0	1	0	0	1	0	0	1	1	0	0	1	0	0	1	0	1	1	0	1	0	1	1	1	0	0	1	1	0	1	1	23
Chicago	1	1	1	1	X	1	1	1	1	1	1	1	1	1	1	1	1	1	1	1	1	1	1	1	1	1	1	1	1	1	1	1	1	1	1	1	1	1	1	1	39
Cincinnati	1	1	1	1	1	X	1	1	1	1	1	0	1	1	1	1	0	1	1	1	1	0	0	1	0	0	1	0	1	0	1	0	1	0	1	1	0	1	1	1	28
Cleveland	1	1	1	1	1	1	X	1	1	0	1	0	1	1	1	1	0	1	1	1	1	0	1	1	0	1	1	0	1	0	1	1	0	1	0	1	1	0	1	1	34
Columbus	1	0	1	1	1	1	1	X	1	0	1	0	1	0	1	0	1	1	1	0	1	0	0	1	0	1	0	0	1	0	1	0	1	0	0	0	1	0	1	1	25
Dallas	1	1	1	0	1	1	1	1	X	1	1	1	1	0	0	1	1	1	1	1	1	1	1	1	1	1	1	1	1	1	1	0	1	1	1	1	1	1	1	1	35
Denver	1	0	1	0	1	0	1	0	1	X	1	1	1	0	0	1	1	1	0	1	1	1	1	1	1	1	1	1	1	1	0	0	1	1	1	1	1	1	0	1	31
Detroit	1	0	1	1	1	1	1	1	1	1	X	1	1	1	0	1	1	1	1	1	1	1	1	1	0	0	1	1	1	1	1	1	1	0	1	1	1	1	1	1	34
Honolulu	1	0	1	0	1	0	1	0	1	1	1	X	1	0	0	1	1	1	0	0	1	1	1	1	0	0	1	0	1	0	0	1	0	0	1	1	1	1	0	1	23
Houston	1	1	1	0	1	1	0	1	1	1	1	1	X	1	1	1	0	1	1	1	1	0	1	1	1	0	1	1	1	0	1	0	1	1	1	1	1	1	1	1	33
Indianapolis	1	0	1	1	1	1	1	1	0	1	1	0	1	X	1	1	0	1	1	1	0	1	0	1	0	0	1	0	1	0	1	0	1	0	0	0	1	0	1	1	25
Jacksonville	1	0	1	1	1	0	1	0	0	0	0	0	1	0	X	0	0	1	1	0	1	1	1	1	0	0	1	0	1	0	1	1	1	1	0	0	1	0	1	1	20
Kansas City	1	1	0	0	1	1	1	1	1	1	1	1	1	1	0	X	1	1	1	1	1	1	1	1	1	1	1	0	0	1	0	1	1	0	1	1	1	1	1	1	31
Las Vegas	1	0	1	0	1	0	1	0	1	1	1	1	0	0	1	1	X	1	0	0	1	1	1	1	1	1	1	1	1	1	0	1	0	1	1	0	1	1	1	1	27
Los Angeles	1	0	1	1	1	1	1	1	1	1	1	1	1	1	1	1	1	X	1	1	1	1	1	1	1	1	1	1	1	1	1	0	1	1	1	1	1	1	1	1	37
Louisville	1	1	1	0	1	1	1	1	1	0	1	0	0	1	1	0	0	1	X	1	1	0	1	0	0	1	0	1	1	0	1	0	1	0	0	0	0	1	1	1	25
Memphis	1	1	1	0	1	1	1	0	1	1	1	0	1	0	1	1	0	1	1	X	1	0	1	1	1	1	1	0	1	0	1	0	1	0	1	0	1	0	1	1	30
Miami	1	1	1	1	1	1	1	1	1	1	1	1	1	0	1	1	0	1	0	1	X	1	1	1	0	1	1	0	1	0	1	1	0	1	1	0	1	1	1	1	35
Minn.-St. Paul	1	1	1	0	1	0	1	0	1	1	1	1	1	1	0	0	1	1	1	0	1	X	1	1	0	1	1	1	1	1	1	0	1	0	0	1	1	1	1	1	30
New Orleans	1	1	1	0	1	0	1	0	1	1	1	1	1	1	1	1	0	1	1	1	1	1	X	1	1	0	1	1	0	1	1	0	1	0	1	1	1	1	1	1	31
New York	1	1	1	1	1	1	1	1	1	1	1	1	1	1	1	1	1	1	1	1	1	1	1	X	1	1	1	1	1	1	1	1	1	1	1	1	1	1	1	1	39
Oklahoma City	0	0	1	0	1	0	0	0	1	1	0	0	1	1	0	1	1	0	1	1	0	1	1	1	X	1	1	0	0	0	0	0	1	0	1	0	1	1	0	1	19
Omaha	0	0	0	0	1	0	1	0	1	1	0	0	1	0	0	1	0	0	0	1	0	1	0	1	1	X	1	0	0	1	0	0	1	0	0	1	1	0	1	1	19
Philadelphia	1	1	1	1	1	1	1	1	1	1	1	1	1	1	1	1	1	1	1	1	1	1	1	1	0	1	X	1	1	1	1	1	0	1	1	1	1	1	1	1	37
Phoenix	0	0	1	0	1	0	1	0	1	1	1	1	1	0	0	1	1	1	0	0	0	1	0	1	0	0	1	X	1	1	0	1	1	1	1	1	1	1	0	1	24
Pittsburgh	1	1	1	1	1	1	1	1	1	1	1	0	1	1	1	0	1	0	1	1	1	1	0	1	1	0	1	1	X	0	1	1	1	1	1	1	1	1	1	1	35
Portland	1	0	1	0	1	0	1	0	1	1	1	1	0	0	1	1	1	0	0	0	1	1	0	1	1	1	0	1	0	X	0	0	1	1	1	1	1	1	1	1	26
Providence	1	0	1	1	1	0	1	1	0	1	0	1	1	1	0	0	0	1	1	1	0	1	0	0	0	1	0	1	X	1	1	0	1	0	0	0	0	0	1	21
Rochester	1	0	1	1	1	1	1	1	1	0	1	0	0	0	0	1	0	0	1	0	1	0	1	0	1	0	1	0	1	0	1	X	0	0	0	0	1	0	1	1	21
St. Louis	1	1	1	1	1	1	1	1	1	1	1	0	1	1	1	1	1	1	1	1	0	1	1	1	1	1	1	1	1	1	1	1	X	1	0	1	1	1	1	1	37
Salt Lake City	0	0	0	1	1	0	0	0	1	1	0	0	0	0	0	1	1	1	0	0	0	1	0	1	0	1	0	1	1	1	1	0	1	X	0	1	1	1	0	1	20
San Antonio	1	0	0	0	1	1	0	0	1	1	0	0	1	0	0	1	0	1	0	1	0	0	1	1	1	0	1	1	1	0	0	0	0	0	X	1	1	0	1	1	21
San Diego	1	0	1	0	1	1	0	1	1	0	1	1	1	0	1	0	1	1	0	0	1	1	0	1	0	1	1	1	0	1	0	0	1	1	1	X	1	1	1	1	29
San Francisco	1	1	1	1	1	1	1	1	1	1	1	1	1	1	1	1	1	1	1	1	1	1	1	1	1	1	1	1	1	1	0	1	1	1	1	1	X	1	1	1	38
Seattle	1	0	1	0	1	0	1	0	1	1	1	1	1	0	0	1	1	1	0	1	1	0	1	1	1	1	1	1	0	1	0	0	1	1	1	1	1	X	0	1	28
Tampa	1	0	1	1	1	1	1	1	1	0	1	0	1	1	1	1	1	1	1	1	1	1	1	1	0	0	1	0	1	0	0	1	1	0	0	1	1	0	X	1	28
Wash.-Baltimore	1	1	1	1	1	1	1	1	1	1	1	1	1	1	1	1	1	1	1	1	1	1	1	1	1	1	1	1	1	1	1	1	1	0	1	1	1	1	1	X	38

Fig. 5.3. *Matrix of Direct Airline Connections. The airline network in Figure 5.2 may be abstracted as a graph and the information on direct jet connections recorded in a matrix. The rows of the matrix are origin cities and the columns are destination cities. The presence or absence of direct jet service between every pair of origin-destination cities is recorded in the cells of the matrix.*

indirect Interstate Highway linkages. Indianapolis is connected to Cleveland by a sequence of three links: Indianapolis to Dayton, Dayton to Columbus, Columbus to Cleveland. In terms of Indianapolis's total accessibility to other Manufacturing Belt cities, these indirect linkages must be taken into account. Even in the case of airline traffic, where direct jet linkages between centers is a plausible indicator of relative importance, the degree of the node is a poor discriminator among centers in the hierarchy. This is obvious in the number of nodes having identical rankings in the example of the forty major air-traffic centers of the United States (Table 5.1). What is needed, therefore, is a measure that takes account of both direct and indirect connections.

Table 5.1. A Hierarchy of Forty Major Air-Traffic Cities

Rank	City	Number of direct connections to other cities
1	Chicago	39
1	New York	39
3	San Francisco	38
3	Washington–Baltimore	38
5	Boston	37
5	Los Angeles	37
5	Philadelphia	37
5	St. Louis	37
9	Atlanta	35
9	Dallas	35
9	Miami	35
9	Pittsburgh	35
13	Cleveland	34
15	Houston	33
16	Denver	31
16	New Orleans	31
16	Kansas City	31
19	Memphis	30
19	Minneapolis–St. Paul	30
21	San Diego	29
22	Cincinnati	28
22	Seattle	28
22	Tampa	28
25	Las Vegas	27
26	Portland	26
27	Columbus	25
27	Indianapolis	25
27	Louisville	25
30	Phoenix	24
31	Buffalo	23
31	Honolulu	23
33	Providence	21
33	Rochester	21
33	San Antonio	21
36	Jacksonville	20
36	Salt Lake City	20
38	Oklahoma City	19
38	Omaha	19
40	Birmingham	18

INDIRECT CONNECTIVITY. It is possible to manipulate the connectivity matrix, which records the elementary structure of a network, to derive two measures of accessibility involving indirect connections—one related directly to structure and one related to topological distance. The number of indirect connections or paths between nodal pairs can be determined by matrix multiplication. Matrix multiplication involves the element-by-element multiplication of the rows in a matrix by the columns of another. To derive a value for the cell of the first row and first column of the matrix, we multiply the first column times the first row—that is,

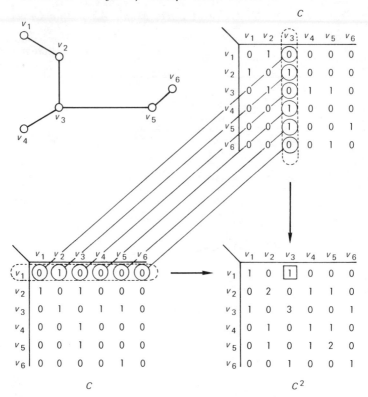

Fig. 5.4. *Matrix Multiplication. To determine if a two-linkage path exists between* v_1 *and* v_3, *each element of the third column of the connection matrix C is multiplied by each element in the first row of matrix C. The sum of the element-by-element products is an enumeration of the number of two-linkage paths between the nodal pair. In this example, one such path exists.*

we multiply the first element in row 1 by the first element in column 1. Then we multiply the second element in row 1 by the second element in column 1, and so on. We record the sum of all the element-by-element products as the value in the first row and first column of a new matrix.

We can also multiply a matrix by itself as shown in Figure 5.4, where the matrix C from Figure 5.1 is multiplied by itself to produce the new matrix C^2. In each individual cell of C^2 we record the value:

$$c_{ij}^2 = \sum_{k=1}^{n} c_{ik} \cdot c_{kj}.$$

What is $c_{ik} \cdot c_{kj}$? It is an indirect connection, or path, of two linkages from node i to node j. Thus nonzero elements in C^2 indicate the presence of two linkage paths between any given pair of nodes on the network.

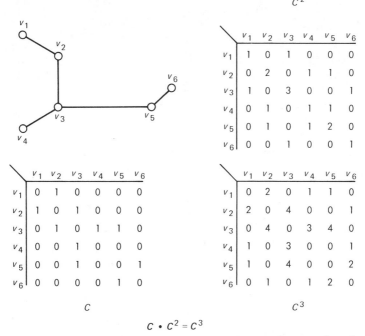

Fig. 5.5. *Three-Linkage Paths. To determine the number of three-linkage paths between nodal pairs, a matrix C^3 is derived by multiplying the matrix C^2 by the original connection matrix C.*

The matrix C^2 (Fig. 5.4) provides a complete enumeration of the number of paths of two linkages in the network. This is not surprising. Consider how we arrived at a particular entry in the matrix and consider the cell entry for the vertices v_1 and v_3. We multiplied the row in the original connection matrix C_j, which gives the number of direct linkages from v_1 to all other nodes in the network, by the column giving the number of direct connections from all other nodes to v_3. In determining if there is an indirect linkage between v_1 and v_3 in C^2, we evaluated: $(0 \cdot 0) + (1 \cdot 1) + (0 \cdot 0) + (0 \cdot 1) + (0 \cdot 1) + (0 \cdot 0)$. In this calculation the second entry pairs two values of unity. This indicates there is a direct connection from v_1 to a node that in turn has a direct connection to v_3. Thus a path of two linkages exists between nodes v_1 and v_3. The complete computation gives the total number of such indirect connections for all nodes.

Suppose we wish to know whether or not two nodes are connected by an indirect linkage passing through two intermediate centers. We need to enumerate paths with lengths of three linkages between the nodal pairs, as in the case of the Interstate linkages from Indianapolis to Cleveland. A matrix C^3 would seem logically appropriate. Consider the way we would find the number of three linkage paths from v_1 to v_5. The

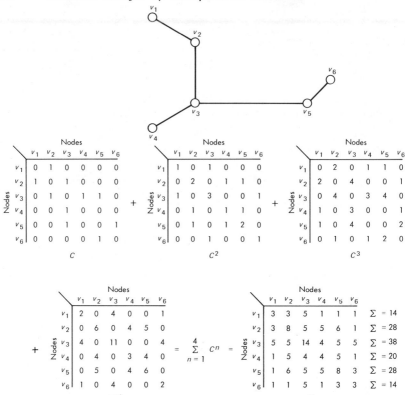

Fig. 5.6.   *The Accessibility Matrix. The accessibility matrix* (T) *is the sum of the connection matrix* (C) *and all matrices that enumerate indirect paths between nodes on the network, or* T = C + C² + C³ + . . . + Cⁿ, *where* n *is equal to the diameter of the network. By summing across the rows of matrix* T, *a column vector is obtained in which the elements are the accessibility of a given node to the network.*

first row of C^2 gives us the number of two linkage connections from v_1 to other nodes. There is a two-linkage path from v_1 to v_3. Looking at the fifth column in the connectivity matrix C, we observe that a direct connection exists between v_3 and v_5. Thus there exists a path of three linkages from v_1 to v_5 that passes through intermediate nodes v_2 and v_3. Numerically the procedure has been to consider $(1\cdot0) + (0\cdot0) + (1\cdot1) + (0\cdot0) + (0\cdot0) + (0\cdot1) = 1$. In similar fashion, the number of paths of three linkages between all the nodes of the network can be determined by the matrix multiplication procedure $C^2 \cdot C = C^3$ (Fig. 5.5).

The procedure we have employed to determine paths with links of two or three linkages can be generalized to determine paths of any length in the network. Generalizing this concept to any power of the connection matrix (C^n), c_{ij}^n is a path of n length between nodes i and j. All nodes will have a path connection to all other nodes when the value n is equal to the diameter of the network (the minimal number of links between the two most distant nodes in the network). For example, the most distant nodes in the network, v_1 and v_6, in Figure 5.6, are first connected when the matrix C is multiplied to the fourth power, since they are four linkages apart. Thus, the diameter of the network is four.

THE ACCESSIBILITY MATRIX T.   If we sum the matrix C with all of the matrices recording indirect paths between the nodes, the result is a matrix specifying all direct and indirect connections between the nodes of the network. In Figure 5.6 the matrices C, C^2, C^3 and C^4 are summed to give a matrix T that enumerates the total of all direct and indirect connections in our sample network. We can refer to this matrix T as a representation of the accessibility surface of the network. The row elements indicate the accessibility of a given node to other nodes in the network. If we sum across the rows of the matrix, we obtain a column vector, the elements of which represent the accessibility of a node to the network.

In determining the accessibility matrix T, the multiplication of the connectivity matrix C is terminated when a matrix C^n is obtained, where n is equal to the diameter of the network. It is mathematically possible to compute matrices of higher powers. However, a network with v nodes can have no sequence of connections greater than $v - 1$ without establishing a path that passes through at least one node more than once. In our simple example, a matrix C^5 can be calculated to enumerate the paths of five linkages. Such a path can be determined between nodes v_1 and v_5 with a linkage sequence from $v_1 \rightarrow v_2$, $v_2 \rightarrow v_3$, $v_3 \rightarrow v_5$, $v_5 \rightarrow v_6$, $v_6 \rightarrow v_5$. The path passes through v_5 more than once, creating a redundancy in the sense that a shorter path is available from v_1 to v_5. Any path of a length greater than $v - 1$ will be redundant because shorter paths exist. It is for this reason that the matrix powering procedure is terminated when the shortest-distance path has been established between the two most distant nodes on the network.

The termination of the matrix multiplication process at a power equal to the diameter of the network does not, however, eliminate all redundancies in the accessibility matrix T. With the exception of the initial connection matrix, all matrices recording indirect connections between nodes will record redundancies. In our example, the matrix C^2 contains an entry indicating a path of two linkages between node v_1 and itself. Such a path is possible in terms of a sequence of linkages from v_1 to v_2 and then from v_2 back to v_1. In the matrix C^3, the entry in the first row, second column, records two paths between nodes v_1 and v_2. These are redundant paths with linkage sequences from $v_1 \rightarrow v_2$, $v_2 \rightarrow v_1$, $v_1 \rightarrow v_2$, and from $v_1 \rightarrow v_2$, $v_2 \rightarrow v_3$ and $v_3 \rightarrow v_2$. Both paths pass through node v_2 more than once.

Using the row sums of the matrix T, we can rank nodes in terms of their relative position (accessibility) on the network. The higher the value of the row sum, the greater the accessibility of the node. In the example of Figure 5.1, node v_3 is the most accessible of all the nodes in the network. It is most accessible in the structural sense that it has the highest level of centrality in the network. Although this measurement of

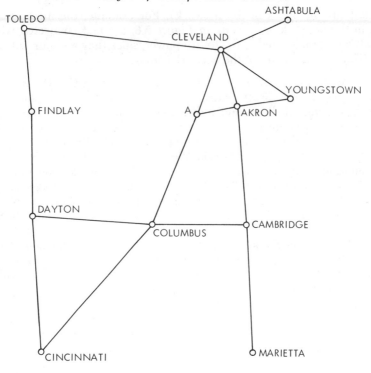

Fig. 5.7.   *The Interstate Highway System in Ohio. The Interstate Highway System in Ohio can be simplified and abstracted as a graph. There are 12 major nodes and 16 linkages.*

accessibility is dependent only on the presence or absence of connections between nodal pairs, it is sensitive to the presence of a spatial clustering of nodes in the network. Consider, for example, the Interstate Highway System in Ohio (Fig. 5.7). The T matrix for this network (Fig. 5.8) shows high levels of accessibility for Cleveland and Akron. Examining the matrices that are summed to the T matrix (Fig. 5.9), it is apparent that redundant connections have contributed to these high values. For example, all of the entries in C^4 for Cleveland are redundant connections. All nodes on the Ohio Interstate System can be reached from Cleveland in a maximum path of three linkages. Akron, for example, is directly connected to Cleveland. Thus the T matrix value of 33 represents 32 redundant connections through two-, three-, and four-linkage paths. The higher the level of nodal clustering, the greater is the role of redundancy in determining accessibility values.

Nodal Accessibility: A Southeastern U.S. Example

An interesting example of the use of the matrix powering procedure to determine nodal accessibility is the study by William L. Garrison of

	Toledo v_1	Cleveland v_2	Ashtabula v_3	Youngstown v_4	Akron v_5	Int. A v_6	Findlay v_7	Dayton v_8	Columbus v_9	Cambridge v_{10}	Cincinnati v_{11}	Marietta v_{12}	$\sum\limits_{v=1}^{12}$ Accessibility
v_1 Toledo	11	11	7	10	12	12	4	7	5	5	3	1	88
v_2 Cleveland	11	43	10	21	33	24	9	5	17	15	5	4	197
v_3 Ashtabula	7	10	6	9	11	10	1	2	3	4	1	1	65
v_4 Youngstown	10	21	9	17	20	20	2	4	6	12	3	2	126
v_5 Akron	12	33	11	20	37	23	5	6	22	13	5	8	195
v_6 Int. A	12	24	10	20	23	28	4	12	13	20	10	3	179
v_7 Findlay	4	9	1	2	5	4	9	7	10	3	7	1	62
v_8 Dayton	7	5	2	4	6	12	7	19	16	11	14	2	105
v_9 Columbus	5	17	3	6	22	13	10	16	31	11	15	8	157
v_{10} Cambridge	5	15	4	12	13	20	3	11	11	20	10	4	128
v_{11} Cincinnati	3	5	1	3	5	10	7	14	15	10	13	2	88
v_{12} Marietta	1	4	1	2	8	3	1	2	8	4	2	4	40

Fig. 5.8. The Accessibility Matrix of the Ohio Interstate Highway. The accessibility matrix T of the Ohio Interstate System records the number of direct and indirect linkages between the 12 nodes on the network. Cleveland ranks as the most accessible city, whereas Marietta ranks as the least accessible city.

the Interstate Highway System in the southeastern United States.[2] The Interstate Highway System, as proposed in 1956, will consist of 41,000 miles of high-speed, low-cost, limited-access facilities linking most of the major cities of the nation. As Garrison recognizes, the concept of the Interstate Highway System is quite different from the concept that governed federal highway policy in the past. Previous policy emphasized the construction of a relatively dense network of highways linking urban centers of all classes with each other and linking urban centers with their tributary areas. The Interstate Highway System may be regarded as a series of trunk lines providing linkages within and between major metropolitan areas. Garrison notes that this concept is more comparable to networks of airline and railroad routes than to present highway networks.

Since the Interstate Highway System represents a marked shift in federal policy, Garrison raises the question of its impact on the accessibility of urban centers in the United States. To measure accessibility

[2] William L. Garrison, "Connectivity of the Interstate Highway System," *Papers* of the Regional Science Association, 6 (1960), 121–38.

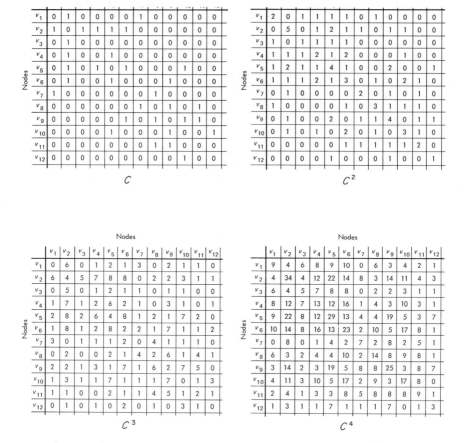

Fig. 5.9. Redundant Connections. An examination of the four matrices that are summed to the T matrix shows that the high levels of accessibility for such nodes as Cleveland and Akron are a result of redundant connections. For example, all of the entries in C^4 for Cleveland are redundant connections.

and its changes, the Interstate Highway System can be abstracted as a graph consisting of 325 linkages associated with 218 vertices. Rather than treat the entire system, Garrison restricts his attention to a subsystem of it—namely, the southeastern United States. This subsystem may be abstracted as a graph consisting of 45 nodes connected by 62 linkages (Fig. 5.10). The elementary structure of this graph may be recorded in a matrix form in which the cell entries indicate whether or not there is a direct Interstate linkage between a given pair of nodes. To determine the

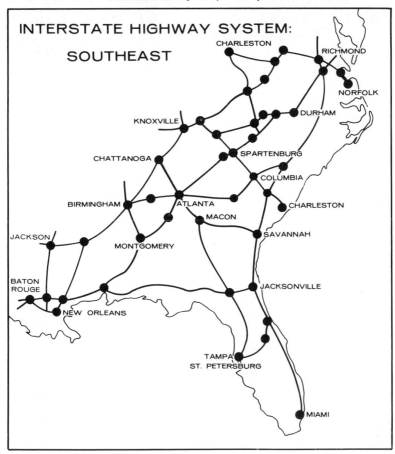

Fig. 5.10. The Interstate Highway System in the Southeast. The Interstate Highway System in the Southeast may be abstracted on a graph and represented in a matrix format to determine nodal accessibility. The abstracted network has 45 nodes connected by 62 linkages. After Garrison, "Connectivity of the Interstate Highway System."

influence of indirect linkages, this connectivity matrix may be powered to the solution time of the system (the diameter). In this example the solution time is a value of 12—that is, the two most distant points in the network require a minimum of 12 linkages for connectivity. It is impossible to get from Norfolk, Virginia, to either Jackson, Mississippi, or Baton Rouge, Louisiana, in less than twelve steps. By summing the values in the connectivity matrix with the values in the 11 matrices recording indirect connectivity, it is possible to obtain a summation matrix T, which may be interpreted as the accessibility matrix of the network. Summing the rows of matrix T gives a vector of values, each element of which represents the total accessibility of a given node to all other nodes on the Interstate Highway System of the Southeast. These values may

Table 5.2.   Hierarchy of Cities on Interstate Highway System of Southeast U.S.: Unweighted Accessibility

Rank	City	Unweighted accessibility value (in 1000s)
1	Atlanta	2,273
2	Columbia	1,986
3	Spartanburg	1,719
4	Macon	1,694
5	Statesville	1,461
6	Florence	1,419
7	Augusta	1,401
8	Savannah	1,397
9	Lake City	1,384
10	Asheville	1,380
11	Chattanooga	1,377
12	Charlotte	1,302
13	Mobile	1,130
14	Gadsden	1,125
15	Columbus	1,106
16	Birmingham	1,105
17	Jacksonville	1,100
18	Montgomery	1,053
19	Meridian	834
20	Greensboro	808
21	Knoxville	763
22	Greenville	762
23	Winston-Salem	744
24	Petersburg	734
25	Tampa-St. Petersburg	581
26	Charleston (S.C.)	544
27	Roanoke	513
28	Charleston (W. Va.)	513
29	Daytona Beach	504
30	Durham	502
31	Jackson	444
32	New Orleans	429
33	Lexington	424
34	Richmond	367
35	Orlando	348
36	Baton Rouge	319
37	Stanton	259
38	Miami	168
39	Newport News	135
40	Norfolk	45

then be ranked to determine a hierarchy of nodal accessibility (Table 5.2).[3]

One of the difficulties recognized by Garrison in determining nodal accessibility by matrix manipulation of the connectivity matrix is that all linkages between nodal pairs, no matter how indirect, are regarded as

[3] The determination of an unweighted accessibility matrix is not part of the analysis by Garrison. In his article, accessibility measures are based on a scalar-weighted multiplication procedure and the Shimbel shortest-path matrix operation.

equal in importance. A more realistic procedure would be to decrease the relative importance of indirect connections between nodes. What is required is a method that takes into account the indirect influences of a sequence (path) of linkages, with each step in the sequence being weighted inversely to its order in the sequence.

A procedure suggested by Garrison is to use a scalar in the multiplication process. Operationally,

$$T = sC + s^2 C^2 + s^3 C^3 + \ldots + s^n C^n$$

where s is a scalar with a value between 0 and 1 $(0 < s < 1)$ measuring the effectiveness of a direct connection. The effectiveness of an indirect connection consisting of two linkages is given by s^2, and the effectiveness of a path of n steps is given by the values s^n, where n is equal to the diameter of the network. For example, if we select a scalar of .3, each direct linkage in the network has the weight .3. Two linkage connections have the weight $.3^2 = .09$; three connection linkages would have the weight $.3^3 = .027$. In this way a distance-decay relationship is introduced into the analysis. The higher-powered matrices are of diminishing importance in determining accessibility.[4]

The impact of introducing a scalar into the matrix multiplication procedure on nodal accessibility is shown in Table 5.3. The ranking of many centers in the hierarchy is scarcely different from the unweighted results. Even though the idea of a scalar reflects a more realistic notion of centrality by using a distance-decay effect, the results are overwhelmed by redundancies in the system. In spite of this limitation, the use of an accessibility measure involving a scalar may be revealing if two different modes of transport are being considered. For example, if this procedure is used to determine accessibility for both the Interstate Highway System and the railroad network in the southeastern United States (Fig. 5.11), it is possible to compare the individual centers in terms of their comparative accessibility on the two networks. As shown in Table 5.4, Atlanta clearly ranks as the most accessible on both networks. Cities such as Montgomery, Petersburg, and Birmingham, which occupy vital positions on the rail network, are relatively less accessible on the Interstate Highway System. On the other hand, cities such as Asheville, Spartanburg, and Statesville have improved accessibility rankings on the Interstate Highway System relative to the railroad network.

The Shortest-Path Matrix

The use of a scalar in the multiplication procedure to determine nodal accessibility is certainly realistic: the importance of a connection between two nodes is inversely related to the number of linkages involved

---

[4] A major problem in using the scalar-weighted multiplication procedure is the selection of an appropriate value for the scalar. In the Garrison study, the scalar value of 0.3 is arbitrary.

Table 5.3.   Hierarchy of Cities on Interstate Highway System of
Southeast U.S.: Scalar-Weighted Accessibility

Rank	City	Scalar-weighted accessibility value
1	Atlanta	12.79
2	Columbia	9.96
3	Spartanburg	9.73
4	Macon	8.50
5	Statesville	8.40
6	Lake City	8.01
7	Asheville	7.51
8	Florence	7.27
9	Savannah	7.24
10	Charlotte	7.20
11	Chattanooga	7.13
12	Augusta	6.74
13	Greenville	6.67
14	Mobile	6.57
15	Jacksonville	6.09
16	Birmingham	6.00
17	Montgomery	5.89
18	Gadsden	5.68
19	Columbus	5.66
20	Meridian	5.33
21	Greensboro	4.97
22	Petersburg	4.81
23	Winston-Salem	4.27
24	Knoxville	4.22
25	Daytona Beach	3.70
26	Lexington	3.70
27	Charleston (S.C.)	3.65
28	Roanoke	3.65
29	Richmond	3.54
30	Tampa-St. Petersburg	3.53
31	Jackson	3.35
32	Durham	3.31
33	New Orleans	3.25
34	Baton Rouge	2.78
35	Stanton	2.66
36	Charleston (W. Va.)	2.63
37	Orlando	2.62
38	Newport News	1.85
39	Miami	1.34
40	Norfolk	0.84

in the connecting path. While this may be an improvement over the multiplication procedure without a scalar, it does not treat the critical problem of redundancies in a network. For certain real-world problems these redundancies are meaningless. In many instances, however, we are interested in paths that pass through any given node only once.

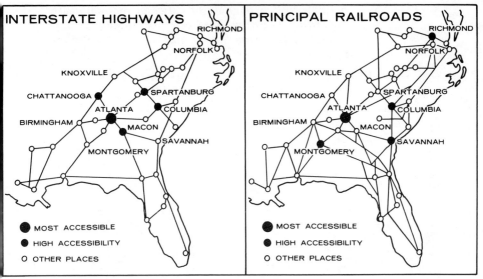

Fig. 5.11.   Highway and Railroad Accessibility in the Southeast. A comparison of scalar-weighted accessibility values for urban centers in the Southeast on the proposed Interstate Highway System (A) and the major regional railroads (B). In both networks, Atlanta is the most accessible center. Some variation is evident between the networks for centers of high accessibility. For example, Birmingham, Montgomery, and Petersburg have high accessibility on the railroad network and relatively less accessibility on the Interstate.

To determine these elementary paths, it is necessary to eliminate redundancies from our computations. A practical procedure for doing this is offered by Shimbel, whereby we are interested not in the total number of paths between any two nodes, but in the length of the shortest path between a pair of nodes.[5] Accessibility is computed in terms of the distance between nodes. To determine the shortest paths in a network, Shimbel has suggested a very simple procedure involving the computation of a matrix D. The elements of the matrix indicate the distance of the shortest path between all pairs of nodes in a network. Operationally this matrix is computed by successively powering the connection matrix C and noting after each iteration whether or not any new nonzero elements occur. If so, the power of that matrix is entered into the appropriate row and column of matrix D. For example, in squaring the connection matrix of the network in Figure 5.12, nonzero elements appear for the indirect connections between $v_1 \to v_3$, $v_2 \to v_4$, $v_2 \to v_5$, $v_5 \to v_6$, and $v_4 \to v_5$. In the shortest-distance matrix D, the value 2 is recorded in the appropriate cells, indicating that these indirect connections occurred for the first time when the original connection matrix was squared. When a power of the

[5] Alfonso Shimbel, "Structural Parameters of Communication Networks," *Bulletin of Mathematical Biophysics*, 15 (1953), 501–507.

Table 5.4. **A Comparative Ranking of Cities in the Southeast According to Scalar-Weighted Accessibility to the Interstate Highway System and the Railroad Network**

| | Interstate Highway System | | Railroad Network |
Rank	City	Rank	City
1	Atlanta	1	Atlanta
2	Columbia	2	Birmingham
3	Spartanburg	3	Jacksonville
4	Macon	4	Montgomery
5	Statesville	5	Savannah
6	Lake City	6	Macon
7	Asheville	7	Mobile
8	Florence	8	Petersburg
9	Savannah	9	Columbus
10	Charlotte	10	Columbia
11	Chattanooga	11	Chattanooga
12	Augusta	12	Florence
13	Greenville	13	Meridian
14	Mobile	14	Gadsden
15	Jacksonville	15	Knoxville
16	Birmingham	16	Lake City
17	Montgomery	17	Tampa-St. Petersburg
18	Gadsden	18	Miami
19	Columbus	19	Charleston (S.C.)
20	Meridian	20	Spartanburg
21	Petersburg	22	Daytona Beach
23	Winston-Salem	23	Orlando
24	Knoxville	24	New Orleans
25	Daytona Beach	25	Roanoke
26	Lexington	26	Charlotte
27	Charleston (S.C.)	27	Richmond
28	Roanoke	28	Greensboro
29	Richmond	29	Norfolk
30	Tampa-St. Petersburg	30	Jackson
31	Jackson	31	Charleston (W. Va.)
32	Durham	32	Asheville
33	New Orleans	33	Statesville
34	Baton Rouge	34	Stanton
35	Stanton	35	Winston-Salem
36	Charleston (W. Va.)	36	Newport News
37	Orlando	37	Durham
38	Newport News	38	Augusta
39	Miami	39	Lexington
40	Norfolk	40	Baton Rouge

matrix C is such that no zero elements can be entered into matrix D, then the procedure is terminated. Again, this final value in the powering procedure will be equal to the diameter of the network. In our example, no zero elements remain in matrix D, other than on the main diagonal, after the connectivity matrix C has been multiplied to the fourth power.

	Nodes					
	v_1	v_2	v_3	v_4	v_5	v_6
v_1	0	1	0	0	0	0
v_2	1	0	1	0	0	0
v_3	0	1	0	1	1	0
v_4	0	0	1	0	0	0
v_5	0	0	1	0	0	1
v_6	0	0	0	0	1	0

C

	Nodes					
	v_1	v_2	v_3	v_4	v_5	v_6
v_1	0	1	-	-	-	-
v_2	1	0	1	-	-	-
v_3	-	1	0	1	1	-
v_4	-	-	1	0	-	-
v_5	-	-	1	-	0	1
v_6	-	-	-	-	1	0

D_1

	Nodes					
	v_1	v_2	v_3	v_4	v_5	v_6
v_1	1	0	1	0	0	0
v_2	0	2	0	1	1	0
v_3	1	0	3	0	0	1
v_4	0	1	0	1	1	0
v_5	0	1	0	1	2	0
v_6	0	0	1	0	0	1

C^2

	Nodes					
	v_1	v_2	v_3	v_4	v_5	v_6
v_1	0	1	2	-	-	-
v_2	1	0	1	2	2	-
v_3	2	1	0	1	1	2
v_4	-	2	1	0	2	-
v_5	-	2	1	2	0	1
v_6	-	-	2	-	1	0

D_2

Fig. 5.12. Shortest-Path Matrix. The shortest-path matrix provides a realistic procedure for eliminating the counting of redundant connections. Rather than enumerating the total number of paths between two nodes, the objective is to determine the length of the shortest path between nodal pairs. In the matrix procedure, the power *of matrix C is recorded in the appropriate cells of the shortest-path matrix when nonzero products occur for the first time.*

The element entries in this final matrix D indicate the lengths of the shortest paths between all pair of nodes on the network (Fig. 5.13).

Summing across the rows of matrix D gives us a vector, the individual elements of which are measures of the shortest-path connections from each node to all other nodes on a network. Shimbel refers to this as the accessibility of a node to the network.

$$A_i = \sum_{j=1}^{n} d_{ij}$$

The smaller the numerical value of a node, the greater is the accessibility of that node to the network. Thus v_3 is still the most accessible node with a value of 7. This means that every other node in the system may be reached from v_3 in a total of only seven steps: two each from v_1 and v_3, one each from the other three. On the other hand, it requires a total of thirteen steps to reach all other nodes from either v_1 or v_6. Therefore an

$C =$

	v_1	v_2	v_3	v_4	v_5	v_6
v_1	0	1	0	0	0	0
v_2	1	0	1	0	0	0
v_3	0	1	0	1	1	0
v_4	0	0	1	0	0	0
v_5	0	0	1	0	0	1
v_6	0	0	0	0	1	0

$D_1 =$

	v_1	v_2	v_3	v_4	v_5	v_6
v_1	0	1	–	–	–	–
v_2	1	0	1	–	–	–
v_3	–	1	0	1	1	–
v_4	–	–	1	0	–	–
v_5	–	–	1	–	0	1
v_6	–	–	–	–	1	0

$C^2 =$

	v_1	v_2	v_3	v_4	v_5	v_6
v_1	1	0	1	0	0	0
v_2	0	2	0	1	1	0
v_3	1	0	3	0	0	1
v_4	0	1	0	1	1	0
v_5	0	1	0	1	2	0
v_6	0	0	1	0	0	1

$D_2 =$

	v_1	v_2	v_3	v_4	v_5	v_6
v_1	0	1	2	–	–	–
v_2	1	0	1	2	2	–
v_3	2	1	0	1	1	2
v_4	–	2	1	0	2	–
v_5	–	2	1	2	0	1
v_6	–	–	2	–	1	0

$C^3 =$

	v_1	v_2	v_3	v_4	v_5	v_6
v_1	0	2	0	1	1	0
v_2	2	0	4	0	0	1
v_3	0	4	0	3	4	0
v_4	1	0	3	0	0	1
v_5	1	0	4	0	0	2
v_6	0	1	0	1	2	0

$D_3 =$

	v_1	v_2	v_3	v_4	v_5	v_6
v_1	0	1	2	3	3	–
v_2	1	0	1	2	2	3
v_3	2	1	0	1	1	2
v_4	3	2	1	0	2	3
v_5	3	2	1	2	0	1
v_6	–	3	2	3	1	0

$C^4 =$

	v_1	v_2	v_3	v_4	v_5	v_6
v_1	2	0	4	0	0	1
v_2	0	6	0	4	5	0
v_3	4	0	11	0	0	4
v_4	0	4	0	3	4	0
v_5	0	5	0	4	6	0
v_6	1	0	4	0	0	2

$D_4 =$

	v_1	v_2	v_3	v_4	v_5	v_6	
v_1	0	1	2	3	3	4	$\Sigma = 13$
v_2	1	0	1	2	2	3	$\Sigma = 9$
v_3	2	1	0	1	1	2	$\Sigma = 7$
v_4	3	2	1	0	2	3	$\Sigma = 11$
v_5	3	2	1	2	0	1	$\Sigma = 9$
v_6	4	3	2	3	1	0	$\Sigma = 13$

$$\Sigma\,\Sigma = 62$$

Fig. 5.13. Shortest-Path Accessibility. No zero elements remain in the shortest-path matrix, except on the main diagonal, after multiplying to the diameter of the network. The entries in the matrix are summed to a column vector, the elements of which are the lengths of the shortest paths from a given node to all other nodes on the network.

inverse relationship exists between the accessibility of the node to the network and the length of the shortest paths connecting it to all other nodes.

Table 5.5.   Hierarchy of Cities in the Southeast According to Shortest-Path Accessibility

Rank	City	Shortest-path accessibility
1	Atlanta	154
2	Macon	162
3	Columbia	163
4	Chattanooga	165
5	Spartanburg	166
6	Greenville	169
7	Savannah	170
7	Augusta	170
9	Florence	173
10	Lake City	178
11	Gadsden	181
12	Columbus	182
13	Knoxville	183
13	Birmingham	183
15	Asheville	184
16	Jacksonville	186
17	Charlotte	188
18	Montgomery	189
19	Petersburg (Va.)	193
20	Mobile	195
21	Meridian	199
22	Statesville	205
23	Greensboro	206
24	Richmond	210
25	Durham	211
26	Baton Rouge	212
27	Charleston (S.C.)	213
27	Stanton	213
29	Tampa	217
29	Newport News	217
31	Roanoke	223
31	Charleston (W. Va.)	223
33	Daytona Beach	224
33	New Orleans	224
35	Winston-Salem	225
36	Jackson	226
37	Lexington	235
38	Norfolk	239
39	Orlando	243
40	Miami	247

Not only are redundancies removed, but a distance-decay relationship is maintained.

Using the procedure suggested by Shimbel, it is possible to compute the shortest paths between the urban centers on the Interstate Highway System of the southeastern United States. The resulting values may be ranked in order and a hierarchy determined (Table 5.5). These results may be computed with those derived from structural measures of accessibility using a scalar weighting. Atlanta continues to be the most accessible center on the System. Centers such as Macon, Columbia, Augusta, and Florence also continue to rank high in accessibility. However, the spatial pattern based on minimum-distance paths shows a stronger spatial organization focusing on Atlanta. Centers having direct connection to this center have high levels of accessibility and consequent high positions in the urban hierarchy. Conversely, centers such as Statesville, Winston-Salem, Charlotte, and Asheville show declines in levels of accessibility. Their lower rankings reflect the elimination of redundancies that affected their rankings based on a scalar weighting. The Shimbel shortest-path procedure is less sensitive to the spatial clustering of centers in North Carolina.

Networks as Valued Graphs

In determining nodal accessibility by the shortest-path matrix procedure, the distance metric was topological. Distance was defined as the number of linkages between nodes. All linkages were assumed to be of equal value. This definition of distance is reasonable when the concern is strictly with the structural properties of a network, or when one has only a minimum amount of information available about that network. If additional information is available, however, it is not necessary to restrict the concept of a distance metric to one that is purely topological. Values may be available that measure the distance between nodes in actual mileage, or, of more practical utility, the information may be a measure of the cost of movement between nodes or of the time required to travel between the nodes. We may use these more refined measures of distance in graph theory to determine nodal accessibility. Again, the network is abstracted as a graph that is represented by a matrix. The structure of the matrix is identical to that of the connectivity matrix C, but the individual cell entries are different. The values entered in each cell are measures of distance, however defined, between individual pair of nodes.

Let us consider the simple hypothetical network in Figure 5.14. The structure of a network remains the same, as in our previous use of this example. However, we now weight the direct linkages between the nodes in terms of the time required to travel between them. The network may be represented as a matrix. Because connections of a node to itself are meaningless, the values of the main diagonal of the matrix are always zero. If there is no direct linkage between two nodes, a value of infinity is entered in the appropriate cell. If a direct connection between two nodes exists, the value of the distance (or time or cost) between those nodes is recorded. The resulting matrix provides no more information on network structure than is provided in a strictly topological matrix. However, it does permit us to obtain measurements of nodal accessibility that are based on a more refined measure of distance.

To move from the initial valued graph L to a graph L^2, depicting two-stage connections, poses few problems in the relatively simple case used in Figure 5.14. By visual inspection it is readily apparent that it takes

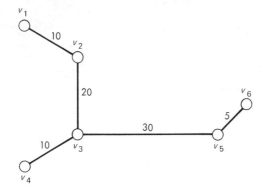

	Nodes					
	v_1	v_2	v_3	v_4	v_5	v_6
v_1	0	10	∞	∞	∞	∞
v_2	10	0	20	∞	∞	∞
v_3	∞	20	0	10	30	∞
v_4	∞	∞	10	0	∞	∞
v_5	∞	∞	30	∞	0	5
v_6	∞	∞	∞	∞	5	0

L

Fig. 5.14. A Network as a Valued Graph. The abstraction of a network as a graph and its representation as a matrix is not limited to the topological properties of the network. In this hypothetical example, the average driving-time on individual linkages is known. This information may be recorded in the appropriate cells of the matrix. If no direct connections exist between a nodal pair, such as v_1 and v_3, a value of infinity is recorded in the matrix cells.

30 minutes to go from v_1 to v_3 in two steps; 35 minutes to go from v_3 to v_6 in two steps; and that it is not possible (time = infinity) to go from v_1 to v_4, v_5, or v_6 in two steps. In the case of a more complex real-world network, however, we cannot rely on visual inspection, and we must have a systematic procedure for developing a matrix of two-stage valued linkages (L^2) from a matrix of direct connections (L).

Figure 5.15 illustrates one way of accomplishing this systematic procedure. Although similar to the matrix-powering procedure used earlier, it differs in two important ways: (1) instead of element-by-element multiplication of row-times-column, we employ element-by-element addition ($x \cdot y = x + y$), and (2) instead of summing the results, we look for the minimum value and insert it in the appropriate cell of the new matrix [$x + y = \min (x \cdot y)$]. Thus the cell ij value in the new

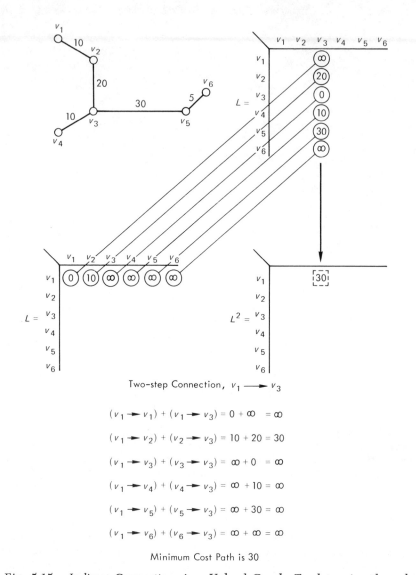

Two-step Connection, $v_1 \longrightarrow v_3$

$$(v_1 \longrightarrow v_1) + (v_1 \longrightarrow v_3) = 0 + \infty = \infty$$

$$(v_1 \longrightarrow v_2) + (v_2 \longrightarrow v_3) = 10 + 20 = 30$$

$$(v_1 \longrightarrow v_3) + (v_3 \longrightarrow v_3) = \infty + 0 = \infty$$

$$(v_1 \longrightarrow v_4) + (v_4 \longrightarrow v_3) = \infty + 10 = \infty$$

$$(v_1 \longrightarrow v_5) + (v_5 \longrightarrow v_3) = \infty + 30 = \infty$$

$$(v_1 \longrightarrow v_6) + (v_6 \longrightarrow v_3) = \infty + \infty = \infty$$

Minimum Cost Path is 30

Fig. 5.15. Indirect Connections in a Valued Graph. To determine the value of a two-stage linkage between v_1 and v_3, each element of the third column of the valued matrix L *is added to each element in the first row of matrix* L. *From the element-by-element addition the minimum sum is determined and inserted in the appropriate cell of the new matrix* L².

matrix is no longer the sum of the products of the links from origin i to all intermediate points k, and from each intermediate point to destination point j:

$$(\sum_{k=1}^{n} 1_{ik} \cdot 1_{kj}).$$

Instead, it is the minimum value of the sums of these two-stage links from origin i to k and then to destination j, or

$$\sum_{k=1}^{n} 1_{ik} \cdot 1_{kj} = \min(1_{ik} + 1_{jk}).$$

To clarify these rules, let us consider indirect connections from v_1 to v_3 as shown in the simple network example (Fig. 5.15). As is evident from the initial valued matrix L, no direct linkage exists between v_1 and v_3. It is necessary to compute the minimum time-path between the nodes. Using Boolean rules, we evaluate the additive relationships between v_1 and all other nodes in the network and between those nodes and v_3. Taking row 1 and column 3 of matrix L, we have

$$(0 + \infty) + (10 + 20) + (\infty + 0) + (\infty + 10) + (\infty + 30) + (\infty + \infty).$$

According to the rule $x + y = \min(x \cdot y)$, we add these values by selecting the minimal one. Hence the path from v_1 to v_3 is equal to 30 minutes of travel-time.

Using these Boolean rules, successive powers of the valued matrix L are calculated, with a typical element (m) indicating the minimum distance required to reach node i from node j in m steps or fewer. When a value of m is reached so that $L^m = L^{m+1}$, a matrix of minimum distance in the network has been obtained. Computing the matrix in Figure 5.15 up to the fourth power (the diameter) gives us a matrix in which there are no nonzero entries except on the main diagonal (Fig. 5.16). The elements in the matrix represent the minimum distance, measured in travel-time, between every pair of nodes. Summing across the rows of this matrix gives us a vector, each element of which is the total minimum distance from a given node to all other nodes on the network. This is a value of nodal accessibility based on distance—in this instance, the minimum travel-time between pairs of centers.

A comparison of the results of the valued-graph procedure with those based on Shimbel's minimum-path procedure indicates strong structural similarities. The power at which a new cell entry is added to the matrix is identical in both cases. The only significant differences between matrices, of course, is the final vector of nodal accessibility. Even here the changes are not dramatic. Node v_3 continues to be the most central in terms of ease of accessibility to all other nodes. Nodes v_1 and v_6 remain the most inaccessible. The effect of weighting linkages according to travel-

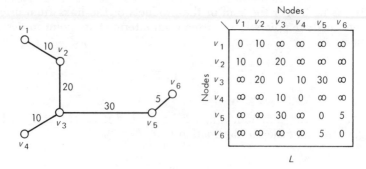

Nodes

	v_1	v_2	v_3	v_4	v_5	v_6
v_1	0	10	∞	∞	∞	∞
v_2	10	0	20	∞	∞	∞
v_3	∞	20	0	10	30	∞
v_4	∞	∞	10	0	∞	∞
v_5	∞	∞	30	∞	0	5
v_6	∞	∞	∞	∞	5	0

L

Nodes

	v_1	v_2	v_3	v_4	v_5	v_6
v_1	0	10	30	∞	∞	∞
v_2	10	0	20	30	50	∞
v_3	30	20	0	10	30	35
v_4	∞	30	10	0	40	∞
v_5	∞	50	30	40	0	5
v_6	∞	∞	35	∞	5	0

L^2

Nodes

	v_1	v_2	v_3	v_4	v_5	v_6
v_1	0	10	30	40	60	∞
v_2	10	0	20	30	50	55
v_3	30	20	0	10	30	35
v_4	40	30	10	0	40	45
v_5	60	50	30	40	0	5
v_6	∞	55	35	45	5	0

L^3

Nodes

	v_1	v_2	v_3	v_4	v_5	v_6	
v_1	0	10	30	40	60	65	= 205
v_2	10	0	20	30	50	55	= 165
v_3	30	20	0	10	30	35	= 125
v_4	40	30	10	0	40	45	= 165
v_5	60	50	30	40	0	5	= 185
v_6	65	55	35	45	5	0	= 205

L^4

Fig. 5.16. *Accessibility in a Valued Graph. Successive power of the valued matrix* L *are calculated until* $L^m = L^{m+1}$, *a matrix of minimum distance in the network, has been obtained. Summing across the rows of the matrix gives a vector in which each element is the total minimum distance from a given node to all other nodes on the network.*

time is evident for nodes v_4 and v_5. In the Shimbel minimal-path matrix, v_5 has a higher level of accessibility. In the valued-graph analysis, v_4 has a higher level of accessibility. The reason for this change is obvious. In the shortest-path matrix, the sequence of linkages $v_1 \rightarrow v_2 \rightarrow v_3 \rightarrow v_4$ is equal to the sequence $v_1 \rightarrow v_2 \rightarrow v_3 \rightarrow v_5$. In both cases two intermediate nodes were involved in the sequence of linkages, and the total number of linkages involved was three. This structural relationship does not change in the use of the valued graph. However, the connection from v_3 to v_4 is no longer equal to the one from v_3 to v_5; they are 10 minutes and 30 minutes respectively. Consequently, the minimum-distance path from v_1 to v_4 is 40 minutes, whereas the minimal distance path from v_1 to v_5 is 60 minutes. Similar differences in time-distance are evident in the paths from v_2 to v_4 and from v_2 to v_5.

Although structural relationships between nodes in a network do not change by using valued graphs, the weighting of linkages according to some distance criteria does give us a more refined measurement of nodal accessibility. Frequently we have raised the issue of the impact of transportation changes on spatial organization. Let us consider the impact of the proposed Interstate Highway System on the accessibility of major urban centers in the American Manufacturing Belt. This network may be abstracted as a graph of 56 nodes connected by 202 linkages (Fig. 5.17). To determine nodal accessibility, we have a 56×56 matrix in which each cell entry records the presence or absence of a direct linkage between every pair of nodes in the network. Using the procedure suggested by Shimbel, we can compute the shortest-path matrix for the network and obtain a vector of values representing nodal accessibility (Table 5.6). An alternative is to use the same information on the structure of the network, but to record in each cell of the matrix the driving-time between nodes that are directly connected. Using the rules for multiplying valued graphs, we can derive a minimum time-distance matrix and a corresponding vector of values of nodal accessibility (Table 5.7).

A comparison of the results suggests the utility of using the more precise measurement of distance for ranking centers according to network accessibility. The Shimbel shortest-path procedure clusters eight of the ten most accessible centers in Ohio. Clearly this clustering is the result of a spatial bias inherent in this method that assigns equal values to all linkages. By contrast, the valued-graph analysis, which is sensitive to the multiplicity of short linkages in the eastern portion of the A.M.B., reveals a spatial organization of high accessibility extending along an axis from Cleveland in the west to Washington, D.C. on the Atlantic Seaboard. Centers located along this axis, or in close spatial proximity to it, have high accessibility to all urban centers in the American Manufacturing Belt (Fig. 5.18).

Valued graphs are a relatively simple way of comparing on the national scale the relative accessibility of urban centers on the Interstate Highway System to their accessibility on the national railroad network.

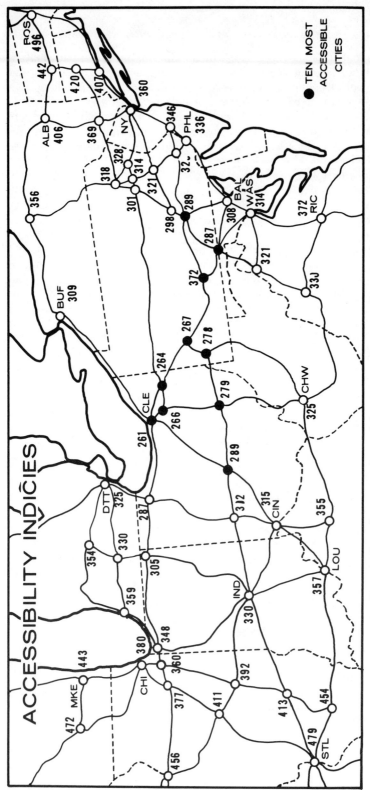

Fig. 5.17. The Interstate Highway System of the A.M.B. as a Valued Graph. The proposed Interstate Highway System in the American Manufacturing Belt is abstracted as a valued graph of 56 nodes connected by 202 linkages. The figure on each linkage is the average driving-time between nodal pairs.

Table 5.6. *Ranking of Selected Cities of the A.M.B. According to Shortest-Path Accessibility*

Rank	City	Shortest-path accessibility
1	Cleveland	192
2	Columbus	206
2	Toledo	206
2	Youngstown	206
5	Cincinnati	210
6	Syracuse	215
7	Akron	220
7	Dayton	220
9	Fremont	221
10	Cambridge	223
11	St. John	225
12	Pittsburgh	228
13	Indianapolis	229
13	Scranton	229
15	Louisville	231
16	Lexington	233
17	Charleston	234
18	Buffalo	242
19	Gary	244
19	Washington	244
21	Hershey	249
22	Albany	251
23	Detroit	254
24	Breezewood	256
25	Danbury	262
26	Staunton	265
27	Champaign	266
28	Stroudsburg	267
29	Marshall	269
30	Hagerstown	271
30	Harrisburg	271
32	Effingham	272
32	Mt. Vernon	272
34	Allentown	275
34	Strasburg	275
36	Homewood	279
37	Lansing	283
38	New York	285
39	Washington	289
39	Richmond	289
39	Benton Harbor	289
42	Baltimore	295
43	Norristown	299
43	Springfield	299
45	St. Louis	301
46	Trenton	308
47	Hartford	310
47	Bloomington	310
49	Boston	320
50	Philadelphia	323
51	Joliet	324
52	Chicago	325
53	New Haven	331
54	Moline	357
55	Milwaukee	378
55	Madison	378

Table 5.7. Ranking of Selected Cities of A.M.B. According to Shortest-Path Driving-Time

Rank	City	Shortest time-path from the city to all others
1	Cleveland	261.1 hrs.
2	Youngstown	264.0
3	Akron	265.6
4	Pittsburgh	267.3
5	Breezewood	271.5
6	Washington	277.5
7	Cambridge	278.7
8	Toledo	287.2
9	Hagerstown	287.4
10	Harrisburg	288.6
11	Columbus	289.4
12	Hershey	297.7
13	Dayton	301.8
14	Fremont	304.9
15	St. John	307.3
16	Baltimore	308.0
17	Buffalo	308.7
18	Washington, D.C.	314.1
19	Cincinnati	315.2
20	Scranton	318.2
21	Allentown	320.9
22	Strasburg	321.3
23	Detroit	324.5
24	Charleston	325.1
25	Norristown	325.2
26	Stroudsburg	327.8
27	Marshall	330.4
28	Indianapolis	330.7
29	Philadelphia	335.7
30	Staunton	339.0
31	Trenton	346.0
32	Gary	348.0
33	Lansing	354.3
34	Lexington	355.1
35	Syracuse	355.8
36	Louisville	357.4
37	Benton Harbor	359.3
38	Homewood	359.9
39	New York	360.9
40	Danbury	368.9
41	Richmond	371.6
42	Joliet	376.9
43	Chicago	379.7
44	Champaign	392.1
45	Albany	406.2
46	New Haven	407.4
47	Bloomington	411.2
48	Effingham	413.9
49	Hartford	420.1
50	Springfield	442.1
51	Milwaukee	442.5
52	Mt. Vernon	454.3
53	Moline	455.6
54	Madison	471.9
55	St. Louis	479.0
56	Boston	496.2

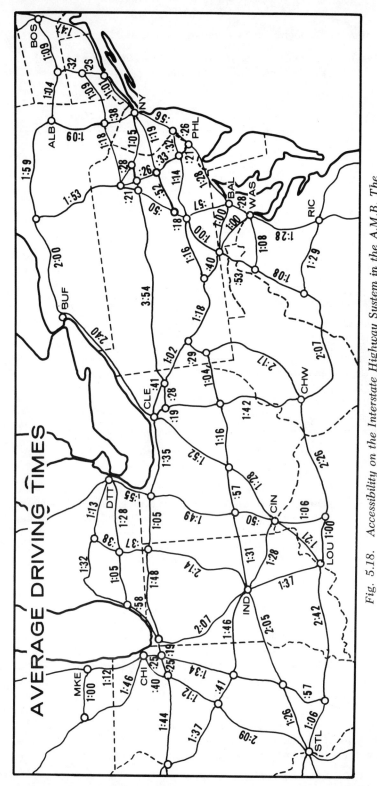

Fig. 5.18. Accessibility on the Interstate Highway System in the A.M.B. The value recorded for each city is the shortest total driving-time from that city to all others on the network. This valued-graph analysis is sensitive to the multiplicity of short linkages in the eastern portion of the region.

Table 5.8.   Accessibility on the Interstate Highway System and the National Railroad Network

Interstate Highways		Railroads	
Rank	City	Rank	City
1	Louisville	1	Indianapolis
2	Nashville	2	Louisville
3	Indianapolis	3	Cincinnati
4	St. Louis	4	Dayton
5	Lexington	5	St. Louis
6	Columbus	6	Chicago
7	Dayton	7	Columbus
8	Knoxville	8	Lexington
9	Cincinnati	9	Toledo
10	Chattanooga	10	Memphis
11	Chicago	11	Spartanburg
12	Atlanta	12	Birmingham
13	Toledo	13	Detroit
14	Memphis	14	Chattanooga
15	Bristol	15	Nashville
16	Akron	16	Little Rock
17	Cleveland	17	Knoxville
18	Birmingham	18	Milwaukee
19	Muskegon	19	Kansas City
20	Charleston, W.Va.	20	Moline
21	Youngstown	21	Atlanta
22	Moline	22	Akron
23	Greenville	23	Cleveland
24	Kansas City	24	Grand Rapids
25	Pittsburgh	25	Muskegon

Figure 5.19 shows each of 100 major urban centers in the United States in terms of its accessibility on both networks according to minimal travel-time. A comparison of the patterns of spatial organization reveals few major variations between the Interstate Highway System and the national railroad network. One major difference is the greater attraction of the western A.M.B., especially Chicago, for the top ten centers of the railroad network as compared to the Interstate Highway System (Table 5.8).

The absence of many obvious differences between urban accessibility on the two networks is not unexpected. As noted earlier in this chapter, the Interstate Highway System was a departure from previous governmental policy on highway development and was similar in several respects to the trunk-line developments of the railroads. We also observed in Chapter 2 that there is a general tendency in transportation development on the national scale for new systems to replicate and thereby reinforce an existing spatial organization. At a more detailed regional scale specific differences between nodal accessibility in the highway and railroad networks may be present, as in the example of the Southeast. The broad patterns of spatial organization, however, are similar even on that scale, as witness the focus on Atlanta.

A Graph-Theory Interpretation of Hierarchies

We observed in Chapter 1 that when a geographer examines the functional organization of a region he stresses the manner in which different points within the region are linked to each other. We said that a functional region consists of a set of centers between which a high degree of association exists. These associations may be in terms of the interactions that occur directly between city pairs or indirectly through one or more intermediary cities. The magnitude of the combined direct and indirect associations is a measure by which centers may be ranked. As a system of centers connected by varying degrees of association, the organization of the functional region may be abstracted as a graph. The centers become points in geographic space and the associations become linkages between the centers. These associations may be weighted according to some magnitude of interaction, both direct and indirect, between the centers.

Nystuen and Dacey have suggested an operational procedure for identifying hierarchical regions by graph-theoretic procedures.[6] To measure the degree of association between nodes, they selected a single index that they regarded as most representative of all functional contacts between centers. This index is long-distance telephone communication. When the functional region is abstracted as a graph, it may be represented in matrix form. The rows of the matrix represent centers from which telephone calls originate, and the columns represent centers at which telephone calls terminate. Unlike our previous examples, however, we cannot assume that the interaction between two centers will be identical in both directions. Consequently, when abstracting a functional region as a graph, we must define it as a directed graph: the number of outgoing telephone messages from a city may be greater or less than the number of incoming telephone messages. The number of telephone messages between two nodes is recorded in the individual cells of the matrix.

To establish dominant centers in the functional region, three properties related to flows are identified. The first property is that a city is independent if its largest flow is to a smaller city. By definition, the measure of size is the total number of messages received by a city from all cities in the study area. A subordinate city is defined as one whose greatest flow is to a larger city. The second property is that of transitivity. This implies that if a given city A is subordinate to city B, and B is in turn subordinate to city C, then city A is subordinate to city C. The third property stipulates that a city cannot be subordinate to any of its subordinates. This is a necessary requirement if a hierarchy is to be established on the basis of node-linkage associations.

To account for indirect influences between centers, the valued matrix is adjusted so that the direct association between each city pair is

[6] John Nystuen and Michael Dacey, "A Graph Theory Interpretation of Nodal Regions," *Papers* of the Regional Science Association, 7 (1961), 29–42.

INTERSTATE HIGHWAY ACCESSIBILITY RANKINGS

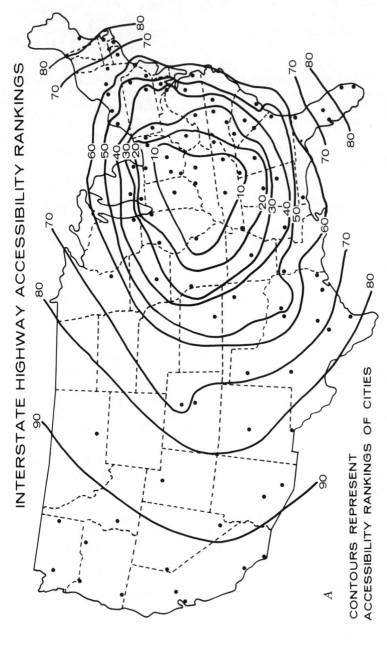

CONTOURS REPRESENT
ACCESSIBILITY RANKINGS OF CITIES

A

Fig. 5.19. Accessibility on the Interstate Highway System and the National Railroad Network. Using valued-graph analysis, the accessibility of 100 major urban centers in the United States can be compared between the Interstate Highway System (A) and the national railroad network (B). On the national scale the patterns of spatial organization reveal few major differences between the two networks.

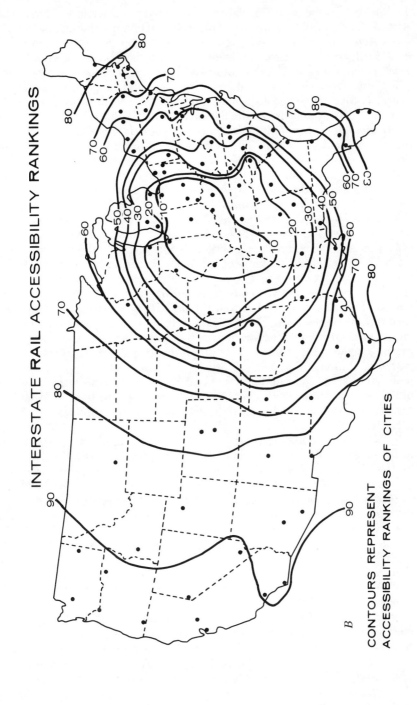

INTERSTATE RAIL ACCESSIBILITY RANKINGS

B
CONTOURS REPRESENT
ACCESSIBILITY RANKINGS OF CITIES

proportional to the total association of the largest center in the area. This is readily accomplished by obtaining the maximum column total of the connectivity matrix and dividing every element by the summation value. As a result of this adjustment, every cell entry will be either equal to or greater than zero and less than unity. Also, the column sum for any center will be greater than zero and less than or equal to one. The adjusted matrix is then subjected to a matrix-powering procedure until the solution time of a system is obtained. Since all of the initial cell entries are fractional values, the multiplication procedure has the effect of introducing a distance-decay effect. The more indirect, or attenuated, the association between centers, the less important it is in determining nodal associations. By summing the adjusted connectivity matrix with the powered matrices derived from it, Nystuen and Dacey obtain a weighted matrix of total nodal associations.

To illustrate this procedure, the authors provide an empirical example for a set of cities in Washington State. If their procedure is reasonable, the nodal structure that emerges should resemble the known hinterlands and hierarchical rankings of the major centers in the study area. The association between centers is defined by the number of long-distance telephone messages between city pairs during one week. (Table 5.9). The results of the analysis are shown in Figure 5.20. Cities are ranked by their total incoming messages. The spatial pattern of organization is determined on the basis of dominant flows between centers. Nystuen and Dacey find that the nodal regions derived by graph-theory analysis agree in general with expectations (Fig. 5.21). Seattle is the dominant center, with nested hierarchies existing around Spokane and Yakima. Portland forms a system of its own by capturing some of the nearby cities in the state of Washington. There are two small and independent hierarchies defined on Pasco and Moses Lake.

The Nystuen and Dacey methodology has been used by M. Miyagi in his investigation of the accessibility changes in the airline network of the United States during the transition period from propeller-driven to jet aircraft, 1959–1965.[7] Miyagi's principal objective is to explore the effects of accessibility changes upon the functional organization of the airline network. Using a 10 percent sample of origin-destination flows between the 100 largest traffic-generating cities in the United States, Miyagi uses dominant-flow analysis to determine functional organization in 1959, 1962, and 1965. The results of his analysis for 1959 and 1965 are presented in Figure 5.22.

A comparison of the nodal regionalization for the three time periods indicates no substantial changes. Miyagi argues that the transition to the new technology of jet aircraft has produced no significant change in the hierarchical organization of the nodal regions. The relative strength of each region has remained rather stable. In the three time periods, there have been no changes in relative importance of the first-order, second-order, and third-order centers. Even for the lowest-ordered centers in the

---

[7] Michihiro Miyagi, "Impact of Jet Aircraft on the Airline Network of the United States, 1959–1965" (Ph.D. dissertation, Ohio State University, 1969), 196 pp.

Table 5.9. A Portion of the Table of the Number of Telephone Messages Between City Pairs in the State of Washington for One Week in June 1958

From City	Aberdeen	Auburn	Bellingham	Lynden	To City Longview	Seattle	Spokane	Couer d'Alene	Portland
Aberdeen	—	24	50	0	246	3671	54	4	1005
Auburn	26	—	35	0	8	7654	42	0	163
Bellingham	55	27	—	782	24	2494	101	3	356
Lynden	4	0	2250	—	4	357	9	0	110
Longview	329	15	32	0	—	1911	87	4	4773
• • • •									
Seattle	3427	4579	3843	308	1268	—	6168	269	16781
• • • •									
Spokane	61	32	119	6	85	9991	—	3842	3838
Couer d'Alene	0	4	4	0	6	254	5104	—	141
Portland, Ore.	802	210	304	22	4190	22179	3310	98	—

Largest column total: Seattle—154,192.

From Nystuen and Dacey, "A Graph Theory Interpretation of Nodal Regions."

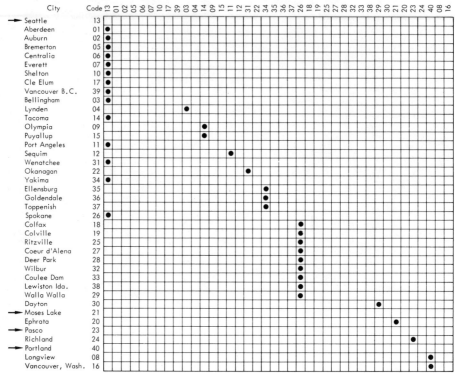

Arrows indicate cities which are terminal points.

Fig. 5.20.   Matrix of Dominant Associations. The matrix represents the pattern of regional organization in the state of Washington as determined by Nystuen and Dacey according to direct flows between centers. Centers marked by an arrow are the dominant nodes in the state, based on direct and indirect associations as measured by telephone messages between cities. The data identify the subordinate cities and the dominant node with which they are associated. From Nystuen and Dacey, "A Graph Theory Interpretation of Nodal Regions," Papers, Regional Science Association, 7 (1961).

hierarchy, changes have been minimal. Thus Miyagi concludes that the increases of scale economies associated with the introduction of direct traffic have had little impact on the hierarchical organization of nodal regions in the American airline network. While there has been an increase in average trip length of air passengers, with a concomitant intensification of the air-passenger fields of each node in the network, these changes have not materially affected nodal regionalization.

It is interesting to note that the dominant-flow analysis of the air-passenger associations between nodes in the United States does not produce a single integrated functional region. This is in contrast to some suggested organizations of space in the United States that have a highest-order region focusing on New York City.[8] Miyagi interprets this variation

[8] Allen K. Philbrick, "Principles of Areal Functional Organization in Regional Human Geography," Economic Geography, 33 (October 1957), 299–336.

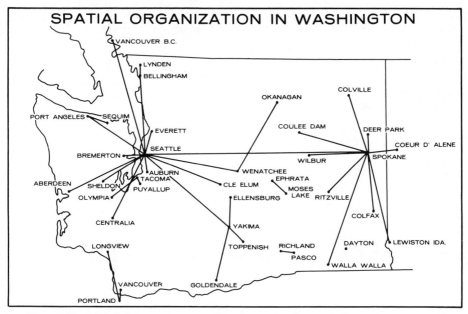

Fig. 5.21. *Spatial Organization in Washington. The map shows the functional organization of the state of Washington as determined by the Nystuen and Dacey analysis of dominant association of spatial interaction. After (Nystuen, Dacey)* "A Graph Theory Interpretation of Nodal Regions."

as an indication that the United States is too large an area to form a single integrated air-passenger region at this point in time, given the present level of interconnections between the metropolises. Rather than having a single integrated functional region, the air-passenger pattern shows three distinct organizations. The system is organized around the major nodes of Los Angeles in the West and New York in the East. Because of its distance from both New York and Los Angeles, Dallas also emerges as a separate first-order center. Chicago is subordinate to New York, and in the West, San Francisco is subordinate to Los Angeles, as is Houston to Dallas in the Southwest. Each of these subordinate centers is in turn a focus for traffic flows from other centers. For example, Kansas City is subordinate to Chicago, and New Orleans is subordinate to Houston. These centers in turn command a hinterland of influence involving a large number of lower-order centers. This pattern is strikingly similar to that observed in the airline dominance map (Fig. 1.25, p. 32).

Summary

In using graph theory to describe and analyze the spatial organization of an area, it is possible to deal with more than the aggregate characteristics of network structure. The component node-linkage relationships of the network may be the basis for determining the accessibility of the nodes to each other. To determine nodal accessibility, the network is

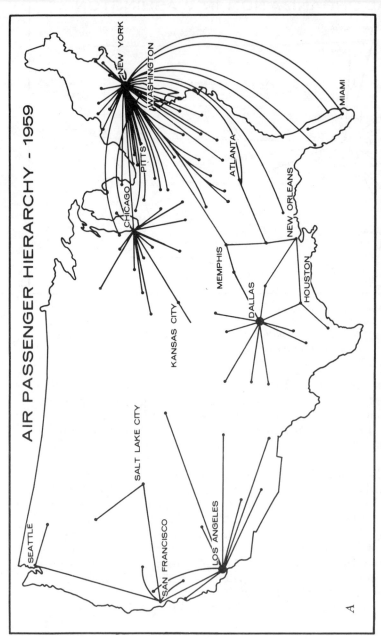

Fig. 5.22. The Air-Passenger Hierarchy of the U.S., 1959 and 1965. A comparison of the air-passenger hierarchy for the 100 major cities in the U.S. in 1959 (A) and 1965 (B) as determined by dominant-flow analysis, this map indicates that the introduction of jet aircraft has had little impact on the pattern of spatial organization. From Miyagi, "Impact of Jet Aircraft on the Airline Network of the United States."

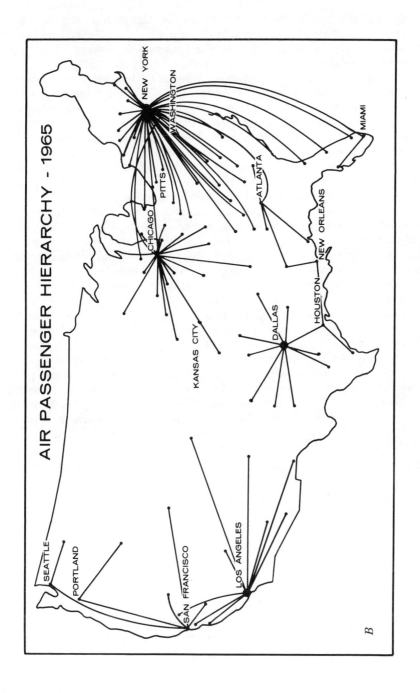

AIR PASSENGER HIERARCHY - 1965

B

abstracted as a graph, and information on the relationship between a pair of nodes is recorded in a matrix. At the simplest level, the cell entries of the matrix may be information on the presence or absence of linkages between a nodal pair.

From the matrix representation of the network it is possible to derive several measures of centrality, or accessibility. By multiplying the original connection matrix to the diameter of the network, successive matrices are derived, which enumerate different-length paths between nodes. Summing the original connection matrix with these matrices gives a matrix that records all direct and indirect connections between nodes on the network. This unweighted accessibility matrix may be used to establish a hierarchy of centers based on their accessibility values. A shortcoming of this procedure is the inclusion of redundant paths between nodes.

To eliminate the counting of redundant paths in determining nodal accessibility, it is possible to employ the shortest-path procedure. The objective is not to enumerate all paths between nodes, but to determine the shortest path between any pair of nodes. A simple and practical matrix procedure for doing this has been provided by Shimbel.

In determining nodal accessibility, it is not necessary to restrict the concept of a distance metric to one that is purely topological. Values that measure actual distance between nodes or the cost of movement or the average driving-time between nodes may be used in valued-graph analysis. The network is still abstracted as a graph and represented as a matrix. However, the cell entries of the matrix now record some measure of the actual distance, cost, or time relationship between nodal pairs. Indirect connections between nodes may be determined by a matrix-powering procedure using Boolean rules. The resulting accessibility matrix of the network does not alter structural relationships between nodes, but it does provide a more refined measurement of nodal accessibility.

CH**6**TER *allocation models*

We considered in Chapters 2 and 3 some of the ways in which geographers identify and describe patterns of spatial organization. In the chapters dealing with the gravity model and graph theory, attention was directed to the forces underlying particular flow and transportation patterns, and to the evaluation of the accessibility of individual nodes and entire networks.

A somewhat different type of analysis will be used in this chapter. The goal is not so much to determine *why* a particular pattern exists, but to determine what the best possible, or *optimal*, pattern would be according to some stated criteria. Such a model will typically allocate flows of goods between producing and consuming areas in a way that minimizes transport costs while still meeting the needs of the areas. A model that will determine such an optimal pattern is called a *normative model*. Some attention was given to optimal patterns in the discussion of potential maps in Chapter 3 where cities of maximum market potential and minimum market potential were identified, and in Chapter 5 where shortest-path measures were developed.

Normative models like the ones in this chapter are not necessarily intended to "fit" an actual flow pattern, as in the case of gravity-model equations; rather, they are intended to determine what the flow *should be* if transport costs are to be minimized. In some cases it may be possible for a traffic manager, dispatcher, or perhaps a regional planner to reallocate flows according to the optimal pattern. More often an investigator might look for reasons why the actual flow pattern *differs* from an optimal allocation, or vice versa. One reason might simply be the failure of certain basic assumptions underlying the normative model to approximate reality. For example, monopolies may exist in reality but not in the model, or everyone in the system may not have perfect knowledge of the comparative shipping costs and market demands. More fundamentally, the economically rational desire to minimize transport costs, or even to maximize profits, may be only a partial explanation of actual market behavior. An examination of the lack of correspondence between optimal and actual patterns may disclose forces other than economic ones at work. These may be political ties, which increase flows between certain regions, or there may be important social gains associated with certain allocations that benefit depressed areas. In the case of social gains, comparison of actual transport costs with the minimal transport costs of the optimal allocation permits a more realistic assessment of the costs associated with these social gains, and these costs may be evaluated against alternative, less costly social programs.

In this chapter we will first discuss and illustrate the simple transportation problem. Then a more complex model, involving optimal flows in a capacitated network, will be discussed. Finally, a brief survey of some of the many possible variations on the basic model will be presented.

The Transportation Model

In the family of normative models dealing with spatial flow patterns, the simplest and most elementary model is the transportation problem.[1] It is basically a static flow analysis intended to allocate flows of goods between different geographic locations in terms of some efficiency criteria. To identify the nature of the problem, consider a simple hypothetical example. Suppose that three factories producing small consumer items are located in St. Louis, Denver, and Indianapolis (Fig. 6.1). These factories can produce 150, 100, 120 appliances per day, respectively. The company operates three warehouses in Chicago, Kansas City, and Dallas. These warehouses can sell 100, 130, and 140 units of the product per day. The company wants to determine the amount of production to be shipped daily from each of the three factories to the three warehouses so that each warehouse obtains the number of units it can sell daily at a minimal total transportation cost.

The problem the company faces is characterized by nine possible activities of shipping the product from each of the factories to each of the warehouses. There are nine unknown activity levels to be determined: these are the amounts to be shipped along the nine routes. The shipping schedule the company follows is subject to a number of constraints. To be feasible, the schedule of shipments must be one that allows each warehouse to receive the required number of units it can sell per day. Also, the schedule cannot require a factory to ship more units than it can produce daily. Thus there is one constraint for each factory and one constraint for each warehouse. Several feasible shipping schedules can be derived that will satisfy these constraints. However, some of the feasible schedules will

---

[1] In spite of its name, this allocation model is not limited to transportation problems. For a discussion of non-transportation applications, see George Dantzig, *Linear Programming and Extensions* (Princeton: Princeton University Press, 1963).

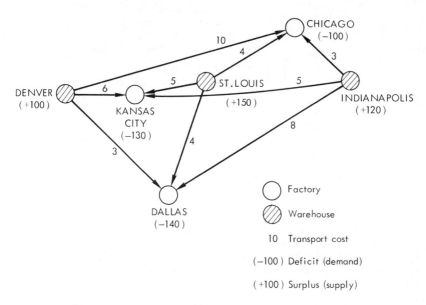

Fig. 6.1. *The Transportation Problem. This is a hypothetical example of a transportation problem involving three factories and three warehouses. The problem is to allocate the production of the factories to the warehouses so that the warehouses obtain at a minimum transportation cost the amount of product they sell daily.*

involve larger shipping costs than others. The problem then is to determine an optimal shipping schedule—one in which the shipment from the factories to the warehouses incurs the smallest aggregate cost. The objective of the problem is to minimize transportation costs. In seeking a solution to the hypothetical transport problem, there are certain known factors: (1) the location of the supplying firms and the location of demand (the warehouses), (2) the production per day of the factories, (3) the amount to be supplied to each warehouse, and (4) the cost of shipping per unit-weight of product from each factory to each warehouse.

We can present this information in matrix form. In Figure 6.2 the rows represent the supplying firms and the columns represent the deficit warehouses. The elements of the matrix are the unknown flows between the individual plants and the individual warehouses. There are nine flows, which we can designate x_{ij}, to be determined. Known information about supply and demand is recorded on the margins of the matrix. A row entry indicates the total production capacity of an individual plant. The allocations made from a given plant to the three warehouses cannot exceed this capacity. For example, the productive capacity of St. Louis is 150 units; the allocation made from this plant to the Chicago, Kansas City, and Dallas warehouses (flows x_{11}, x_{12} and x_{13}) must not exceed 150 units. A column entry indicates the demand of the individual warehouse. The allo-

Warehouses

		(1) Chicago	(2) Kansas City	(3) Dallas	Surplus
	To From				
(1)	St. Louis	4 x_{11}	5 x_{12}	4 x_{13}	150
(2)	Denver	10 x_{21}	6 x_{22}	3 x_{23}	100
(3)	Indianapolis	3 x_{31}	5 x_{32}	8 x_{33}	120
	Deficit	100	130	140	370

(Factories — row label along left side)

Fig. 6.2.   *Matrix Representation of the Hypothetical Problem. In the matrix format, the rows represent the supplying factories and the columns represent the deficit warehouses. The elements of the matrix are the unknown flows to be determined between the factories and the warehouses. These flows are constrained by production capacities at the factories and by demand requirements at the warehouses.*

cations made from the three plants to a given warehouse must equal this demand. For example, the demand at the Chicago warehouse is 100 units. Therefore, allocation made from the St. Louis, Denver, and Indianapolis plants to this warehouse (flows x_{11}, x_{21}, and x_{31}) must equal 100 units. In this particular example the sum of the supply capacity of the plants is equal to the demand of the warehouses.

Knowing the location of the plants and the warehouses, as well as the respective supply and demand, we need to record the information on the cost of shipping a unit-weight of product from each factory to each locality. This information may also be represented in matrix form. For example, the entry (enclosed in the upper left-hand corner of the cell) for the first row, first column in Figure 6.2 states that it costs $4 per unit of weight to ship the small consumer appliances from St. Louis to the warehouse in Chicago. Knowing the cost of shipping the product from the plant to the firm, it is now necessary to determine actual flows from the plant to the warehouses. These flows are subject to certain constraints: (1) the shipments planned from each factory must not exceed the productive capacity of that factory, and (2) the shipments planned for each warehouse must equal its requirements. Many possible routings can meet these constraints. Our problem is to find the routing that accomplishes this objective with the least possible total transport cost.

A FEASIBLE SOLUTION.   To find a feasible solution for the hypothetical problem, let us begin by allocating production of the first plant to the individual warehouses as cheaply as possible. Then we will allocate the surpluses of the other two plants to the warehouses in a manner that satisfies our constraint to balance production and demand. The matrix

Warehouses

To From	Chicago	Kansas City	Dallas	Surplus
St. Louis	4 100	5 0	4 50	150
Denver	10 0	6 10	3 90	100
Indianapolis	3 0	5 120	8 0	120
Deficit	100	130	140	370

Factories (row label at left)

Fig. 6.3. An Initial Allocation. An initial allocation is made so that the flows between the factories and the warehouses meet the supply-and-demand constraints. While the allocation is feasible, it is not necessarily optimal.

(Fig. 6.2) shows that the production of the plant at St. Louis can be allocated either to the warehouse in Chicago or to the one in Dallas—the per-unit transport costs are identical. Let us allocate 100 units of product from St. Louis to Chicago. This completely satisfies the demand at the Chicago warehouse. The remaining 50 units we allocate to the Dallas warehouse. This allocation exhausts the production at St. Louis but does not satisfy the total demand of the warehouse in Dallas. An additional 90 units is needed, which can be obtained from the Denver plant at a cost of $3 per unit-weight. The allocation of the 90 units from Denver to Dallas satisfies the demand at Dallas but does not exhaust the supply produced at Denver. The remaining 10 units may be allocated from Denver to Kansas City. This exhausts the supply at Denver but does not satisfy the demand at Kansas City. An additional 120 units is necessary to meet the demand, and since all other possibilities have been exhausted, it is necessary to supply Kansas City from Indianapolis. (Note that our constraints now force us to use this route even though it is not the lowest-cost route from Indianapolis.) The results of this allocation procedure are presented in Figure 6.3.

The above allocation is a feasible one—that is, the constraints on the problem have been met. No firm is supplying more than it can produce, and the demand at each warehouse is being totally satisfied. While this is a feasible solution, it may not be the optimal one. An alternative shipping schedule may exist that will also satisfy the supply and demand requirements at an even lower total transport cost. The total transport cost in this initial allocation is determined simply by multiplying the amount shipped from a warehouse to a destination site by the per-unit cost of shipment. Thus, for the shipment from St. Louis to Chicago we allocated 100 units at a per-unit cost of $4, so the total transport bill is $400. From St. Louis to Dallas we allocated 50 units at a unit cost of $4, for a total transport charge of $200. Similarly, the allocation from Denver to Kansas City costs $60, from Denver to Dallas $270, and finally, from Indianapolis to Kansas City is $600. The total transportation cost on the proposed shipping schedule is $1,530.

AN OPTIMAL SOLUTION.   Is the total transportation cost obtained from this first allocation the lowest possible in this system? One way of answering this question is to formulate a companion problem to the one we have posed. So far we have concerned ourselves with allocating shipments from supply to demand areas in order to minimize transport costs. This problem is referred to as the *primal* of the transportation problem. A companion problem is the *dual*, which is formulated in terms of a maximum objective. The maximum objective in this case is the economic return to be realized from allocating the small consumer products from the supply to the demand areas. Every transport problem has a primal and a dual component that are interrelated. If the objective of the primal is to be minimized, then the objective of the dual is to be maximized. The solution of the dual component has important economic implications because it represents imputed values, thereby providing a way to place an economic value on the allocation that has been made. The function of the dual in the transport problem is to maximize the difference between the price of a product at the factory and the price received for those products at the warehouse. These relative differences in factory price and warehouse price among the different producers and consumers are referred to as *shadow prices*. In this case the factory and delivered price will correspond to the optimal pattern of shipment based upon a minimum total transport cost. If the flow is optimal, the dual provides a set of equilibrium prices, which means that the difference between the price at the destination will differ from the price at the origin by the amount of the transportation costs between them.

In Chapter 2 we stated that in order for trade in a particular commodity to take place between two regions (i and j), the cost of transportation (c_{ij}) must be less than or equal to the price differential between the two regions—or, $c_{ij} \leq p_j - p_i$. Now we are saying that if the whole system is in balance or at equilibrium, the cost of transportation over the routes actually used between each surplus and deficit area is exactly equal to the price differential.

In the hypothetical example we used five of the nine possible shipping routes. We can now determine the opportunity costs, or the costs of not allocating shipments over the unused routes. If the difference between delivered price and factory price is *less* than the transportation cost between the factory and warehouse, we would have incurred losses by using these unused routes, so the opportunity cost is negative. However, if the price differential between the factory and the warehouse is higher than the transportation costs over an unused route, then we could have shipped over that route and made a profit; therefore, a positive opportunity cost exists in the system. Logically, there should be an allocation from the factory to the warehouse over any route for which the price

Warehouses

u	To / From	Chicago	Kansas City	Dallas	Surplus
v →		4	7	4	
0	St. Louis	4 / 0	5 / +2	4 / 0	150
1	Denver	10 / −7	6 / 0	3 / 0	100
2	Indian-apolis	3 / −1	5 / 0	8 / −6	120
	Deficit	100	130	140	370

(Factories)

Fig. 6.4. *The Dual. The dual of the transportation problem is used to determine if the allocation is optimal. If it is, the differences in shadow prices will be less than or equal to the transportation costs between the factories and the warehouses.*

differential is greater than the transport cost. An optimal solution is one in which all opportunity costs are negative.

To determine these price differentials, we begin by arbitrarily assigning a value to a given plant, as shown in Figure 6.4. Let us arbitrarily assign a value of zero to St. Louis.[2] Since a shipment has been made from St. Louis to Chicago at a unit rate of $4, the shadow price of the product at Chicago is set at $4. Similarly, a shipment has been made from St. Louis to Dallas at a unit rate of $4, so a shadow price at Dallas is set at $4. The Dallas warehouse also received a shipment from the Denver plant. Since the shadow price at Dallas is $4, and the transportation cost is $3 per unit, then the shadow price at Denver must be $1. From Denver, shipments were made to Kansas City. The shadow price at Denver is $1, and the transport charge is $6, so the shadow price at Kansas City is $7. Shipments were also made to the Kansas City warehouse from the Indianapolis plant at a cost of $5 per unit. Since the shadow price at Kansas City is $7, the shadow price in Indianapolis will be $2. Having established these shadow prices for the origin and destination places over routes that were actually used, we can now consider whether or not the positive opportunity costs exist on the unused routes. For example, no shipment was made between Denver and Chicago. The difference between the

[2] The procedure used in this section was utilized by Richard Morrill for solving similar types of allocation problems. The student should recognize that the procedure is not computationally useful but does illustrate quite clearly the relationship of dual values to the primal allocation. Although a value of zero is used to initiate the determination of shadow prices in this example, any arbitrary value is appropriate since we are interested only in price differentials, not actual prices. For those interested in operational procedures, an excellent introduction is provided by Allan J. Scott, *An Introduction to Spatial Allocation Analysis,* Commission on College Geography, Resource Paper Number 9, Association of American Geographers (1971).

Warehouses

To From	Chicago	Kansas City	Dallas	Surplus
St. Louis	4 0	5 110	4 40	150
Denver	10 0	6 0	3 100	100
Indianapolis	3 100	5 20	8 0	120
Deficit	100	130	140	370

Factories

Fig. 6.5. *A Second Allocation. As the initial allocation is not optimal, a second assignment of flows is necessary. Shipments are made between factories and warehouses where positive opportunity costs exist.*

shadow prices is a value of $3, whereas the transport charge between the two places is a value of $10 per unit-weight. Clearly the price differential between the Chicago warehouse and the Denver supplying plant is less than the transportation charge between the two points. Under these circumstances, no shipments are justified.

Similarly, the transportation costs between Indianapolis and Chicago and between Indianapolis and Dallas are greater than the difference between the delivered price at the warehouses and the factory price at the Indianapolis plant. No shipments are justified. The transportation charges over this route are less than the difference in shadow prices. However, the unused route between St. Louis and Kansas City indicates that our allocation schedule is not optimal. The price of the commodity at St. Louis is zero, but the transport cost to Kansas City is $5. Since the price at Kansas City is $7, the firm will make a profit of $2 by using that route.

To obtain a shipping schedule that minimizes our total transportation cost, another allocation between the plants and warehouses must be found. The evaluation by the dual of the initial allocation suggests that a flow should occur between St. Louis and Kansas City. In reallocating our shipments, we might begin by considering that the demand at the Chicago warehouse can be more economically served from Indianapolis than St. Louis. The per-unit transport costs are lower. We can allocate 100 units from Indianapolis to Chicago (Fig. 6.5), which exhausts the demand in Chicago and leaves 20 units of production in Indianapolis that we can distribute to Kansas City. In evaluating shipments from St. Louis and Denver, the lowest route costs are from Denver to Dallas. We might allocate 100 units of production from Denver to Dallas, which will completely exhaust the supply at Denver. The remaining 40 units of demand at Dallas must be allocated from St. Louis to Dallas. To satisfy the remaining demand at Kansas City it is necessary to ship 100 units from the St. Louis plant. This proposed allocation is feasible and is in accord with

u	From \ To	v=3 Chicago	v=5 Kansas City	v=4 Dallas	Surplus
0	St. Louis	4 / −1	5 / 0	4 / 0	150
1	Denver	10 / −8	6 / −2	3 / 0	100
0	Indian-apolis	3 / 0	5 / 0	8 / −4	120
	Deficit	100	130	140	370

Fig. 6.6. An Optimal Allocation. The dual indicates that the second allocation is both feasible and optimal. All the differences in shadow prices are less than or equal to the transportation costs between the factories and warehouses. There are no positive opportunity costs.

the dual evaluation, which suggests a flow from St. Louis to Kansas City. The total transport cost is $1,415, or $115 less than in our initial allocation. This solution is optimal, as shown in Figure 6.6. All opportunity costs are negative—that is, the difference in shadow prices between warehouses and plants over all unused routes are less than the transportation costs between the plant and the warehouse.

Notation. To make the transportation problem more explicit, we can use a compact mathematical notation to summarize the previous exposition in a series of linear relationships. Figures 6.7 and 6.8 show the

Deficit Areas

i \ j	1	2	3	4	j	•	m	s_i
1	x_{11}	x_{12}	x_{13}	x_{14}	x_{1j}	•	x_{1m}	s_1
2	x_{21}	x_{22}	x_{23}	x_{24}	x_{2j}	•	x_{2m}	s_2
3	x_{31}	x_{32}	x_{33}	x_{34}	x_{3j}	•	x_{3m}	s_3
4	x_{41}	x_{42}	x_{43}	x_{44}	x_{4j}	•	x_{4m}	s_4
i	x_{i1}	x_{i2}	x_{i3}	x_{i4}	x_{ij}	•	x_{im}	s_i
•	•	•	•	•	•	•	•	
n	x_{n1}	x_{n2}	x_{n3}	x_{n4}	x_{nj}	•	x_{nm}	s_n
d_j	d_1	d_2	d_3	d_4	d_j		d_m	$\sum_i s_i = \sum_j d_j$

(Surplus Areas — left axis label)

Fig. 6.7. Matrix of the Transportation Problem. The elements of the transportation problem are generalized in mathematical notation. There are n surplus areas and m deficit areas. The unknown shipment activities (x_{ij}) are constrained by known supply (s_i) and demand (d_j) requirements.

Deficit Areas

j	1	2	3	4	j	•	m
1	c_{11}	c_{12}	c_{13}	c_{14}	c_{1j}	•	c_{1m}
2	c_{21}	c_{22}	c_{23}	c_{24}	c_{2j}	•	c_{2m}
3	c_{31}	c_{32}	c_{33}	c_{34}	c_{3j}	•	c_{3m}
4	c_{41}	c_{42}	c_{43}	c_{44}	c_{4j}	•	c_{4m}
i	c_{i1}	c_{i2}	c_{i3}	c_{i4}	c_{ij}	•	c_{im}
•	•	•	•	•	•	•	
n	c_{n1}	c_{n2}	c_{n3}	c_{n4}	c_{nj}		c_{nm}

(left-side label: Surplus Areas)

Fig. 6.8.   *Transport-Cost Matrix. The cell entries in the matrix are the transport costs* (c_{ij}) *between the ith surplus area and the jth deficit area. The objective is to find a set of flows* (x_{ij}), *such that the total transportation costs are minimized.*

matrix format for the simple transport problem. In the first matrix, surplus points are listed in the far left-hand column and deficit areas are listed along the top row. In the last column, s_i represents the amount of the given commodity that is available for export from the ith surplus region. The sum of the s_i, represented by Σs_i, is the total amount of the commodity available for export from all of the surplus regions. In the last row, d_{ij} represents the amount of a commodity demanded by the jth region. The total amount of the commodity demanded by all the deficit regions is Σd_j. As the total demand is equal to the total supply, we have $\Sigma s_i = \Sigma d_j$. In the body of the table, x_{ij} represents flow from the ith to the jth region. These are the unknown levels of activity in the problem. In the second matrix, the surplus regions are listed in the left-hand column and the deficit regions along the top row. The cell entries in the matrix are the unit transportation cost (c_{ij}) between the ith origin region and jth destination region. The objective of the transportation problem is to find a set of x_{ij} (flows) so that T, total transport cost, is minimized. Since T is equal to the sum of each shipment times the cost of that shipment, or $\Sigma\Sigma\, c_{ij}\, x_{ij}$, we can say that the objective of the transportation problem is
$$i\,j$$
to minimize

$$T = \Sigma\Sigma\, c_{ij}\, x_{ij}$$
$$i\ j$$

This objective is subject to the following restrictions or constraints:

$$\Sigma\, x_{ij} = d_j$$
$$i$$

i.e., the flow from all i origin points to destination j is equal to the demand at a given j destination;

$$\sum_j x_{ij} = s_i$$

i.e., the flow to all j destination points is equal to the supply of a given ith origin;

$$\sum_i s_i = \sum_j d_j$$

i.e., total surpluses are equal to total deficits;

$$x_{ij} \geqslant 0$$

i.e., there will be no negative flows in the solution since negative flows have no meaning in this problem.

The objective function and the associated constraints together form the primal transportation problem. The dual of this primal problem has direct economic interpretation. If v_j is the imputed value (shadow price) for the product at the destination j, and u_i is the imputed value (shadow price) of the product at origin i, the dual problem is to maximize S, the value added to the product by the transfer between origin and destination:

$$\text{Max } S = \sum_j d_j v_j - \sum_i s_i u_i$$

This is subject to the constraint that the difference in price between origin and destination must be less than or equal to transportation costs:

$$v_j - u_i \leqslant c_{ij}$$

In the optimal solution, S, the total value added to the product, is exactly equal to T, the minimum total value of transfer. The constraint in the dual illustrates the economic restriction of pure competition; the value per unit that is added to the product by its transfer from the ith origin region to the jth destination region cannot be greater than the cost per unit of that transfer. For the shipments that actually occur in the optimal solution, the value added is equal to the transfer cost.

In treating allocations from origin to destination points in terms of the transportation problem, certain assumptions are made. These include: (1) an economy operating under conditions of perfect competition, (2) product homogeneity, (3) the transfer rate per unit of product is independent of the distance the product is shipped, and (4) the amount of product produced and the amount of product consumed are fixed.

Empirical Examples of the Transportation Problem

THE SOVIET WOOD-PROCESSING INDUSTRY. An example of the use of the basic transportation problem is provided by Brenton Barr in his recent study of transport costs as a factor in the location of the Soviet wood-processing industry.[3] One phase of the study is concerned with determining the efficiency of the pattern of interregional flows of roundwood lumber within the Soviet Union. The transport problem is used to determine the optimal pattern of flows between the regions of supply and demand. To determine this optimal pattern of interregional flow, certain information is needed: (1) the sources of supply of roundwood, (2) the major markets for this product, and (3) the transportation costs per cubic meter of product between regions of supply and regions of demand. Barr calculated surpluses and deficits of roundwood for 34 regions in the U.S.S.R. as well as rail transport costs between them. His objective was to allocate the roundwood shipments from the sources of supply to the deficit areas so that total transportation costs would be minimized. The allocation must be such that no producing area is asked to supply more than its present level of output, and the demand in the consuming areas must also be met. The primal solution to this problem provided a pattern of flows with a minimal aggregate cost of transport. This allocation was then evaluated in terms of the secondary solution, the dual, which provided a system of imputed prices for the commodities being analyzed. The actual flow pattern of roundwood in the Soviet Union is shown in Figure 6.9. The optimal or theoretical flow pattern obtained by the transportation problem is shown in Figure 6.10. A comparison of the actual and theoretical flow patterns shows that the actual pattern corresponds generally with the optimal pattern. The correspondence is greatest when shipments of less than 2.5 million cubic meters per annum are removed from the analysis. Barr argues that a pattern that includes these smaller flows becomes confused by cross- and back-hauls, features of transportation that are not taken into account in the transportation problem. As there is less evidence of cross- and back-hauling for shipments greater than 2.5 million cubic meters per annum, the correspondence between such flows and the optimal flows increases. Another reason for a discrepancy between actual and optimal shipments is product heterogeneity. Some types of roundwood move primarily to specialized processing centers not found in all destination regions, as in the case of birch or aspen moving to plywood plants. This too is reduced when small shipments are excluded, since shipments of more than 2.5 million cubic meters are more homogeneous. Despite the general similarity of the two patterns, Barr concludes that Soviet planners could achieve a more economic allocation of roundwood between regions by bringing the actual patterns closer to the optimal patterns that are based on minimal transport costs. He estimates that a 20 percent saving (55 million rubles) could be effected in roundwood shipments. Barr also derives a series of relative shadow prices for the regions, which should be equivalent to f.o.b. prices at origins and delivered prices at destinations. He was unable, however, to compare these differentials with actual price differentials.

[3] Brenton Barr, *The Soviet Wood-Processing Industry* (Toronto: University of Toronto Press, 1970).

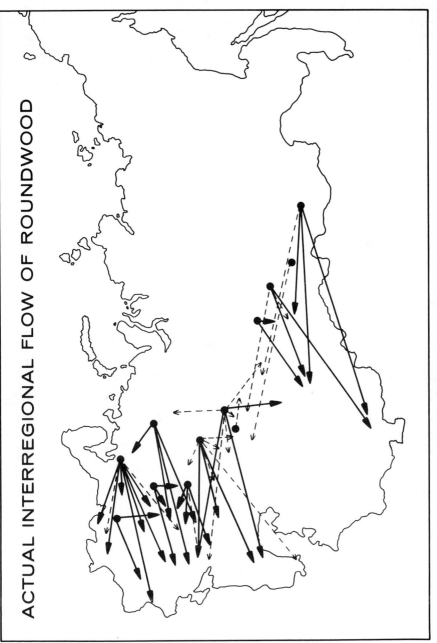

ACTUAL INTERREGIONAL FLOW OF ROUNDWOOD

Fig. 6.9. Major Interregional Flows of Roundwood in the Soviet Union, 1964. After Brenton Barr, The Soviet Wood-Processing Industry, Toronto: University of Toronto Press, 1970.

OPTIMAL INTERREGIONAL FLOW OF ROUNDWOOD

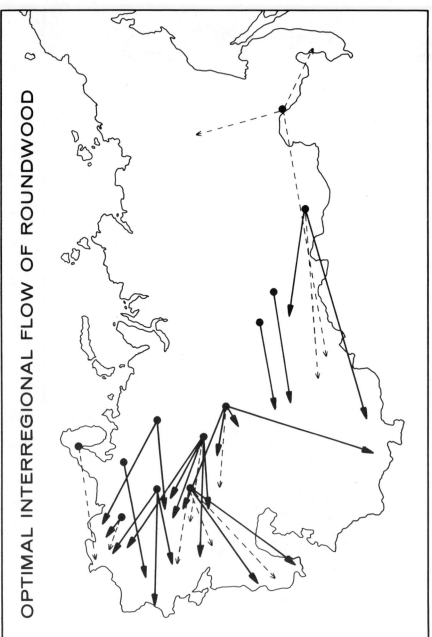

Fig. 6.10. Optimal Interregional Flows of Roundwood in the Soviet Union, 1964. After Brenton Barr, The Soviet Wood-Processing Industry, Toronto: University of Toronto Press, 1970.

HINTERLAND DELIMITATION. We discussed in earlier chapters the importance of the hinterland concept in understanding the spatial organization of the region. In Chapter 3 we examined some ways in which the gravity model could be used to delineate hinterlands. The transportation problem also provides a technique for constructing hinterlands based upon optimal criteria. These optimal hinterlands can be compared to actual ones—for example, one might group a number of interior centers in such a manner that the total cost of transport commodities from these centers to a limited number of ports is at a minimum. These optimal port hinterlands might be compared with the actual hinterlands, and efforts could be made to explain the variations.

While we have emphasized transport-cost minimization as the principle objective of the transport problem, it is easy to substitute other variables for transport costs. Maurice Yeates, in a study of school districts in Grant County, Wisconsin, uses the transportation problem to delimit hinterlands in which the objective is to minimize the distance that the students must travel from their homes to high school.[4] These optimal school districts for the high schools can be compared with actual school districts. If it is assumed that minimizing the distance students travel from home to school will minimize the cost involved in transporting students, then it is possible to conclude that the school districts that do not yield the minimal aggregate distance are not efficient, for cost savings are possible that are not being realized.

Yeates divided Grant County into 1,160 mile-square sections. He tabulated the number of high-school students in each section, and he measured the straight-line distance from the center of each section to each of the thirteen high schools in the county. The problem was

$$\min T = \sum_i \sum_j s_{ij} d_{ij}$$

where s_{ij} equals the students to be transported from the ith mile-square cell to any jth high school, and d_{ij} equals the distance from the ith cell to the jth high school. To solve this problem there are certain constraints—namely,

$$\sum_j s_{ij} = a_i$$

i.e., the number of students assigned from the ith mile-square section must equal a_i, the number attending high school from that section,

$$\sum_i s_{ij} = b_j$$

i.e., the number of students assigned to the jth high school must equal b_j, the classroom capacity of that high school,

$$\sum_i a_i = \sum_j b_j$$

[4] Maurice Yeates, "Hinterland Delimitation: A Distance Minimizing Approach," *The Professional Geographer,* 16 (1963), 7–10.

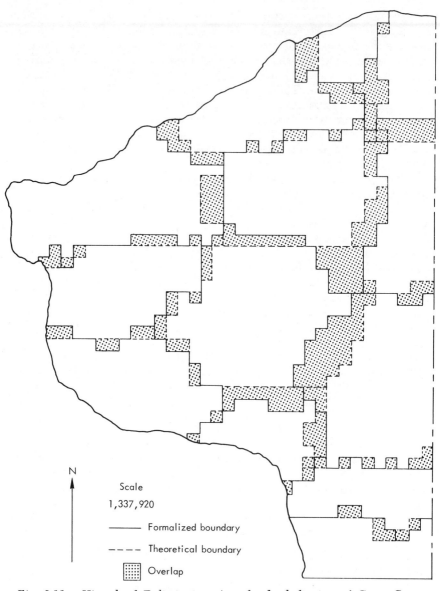

Fig. 6.11.   Hinterland Delimitation. Actual school districts of Grant County, Wisconsin, may be compared with those based on optimality criteria. An optimal district is one that minimizes the distance students must travel to high school. From M. Yeates, "Hinterland Delimitation: A Distance Minimizing Approach," The Professional Geographer, 9 (1961).

i.e., the total supply of students must be equal to the classroom capacity to serve their demand for education.

The minimum-distance solution to this allocation problem results in the school districts illustrated in Figure 6.11. This optimal division of school districts can be compared with the actual school boundaries to indicate the degree to which the 1961 school districts in Grant County minimized the distance between students and schools. The results suggest a high degree of correspondence between the actual and theoretical school districts. Yeates observes that of the 1,160 mile-square cells, only 209 need to be reassigned to achieve the spatial efficiency called for in the optimal solution.

Flows in a Capacitated Network

In the transportation problem the allocation of flows from surplus areas to deficit areas is made on the assumption that a direct linkage exists between each surplus and deficit area and that an unlimited amount of flow can occur over that linkage. The occurrence of this situation in the real world is rare. More commonly, flows must pass through a series of intermediate areas, or nodes, between the origin and destination points. Moreover, there are restrictions on this flow posed by the capacity of the linkages that connect the points of origin to intermediate points, the intermediate points to other intermediate points, and the intermediate points to other destination points.

An allocation model that includes a consideration of intermediate nodes, as well as capacity constraints, is the general transportation problem. The objective function is still to find a maximum flow that minimizes cost from a given origin point to a given destination point. This flow, however, is constrained by the capacity of the network. The maximal flow that can occur between two points is determined by the minimal capacity of the linkages in the network.

A HYPOTHETICAL EXAMPLE. To illustrate the general transportation problem, consider the network in Figure 6.12. There are eleven nodes and twenty-one linkages. A manufacturer located in Los Angeles wishes to ship his product to a number of marketing outlets in New York City. Given the available transportation facilities, he finds he is unable to ship his production directly from Los Angeles to New York. Consequently, the flow must pass through a series of intermediate points between Los Angeles and New York. The amount of product that he can supply to the New York distributors is restricted by (1) the cost of movement over the linkages of the network and (2) the capacity of the individual linkages. In this case the linkage capacity is equal to the availability of cargo space between centers. In Figure 6.12 each link of the network is identified by two values: the first is the unit cost of transportation, and the second is the capacity (cargo-space availability) of that linkage. A problem facing the producer is to ship a maximal amount of product from Los Angeles to New York given these cost and capacity constraints.

Since linkage capacity is greatest from Los Angeles to Denver, and the per-unit transport cost is the lowest over this route, the manufacturer may consider, as an initial move, sending 500 units of product to Denver at a per-unit charge of 30¢. From Denver it is impossible for him to move the entire 500 units directly to St. Louis because the capacity on that route is less than the capacity on the initial route from Los Angeles to

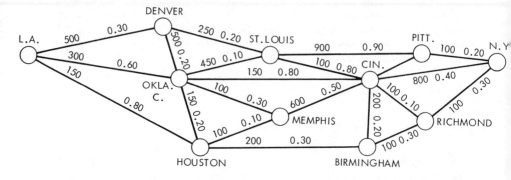

Fig. 6.12.   *The General Transportation Problem. A hypothetical example of the general transportation problem involving eleven cities and two linkages. The problem is to ship the maximum amount of product to New York from Los Angeles over the capacitated network at minimal total transportation costs. The first figure on a linkage is its capacity; the second is the transportation cost.*

Denver. An alternative route from Denver to Oklahoma costs the same as the route from Denver to St. Louis and can accommodate the 500 units of product. Thus the route from Denver to Oklahoma City becomes the second linkage in the shipping schedule. What is being sought, of course, is a path of linkages from Los Angeles to New York that will permit the manufacturer to move a maximal amount of his product at a minimal cost.

There is no linkage from Oklahoma City toward New York that has a capacity of 500 units. The shipper may consider dividing the 500 units and sending 450 of them to St. Louis and the remaining 50 from Oklahoma City to Cincinnati. However, this strategy has certain disadvantages. The cost of shipment from Oklahoma City to Cincinnati is high. Also, a flow from Oklahoma City to St. Louis poses a subsequent difficulty for the shipper because the linkages from St. Louis to Pittsburgh or to Cincinnati are high-cost routes. In trying to minimize cost, the most economical route is from Oklahoma City to Houston. However, the capacity on that route is only 150 units. If the shipper moves the 150 units from Oklahoma City to Houston, then he can ship from Houston to Birmingham, and from Birmingham to Cincinnati. At Cincinnati the 150 units could be moved directly to New York City over a route of more than adequate capacity. However, the Cincinnati to New York linkage is more costly than the combined linkage from Cincinnati to Pittsburgh to New York. If the shipper selects the lower-cost route, the capacity limitation on flow is 100 units. Consequently, if the shipper seeks the least-cost path from Los Angeles to New York, given the capacity constraints on the linkages, he is able to move only 100 units of product at a total cost in New York of $150 in transportation charges (Fig. 6.13). The maximal flow on this minimal-cost path is equal to the minimal capacity of linkages on it.

The maximal flow in this case is limited by the capacity of the

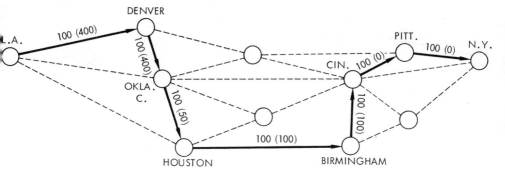

Fig. 6.13.   An Initial Shipment. An initial shipment of 100 units of product is made by the least-cost path from Los Angeles to New York. The figure in parenthesis is the unused capacity of a linkage.

linkages from Cincinnati to Pittsburgh, and from Pittsburgh to New York. Both of these linkages are saturated by a flow of 100 units of product; however, other linkages in this path have not been saturated. Consequently, they constitute an opportunity for additional flow, but at a slightly higher cost. The shipper could consider shipping from Los Angeles to Denver–Oklahoma City–Houston–Birmingham–Cincinnati–New York. The Cincinnati–New York linkage replaces the saturated one from Cincinnati to Pittsburgh and Pittsburgh to New York. However, the cost of using that linkage is 10¢ more per unit of product, and the amount of additional product that can be moved over this path is only 50 units. This maximal flow is determined by the capacity of the linkage from Oklahoma City to Houston. This linkage becomes saturated with the addition of 50 units to the 100 that had been assigned to it previously. The delivered price to New York for these 150 units of product is $240, or $1.60 per unit (Fig. 6.14).

If the shipper is willing to incur additional costs, he can consider alternative flows from Los Angeles to New York. For example, the remaining capacity on the Los Angeles–Denver linkage, 350 units, can be used in the following fashion. At Denver 250 of these units may be shipped to Oklahoma City, increasing total flow over that linkage to 400 units. The remaining 100 units may be shipped from Denver to St. Louis and from St. Louis to New York via Cincinnati. Of the 250 units at Oklahoma City, 150 may be shipped directly from Oklahoma City to Cincinnati and then on to New York. The convergence of the three paths on Cincinnati increases total flow over the Cincinnati–New York linkage to 400 units. The remaining 100, due to capacity constraints, must be shipped from Oklahoma City to Memphis to Cincinnati and then to New York. Using these three paths of flow from Los Angeles to New York results in a total transportation cost of $850 for the 500 units, or a unit cost of $1.70 (Fig. 6.15).

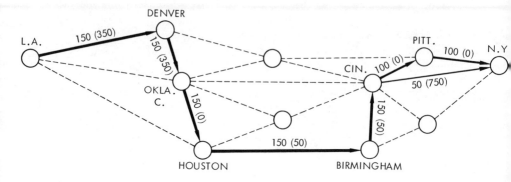

Fig. 6.14.   *Augmenting Flow. An additional shipment of 50 units of product is made by using the linkage between Cincinnati and New York.*

In this fashion we have exhausted a shipment of 500 units from Los Angeles along the least-cost routes. However, there is an additional capacity at higher costs from Los Angeles to Oklahoma City and from Los Angeles to Houston. The amount of flow that would take place by these additional routes is of course determined by the transport costs on the individual linkages and by the capacity remaining after the above allocations have been made. Obviously the allocation procedure we have been using is one of exhaustive trial and error. While it would be possible to eventually find the maximal flow at minimal cost over this capacitated network, a more systematic search routine is necessary for efficient allocation.

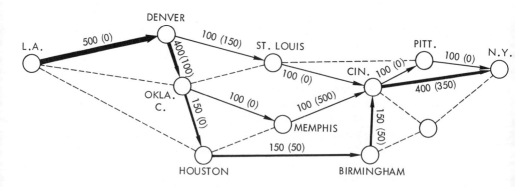

Fig. 6.15.   *Exhausting Linkage Capacity. The capacity of the linkage between Los Angeles and Denver is saturated by allocating shipments over several alternative paths between Los Angeles and New York.*

THE OUT-OF-KILTER ALGORITHM. An efficient algorithm, or set of rules, for solving the general transportation problem has been developed by Fulkerson.[5] Called the out-of-kilter algorithm, it generalizes the primal-dual transportation problem so that it can be initiated with an infeasible dual solution as well as an infeasible primal solution. The algorithm begins with an arbitrary flow, feasible or not, together with an arbitrary set of prices, and then uses a systematic search procedure to adjust the flow over a linkage of the network that fails to satisfy certain optimality properties. The freedom to begin with any flow and pricing vector, rather than starting with particular ones that satisfy certain optimality properties, is the most attractive feature of this algorithm.

A flow is feasible if it satisfies the relationship $l_{ij} \leqslant x_{ij} \leqslant g_{ij}$ where $l_{ij} = $ a lower limit on the amount of flow on a linkage, where $g_{ij} = $ an upper limit on the amount of flow on a linkage, and where $x_{ij} = $ the unknown level of flow to be determined in the problem. A feasible flow that minimizes the cost relationship $\Sigma\Sigma\limits_{i\,j} c_{ij}\, x_{ij}$ over all feasible flows is optimal.

Let us associate with each node a variable u_i or v_j, which are imputed prices (shadow prices) for a unit of flow at a node. We can define a net linkage cost $c_{\overline{ij}}$ as $c_{\overline{ij}} = c_{\overline{ij}} + u_i - v_j$. This represents the total cost to the system of transporting one unit of product from node i to node j. If the price of the unit of product at node i plus the cost of moving it to node j is greater than the price at j, then it does not pay to ship a unit of product from node i to node j—under these conditions, $c_{\overline{ij}} = c_{ij} + u_i - v_j > 0$. If a unit of product at node j costs more than the unit of product at node i plus the transportation costs from i to j, then it is profitable to ship a unit of product from node i to node j—under these conditions, $c_{\overline{ij}} = c_{ij} + u_i - v_j < 0$. If the price at node j is equal to the price at i plus the transportation cost from node i to j, then we are indifferent to additional flows from node i to node j—under these conditions, $c_{\overline{ij}} = c_{ij} + u_i - v_j = 0$.

Limitations on permissible flows ($l_{ij} \leqslant x_{ij} \leqslant g_{ij}$) together with the possible levels of system cost ($c_{\overline{ij}} = c_{ij} + u_i - v_j$) yield the conditions that will be satisfied by an optimal solution: a maximal flow at minimal costs. The first of these optimality conditions states that when the linkage cost is negative (it is profitable to send a commodity from node i to node j), then the flow on that linkage ought to be as large as possible: $c_{\overline{ij}} < 0 \rightarrow x_{ij} = g_{ij}$. The second condition of optimality states that when the linkage cost is zero, we are indifferent to flow levels as long as they meet the constraint that no flow can be less than the lower capacity on a linkage nor greater than the upper capacity on that linkage: $c_{\overline{ij}} = 0 \rightarrow l_{ij} \leqslant x_{ij} \leqslant g_{ij}$. The third condition of optimality states that when the linkage cost is positive (a loss is incurred by sending the commodity from node i to node j), then the flow ought to be at the minimum level possible: $c_{\overline{ij}} > 0 \rightarrow x_{ij} = l_{ij}$.

[5] D. R. Fulkerson, "An Out-of-Kilter Method for Minimal Cost Flow Problems," *Journal of the Society for the Industrial Application of Mathematics*, 9 (1961), 18–27.

Any linkage meeting these optimality conditions is defined by Fulkerson as being *in-kilter*. Linkages that do not meet these conditions are termed *out-of-kilter*—hence the name of the algorithm. To get all linkages in-kilter, Fulkerson uses a modified labeling procedure that searches for a flow-augmenting path from one node to another.[6] This labeling procedure terminates in one of two ways, called a *breakthrough* and a *nonbreakthrough* respectively. If a breakthrough occurs, then a path exists from the point of origin of the flow to the point of destination that can be flow augmented, the increase in flow being determined by the out-of-kilter state of the linkage. If a nonbreakthrough results, it is impossible to increase the flow between the point of origin and the point of destination. By alternate applications of the labeling and flow-augmenting process, all linkages are brought to an in-kilter state. When all linkages are in-kilter, the flow is feasible and optimal in terms of minimal costs.

SOLUTION FOR THE HYPOTHETICAL EXAMPLE.   In seeking an optimal solution for the hypothetical example, we know all the information that is required for the out-of-kilter algorithm. The upper limit on each linkage (g_{ij}) is the amount of transportation service available over that linkage to the shipper in Los Angeles. The shipper is not obligated, however, to use any or all of the transportation service that is available, so the lower limit on each linkage (l_{ij}) may be set equal to zero. We seek a solution whereby the flow over the linkages (x_{ij}) is either equal to or greater than the lower limit of zero, and equal to or less than the upper limit imposed by the availability of transportation services. We are seeking a flow that is maximal in quantity without violating the capacity limits of network linkages. This flow is further constrained by the requirement that the related transportation costs be as low as possible. To determine the cost relationship, we know the per unit product charges on each linkage (c_{ij}).

To apply the out-of-kilter algorithm, we may begin with any flow assignment, feasible or not, or any series of shadow prices. Let us consider the flow assignments in Figure 6.15. Additional flows from Los Angeles may also be assigned to Oklahoma City and Houston consistent with the requirement that the capacity on the linkages not be exceeded. Assigning a shadow price of zero at Los Angeles, the shadow prices may be calculated and used with the per-unit cost of transportation (c_{ij}) to determine the net linkage cost $(c_{\overline{ij}})$. If this net linkage cost is negative, we assign the maximal amount of flow possible on a given linkage (g_{ij}). If the value is positive, we assign the minimal value to an individual linkage (l_{ij}). If the net linkage cost is zero, we are indifferent to the flow, provided it is consistent with our upper and lower capacity limits.

The optimal primal and dual solutions for the hypothetical example are shown in Figures 6.16 and 6.17 respectively. Comparing the optimal primal allocation with Figure 6.15, it is apparent that our initial efforts were feasible but not optimal. The optimal allocation calls for fewer

---

[6] For a detailed discussion of the operational procedures involved in the out-of-kilter algorithm, see E. P. Durbin and D. M. Kroenke, "The Out-of-Kilter Algorithm: A Primer," *Rand Corporation Memorandum*, RM 5472-PR (December 1967).

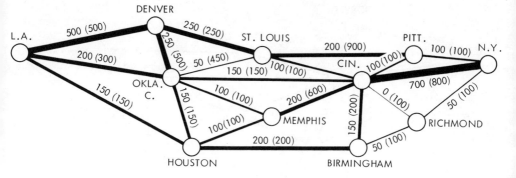

Fig. 6.16. *The Out-of-Kilter Algorithm. The out-of-kilter algorithm is an efficient procedure for allocating flows so that a maximal flow over the capacitated network is achieved at a minimal total transport cost. The first figure on a linkage is the flow allocated by the algorithm. The figure in parenthesis is the capacity of the linkage.*

shipments between Denver and Oklahoma City and higher levels of shipments from Denver to St. Louis and from St. Louis to Pittsburgh. The latter is achieved by reversing the original allocation between Cincinnati and Pittsburgh. This reversal permits greater shipments at a lower total transport cost. In total, 850 units of product are shipped from Los Angeles

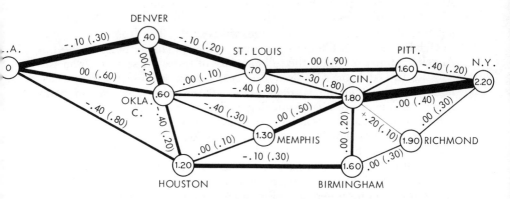

Fig. 6.17. *The Dual of the OKA. The first figure on a linkage is the net linkage cost, c_{ij}; the second figure is the transportation cost per unit of product, c_{ij}; the figure within the city circle is a shadow price, u_i or v_i. Under conditions of optimality, the flow over a linkage will equal the upper limit of its capacity if the net linkage cost is negative; the flow will equal the lower limit of capacity if the net linkage cost is positive. If the net linkage cost is zero, the flow will range between the lower and upper limits of capacity.*

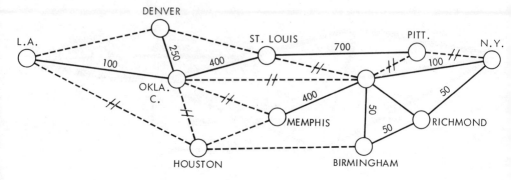

Fig. 6.18.   Bottlenecks. Although there are linkages with unused capacity, none of them can be arranged in a path sequence from Los Angeles to New York. The saturated linkages, indicated by crosshatches, are bottlenecks to any increased utilization of the network.

to New York. Of this amount, 500 units are shipped to Denver and then to New York through a series of intermediate nodes. An additional 200 units are shipped from Los Angeles to Oklahoma City and then to New York through a series of intermediate points. From Los Angeles to Houston 150 units of product are shipped, and by a series of intermediate nodes these reach New York. These 850 units are transported at a total cost of $1,520 or $1.79 per unit. This level of shipping activity and related cost is possible because the only constraint on shipments from Los Angeles is the availability of transport services (route capacities).

It may be observed that the flow from Los Angeles to Houston is equal to the capacity of that linkage, whereas the flow from Los Angeles to Oklahoma City is 100 units less than capacity. The inability of the Los Angeles shipper to utilize the full capacity of transport services from Los Angeles to Oklahoma City is due to restrictions on linkages from Oklahoma City to other intermediate nodes. There exists no series of paths from Los Angeles to New York that will permit the shipper to ship the full-capacity amount of 950 units from Los Angeles to Denver, Oklahoma City, or Houston. The paths of the network are saturated with a flow of 850 units. Although there are linkages with unused capacity, none of these can be arranged in a path sequence from Los Angeles to New York. The saturated linkages constitute bottlenecks to the increased utilization of the transportation network (Fig. 6.18).[7]

[7] The presence of bottlenecks is a direct consequence of the max-flow min-cut theorem upon which the out-of-kilter algorithm is based. Simply, the max-flow min-cut theorem states that the maximal flow that can occur within a network is exactly equal to the minimal capacity of a cut set of linkages which separate the source node from the destination node. See G. B. Dantzig and D. R. Fulkerson, "On the Max-Flow Min-Cut Theorem of Networks," *Linear Inequalities and Related Systems, Annals of Mathematic Study,* 38 (Princeton: Princeton University Press, 1956), 215–21.

In Figure 6.17 the shadow prices and the net linkage costs in the optimal solution are given. It may be observed that of the twenty-one linkages, ten have net linkage costs that are negative, ten have zero values, and one has a positive cost. In accordance with the conditions of optimality, those linkages with negative costs are loaded at their upper capacity and the one linkage of positive cost (Cincinnati to Richmond) is loaded at its lower limit. Those linkages which have zero cost value may load from the lower limit to the upper limit. Of the ten that are in this category, nine load at levels intermediate to the lower and upper limits of capacity. Of the ten linkages having negative cost, seven comprise a set having the minimum capacity for all paths from Los Angeles to New York (Fig. 6.18). These are (1) Los Angeles to Houston, (2) Oklahoma City to Houston, (3) Oklahoma City to Memphis, (4) Oklahoma City to Cincinnati, (5) St. Louis to Cincinnati, (6) Cincinnati to Pittsburgh, and (7) Pittsburgh to New York.

Empirical Studies

CAPACITATED NETWORK IN BRAZIL. The out-of-kilter algorithm has been used to evaluate the program of transportation construction and improvement being undertaken by the state of São Paulo in Brazil.[8] This program calls for the replacement of many gravel-surfaced arterial roads in the state with paved ones. Much of the new construction, as well as the upgrading of existing road ways, is either focused directly on the capital city of São Paulo or is in the form of extensions to roads that focus on São Paulo. As a consequence, the capital city has been connected with the major regional centers of the state by a series of high-capacity, low-cost highways (Fig. 6.19).

The out-of-kilter algorithm provides a convenient way for recognizing bottlenecks that restrict the utilization of these high-capacity highways and force traffic flows to lower-capacity, higher-cost routes. The presence of such bottlenecks is of high economic cost to the state. The transport savings to be derived from the high-capacity highways cannot be realized until the bottlenecks are eliminated. Thus the identification of these bottlenecks permits one to evaluate critically the priorities that the planners are setting in attempting to develop a statewide system of high-capacity, low-cost roads. In the study, an optimal flow pattern is determined between São Paulo and the two regional centers of Riberão Prêto and Baru, and between the two regional centers themselves. The impact of new road projects is evaluated in terms of both the increases to potential flow between the centers and the resulting reductions in transport costs. Bottlenecks that restrict flows and increase total costs are identified, and a series of highway-improvement priorities are suggested as the basis for obtaining a higher economic return from the highway construction program.

[8] H. L. Gauthier, "Least-Cost Flows in a Capacitated Network: A Brazilian Example," in *Geographic Studies of Urban Transportation and Network Analysis*, ed. Frank Horton, Northwestern University Studies in Geography, No. 16 (1968).

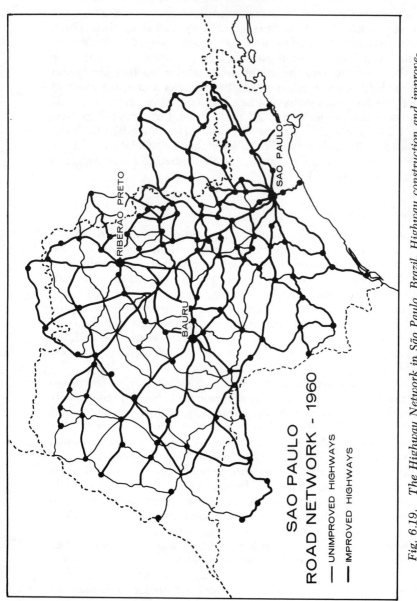

SAO PAULO
ROAD NETWORK - 1960

— UNIMPROVED HIGHWAYS
— IMPROVED HIGHWAYS

Fig. 6.19. The Highway Network in São Paulo, Brazil. Highway construction and improve-
ment are important components of the development program of the state of São Paulo. The
overall developmental objective is to increase the attractiveness of regional centers, such as
Riberão Prêto and Baru, as locations for industry, which has tended to concentrate in the São
Paulo metropolitan area. After H. Gauthier, "Transportation and the Growth of the São
Paulo Economy," Journal of Regional Science, 8 (1968).

The need to derive direct economic benefit from the highway construction program relates to the overall objective of increasing the attractiveness of regional centers as industrial locations. Industry has tended in the past to concentrate in the São Paulo metropolitan area. It is virtually impossible for this objective to be achieved under programs that provide high-capacity, low-cost connection between the regional centers and São Paulo but not between the regional centers themselves. Such a program only increases the attractiveness of the São Paulo metropolitan area as an industrial location at the expense of the regional centers.

Increasingly aware of the difficulties involved in establishing regional centers as secondary targets for the factor movements of labor and capital that have focused on São Paulo, the state government is concerned that the spatial interaction between the regional centers be improved. Indications of this concern are present construction plans to improve highway connections between many regional centers. Theoretically these improvements should create conditions that increase the attractiveness of the regional centers for capital investment, given the permissive role of transportation in the process of economic development. However, as this study suggests, this may prove to be an unwarranted expectation. The results of the analysis suggest that while improvements between the regional centers do increase the flow between these centers and reduce substantially the average transportation costs, the cost reductions between the regional centers and São Paulo are greater than between the regional centers themselves. Thus one consequence of the plan to improve the potential for spatial interaction between the regional centers will be a greater reduction in the transport barrier between those centers and the metropolis of São Paulo. This should increase the locational advantages of the capital city of São Paulo relative to the regional centers. These results emphasize the necessity of considering improvements in transportation in terms of their systemwide impact.

OPTIMAL TRANSPORTATION PATTERNS OF COAL IN THE GREAT LAKES REGION. In a recent study by King, Casetti, Odland, and Semple, the out-of-kilter algorithm is used to determine the optimal transportation pattern of bituminous coal throughout the Great Lakes Region.[9] The study area encompasses the bituminous coal-producing areas and the coal-receiving centers of the Midwest and Great Lakes regions of the United States and Canada. In the study, two major sources of coal demand are considered: thermal-electric generating plants and the coking ovens of the steel industry. Together these two sets of customers account for approximately three-quarters of the coal consumed in the region. For purposes of analysis, these electric generating plants and coking oven centers are aggregated into nineteen major coal-receiving centers. Within each coal-producing region the major transportation center is identified as the source of coal production. The productive capacity of each of these nodes is defined as the sum of the bituminous coal shipments for a given year

[9] L. King et al., "Optimal Transportation Patterns of Coal in the Great Lakes Region," *Economic Geography*, 47, No. 3 (July 1971), 401–13.

from the counties included in the region. A total of fifteen composite nodes are used to represent the coal-mining districts.

As formulated, this study investigates the least-cost flows of bituminous coal from the fifteen major producing centers to the nineteen receiving centers surrounding the Great Lakes area. The origin points are considered to be directly connected to the destination points by a 104-link network. The end points of each linkage are a receiving node and a shipping node. Associated with each linkage are three values: (1) an upper capacity that is equal to the production of a shipping node, (2) a lower capacity equal to the demand of a receiving node, and (3) a cost of shipment from a supplying to a consuming node. For transportation costs the authors use the volume and trainload rates that apply to most major coal shipments. For each route, the lowest rate for coal shipments is applied. As the authors note, these rates reflect competition and are not related simply to the distance of the haul. The volume and unit train rates have been established to be consistent with the marketing strategies of the companies involved.

The out-of-kilter algorithm is used to determine an optimal set of flows that involves the minimal total transport cost. These flows are subject to the three constraints that (1) the demands for coals at the various destinations are met, (2) shipments from the various origins are equal to or smaller than the supplies of coal available, and (3) the capacity limitations on the transport linkages are not violated.[10] The flow pattern that satisfies those requirements is shown in Figure 6.20. Operating under conditions of optimality, four coal regions produce at full capacity, whereas four others would be completely inactive. Also, the coal-producing regions of the midcontinent section of Illinois and Indiana would serve only the Chicago and Milwaukee consuming areas. The coal-producing regions in the eastern section of the region would be able to capture the remainder of the markets for coal in the Great Lakes region.

Variations of the Basic Transportation Problem

THE PHANTOM REGION.   When allocating flows in the transportation problem, the objective is to minimize the total transportation cost. This objective is subject to a number of constraints relative to supply-and-demand equalities. When applying the transportation problem to an empirical case study, it is frequently not reasonable to abide by such supply-and-demand equalities. For example, a real-world problem may exist in which the productive capacity of the supply regions exceeds the demand requirements of the receiving regions. Under these circumstances the surpluses available for allocation will exceed the deficits that must be satisfied. This problem of excess supply relative to demand may be solved within the framework of the transportation problem by utilizing slack variables. The most frequent use of the slack variable is the phantom-

---

[10] When used without concern for intermediate nodes, the out-of-kilter algorithm generates a solution identical to the simple transport problem.

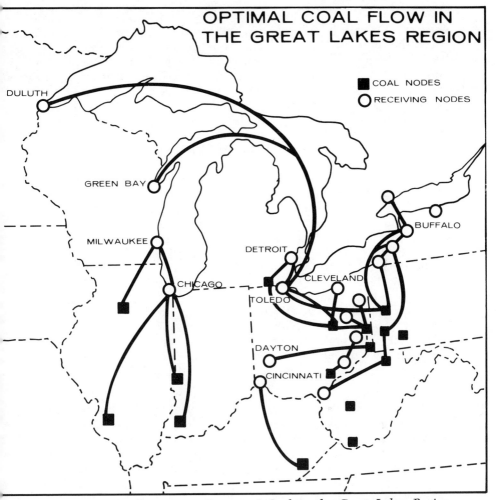

Fig. 6.20. *Optimal Transport Pattern of Coal in the Great Lakes Region. Under conditions of transport-cost minimization, the bituminous-coal-producing centers of Pennsylvania and Ohio supply most of the markets in the Great Lakes Region. The coal-producing centers of Illinois and Indiana serve only Chicago and Milwaukee consuming areas. After King et al., "Optimal Transportation Patterns of Coal in the Great Lakes Region,"* Economic Geography, *47 (1971).*

region allocation. An artificial region is created to which the surplus supply is allocated. This mathematical allocation satisfies the equality requirements of the original transportation problem. No actual shipments occur, of course—the unrequired surplus remains at the factory. Using the slack variable of the phantom region permits us to solve an optimal allocation problem under conditions where supply requirements do not equal demand.

BACKHAULS.   The problem of backhauls is a familiar one in transportation. Frequently we are confronted with the real-world situation in which the transportation of several goods and one good is shipped as a backhaul from a previous shipment of another good. For example, it is very common for coal to be backhauled on the Great Lakes for the iron ore that has been shipped from the Minnesota region to the major steel-producing areas in Ohio and Pennsylvania.

The problem of dealing with the efficient transportation of several goods involving a backhaul relationship has been discussed by Goldman.[11] He proposes a hypothetical problem in which we have three islands: one island produces coal, another produces iron ore, and the third has limestone, and each demands steel products. The problem he raises deals with the location of steel production and with the flow pattern that provides steel in the desired amounts at the least transportation cost. This is obviously a complex problem. The location of steel production on any one island will make empty cargo capacity available for shipping either raw materials or finished products from that island. The problem is to establish a steel-producing center that can produce an adequate amount of steel products to meet existing demands and ship them so that transportation costs are minimized. Goldman offers an algorithm whereby this can be accomplished so that the number of empty backhauls is minimized. The advantage of this algorithm is that it considers transportation shipments in terms of round-trip characteristics and emphasizes an allocation that minimizes the number of empty backhauls. This extension of the transportation problem permits application of the model to more realistic problems.

LOCATION.   Casetti utilizes a variation of the Goldman algorithm to determine the optimal location of steel mills serving the Quebec and Southern Ontario steel markets.[12] This study is an attempt to analyze the impact on the optimal location of steel mills supplying the Canadian market of (1) the flow of iron ore from the Seven Islands via the St. Lawrence Seaway to the steel centers around the Great Lakes and (2) the increase of steel consumption in Canada. The problem he formulates is one of determining the patterns of steel production, steel transportation, raw-material transportation, and empty-carrier movement, that minimize cost and satisfy both the steel requirements of the Canadian market and the ore requirements of the U.S. markets. As complex as this problem is, Casetti recognized that critical variables related to actual location decisions in the steel industry are not considered. Thus, the study is regarded as an exploratory example of a transportation allocation procedure that may be useful in formulating policies and decisions on the establishment of new, large-scale steel capacity in the St. Lawrence region.

[11] T. A. Goldman, "Efficient Transportation and Industrial Location," *Papers of the Regional Science Association*, 4 (1958), 91–106.

[12] Emilio Casetti, "Optimal Location of Steel Mills Serving the Quebec and Southern Ontario Steel Market," *Canadian Geographer*, 10 (1966), 27–39.

SPATIAL PRICE EQUILIBRIUM. The spatial-price-equilibrium problem is similar to the transportation problem in that it is concerned with the optimal allocation of flows between regions at a minimal transportation cost. Unlike the transportation problem, however, spatial price equilibrium requires that the amounts to be supplied and received, as well as regional prices, are to be determined by the model. In spatial price equilibrium the location of supplying and receiving points as well as transportation costs are known. In satisfying the objective of allocating flows between supplying and receiving areas under least-cost transportation conditions, the problem is subject to the constraints that all supplies must be shipped and that all demands be met. Also, supplies and demands are considered as functions of prices, and this relationship is known. Unlike the transportation problem, the initial allocation of flows from surplus to deficit areas has an impact on relative prices in both the shipping and receiving regions. The rapidity with which these prices shift affects the relative supply-and-demand conditions for the product. Thus as a result of trade, the supply and demand requirements are altered until a new equilibrium is established. A useful feature of spatial price equilibrium is that the impact of trade upon consumption prices is immediately determined. Any improvements in consumption prices are obtained at some transportation cost. The extent to which these benefits exceed the increase in cost is termed the *net social payoff*. Many studies labeled as spatial-price-equilibrium analyses are actually cross-sectional determinations of supply and demand and their related prices. The impact of trade upon consumption prices and net social payoff is treated in a static fashion, not as a dynamic process leading to a price equilibrium.

SENSITIVITY ANALYSIS. Perhaps one of the most productive uses of allocation models is in sensitivity analysis. The objective is to determine how sensitive the model is to changes in its parameters. Frequently we are interested in knowing what the consequences will be of a change in transportation costs on flow allocations between areas. The generalized transportation problem permits us to consider the regional impacts of different proposals for rate increases or decreases. Of course, sensitivity analysis is not restricted to changes in transportation costs: all the parameters involved in the model may be changed in order to consider their impacts on the allocation of flows. In the initial example in this chapter it would be possible to experiment with the effects of changing warehouse or production capacities on both the nature of the optimal allocation and the resultant transport costs. This experiment could include the elimination of warehouses or producing units. In evaluating agricultural shipments from producing to consuming areas, studies have been made of the effects of drought in certain parts of the country. In the school-district example the effects of school consolidation on allocation and costs could be considered by solving the model with varying numbers of schools. School busing costs might be more realistically compared with minimal costs by requiring that certain quotas from an area be assigned to specific schools regardless of proximity. In the case of the Brazilian highways, alternate networks might be examined until the costs of a pattern that is more advantageous to the regional centers than to São Paulo is determined. Thus policymakers might have a basis for evaluating the trade-offs of economic costs against socio-political needs. In the Great Lakes coal study, King et al. performed a sensitivity analysis by using an intertemporal model in which variations in coal shipments and shipment costs during the summer period and the winter period were taken into account. Since shipments in winter are restricted on the Great Lakes system, the authors considered the consequences of either being forced to use the higher-cost rail routes to serve the thermal-electric plants and the coking ovens of the steel industry or storage during the winter season at certain lake ports. The impact upon shipment patterns of variable storage charges also had to be taken into account.

Summary

The objective of this chapter was not to describe or explain why a particular flow pattern exists, but to determine what the best possible, or optimal, pattern will be according to some stated criteria. The determination of such an optimal pattern involves a normative model. One of the simplest normative models is the transportation problem.

The objective of the primal of the transportation problem is to allocate flows to minimize total transport costs. To do this, the locations of both deficit and surplus areas are known, as well as the cost of transportation per unit of product. The allocation of goods from the surplus to the deficit areas is constrained by the three requirements that (1) no shipments in excess of the available supply may be made, (2) all deficit needs must be met, and (3) the total supply available for shipment must equal the total demand. For purposes of empirical interpretation, no negative shipments can be made.

An allocation that satisfies the constraints of the primal is a feasible one. To determine if a feasible allocation is optimal requires a consideration of the dual of the transportation problem. The objective of the dual is to maximize the economic return to be realized from the allocation in the primal. The dual is subject to the constraint that the difference between the imputed values (shadow prices) of the goods at the surplus and deficit areas must be less than or equal to the transport costs between them. If the flow is optimal, the dual provides a set of equilibrium prices.

A more complicated normative model is the generalized transportation problem. Whereas the simple transportation problem assumes that a direct linkage exists between each surplus and each deficit area, the generalized transportation problem treats the allocation of flows that pass through a series of intermediate nodes between the points of origin and destination. Moreover, there are restrictions on this flow posed by the capacity of the linkages in the network. The objective is to find a maximal flow at a minimal cost that does not exceed the capacity limits. The maximal flow that can occur between two points is determined by bottlenecks, or the minimal capacity of the linkages in the network.

It is recognized that an actual flow pattern may differ from an optimal one. This may be due to the failure of the basic assumptions of a normative model to replicate the underlying causes of actual flow patterns. More likely, however, this variation reflects the fact that the economically rational desire to minimize transport costs, or to maximize profits, is only a partial explanation of actual market behavior.

CHAPTER *7* *summary and*
some unanswered questions

An attempt will be made in this chapter to summarize the aspects of transportation geography set forth in this introduction to the field. Perhaps more important, some of the topics not treated in the text at all will be identified. In the first portion of the chapter the summary of the different models is in the form of a discussion of their possible application to a hypothetical region. The second part of the chapter provides a brief survey of several of the neglected topics, such as transportation investment as an aspect of regional development, the role of perception in transport study, and the question of values implicit in decisions relating transportation and public policy.

Transport Analysis of a Hypothetical Region

Figure 7.1 represents a hypothetical region of six states with eleven cities represented by circles that are graduated in size according to population and connected by lines representing transportation linkages. Table 7.1 lists some of the types of data available for the region. The data is typical of the data available for studies related to U.S. transportation.

Looking at this region, how would the beginning student of transportation geography view such a region in light of the concepts and models developed in this text? What might he look for in the transport pattern? What aspects of the area's transportation might he study, and how would he approach such a study?

STRUCTURAL DESCRIPTIONS. First, it seems clear that descriptions of the transport network's structure, and to a lesser extent, the processes involved in its evolution as discussed in Chapters 1 and 2, could be a first step in a better understanding of the transportation geography of the

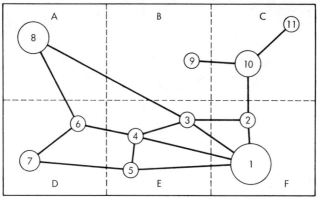

Fig. 7.1. Hypothetical Region. This is a region of six states and eleven cities. The cities are represented by circles graduated in size according to population, and they are connected by lines representing transportation linkages.

area. A probable trunk line is the connection between cities 1 and 8 via city 3. The 1→7 and the 1→10 routes might also be trunk lines, and the rest are probably feeders. City 1 obviously functions as a gateway, and cities 6 and 10 probably do also. Clearer identification of trunk lines, feeder lines, and gateways could be based on traffic-flow information as well as on such route-capacity information as schedules and types of vehicles. Hinterland structure could be approached directly at the metropolitan level, using the commuting information for the cities, and at the national level with intercity air-passenger figures. A possible set of first-order hinterlands, possibly from air-traffic figures, for the three largest cities (1, 8, and 10) is shown in Figure 7.2. More localized studies involving phone calls and various forms of highway traffic could be added to the commuting and airline-linkage information in order to establish the hierarchical nature of the area's organization in the form of low-order hinterlands around the middle-sized as well as large centers.

Table 7.1. Data Available for Hypothetical Region

Cities (1–11)	States (A–F)
Population	Population
Income	Commodity Production
Retail Sales	Commodity Consumption
Manufacturing Production	Commodity Shipments to
Air-Passenger Traffic to	All Other States
All Other Cities	Transport Costs for
Air, Bus, and Rail	All Commodity Shipments
Schedules and Fares	
Highway Traffic Flow	
Highway Traffic Capacity	

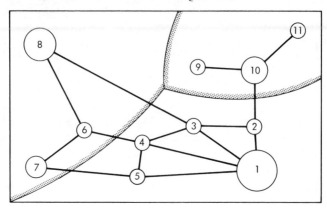

Fig. 7.2.   Hinterlands. The diagram shows a possible set of hinterlands for the three largest cities.

In terms of an idealized sequence of development, the transport network seems to be in the early phase of interconnection. Port concentration has already taken place, and city 1 has established its dominance over small nearby cities, no longer shown on the map. The route from city 1 to city 8 was probably the first penetration line, followed by the route from city 1 to city 7 and then to city 10. Interconnection is best developed near city 1 in the lower part of the diagram.

APPLICATION OF MODELS.   The three models discussed in the text (gravity, graph theoretic, and allocation) could be applied to the hypothetical area in Figure 7.1 to analyze such transportation characteristics as commodity flow, passenger flow, accessibility, and additional ramifications of hinterland structure.

Commodity-flow studies could be based on modifications of the gravity model. If one were analyzing state-to-state commodity shipments, for example, the attractive-force portion of a gravity model would probably not be a population product $(P_i P_j)$. If state A, for example, were the only wheat-producing area, the attractive force in the gravity model could be $S_A D_j$, where S_A equals the surplus wheat in state A, and D_j represents the wheat-consumption needs in each of the other five states ($j = D$ through F) based on average per-capita wheat-consumption figures and the population of each state. The impedance force in the gravity model could either be distance (d_{Aj}) or the actual transport cost for shipping wheat between state A and each of the other states (t_{Aj}). The initial form of a gravity-model analysis would probably be a regression equation describing the average relation between actual and expected flow of wheat between state A and the other five states. If distance were used and transformed into logarithms, an empirically derived exponent of distance ($\propto$) would be obtained. Among the first modifications perhaps derived from an examination of a map of residuals would be the inclusion of effects of complementarity or of intervening opportunity, either in the form of competitive commodity production for state A (a substitute for wheat) or

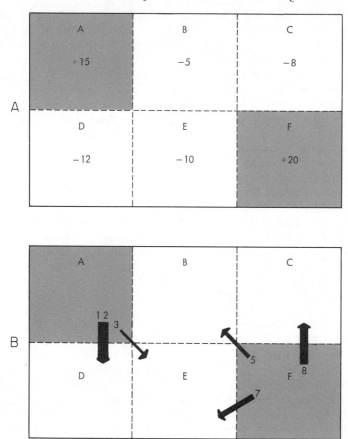

Fig. 7.3. Optimal Flow Patterns. Wheat surpluses and deficits are shown in A. A possible optimal allocation is shown in B, whereby states A and B distribute their surpluses to the four deficit states in a way that minimizes transportation costs.

intervening markets to compete with states B through F. Commodity-flow studies could also be based on the transportation problem or some of its variations. An optimal flow pattern for a given commodity could be obtained by distributing surpluses to all deficit states in a fashion that minimizes the total transport costs. As illustrated in Figure 7.3A, for example, states A and F might have wheat surpluses available for shipment to deficit states B, C, D, and E. The optimal allocation might be represented by the shipments indicated in Figure 7.3B. This optimal commodity-flow pattern could then be compared with the actual flow pattern and the discrepancies interpreted. If information on traffic capacity were available, it would be possible to determine the maximal profitable flow at minimal cost from city 1, for example, through a series of intermediate cities to city 8. The upper capacity on the network linkages could be the availability of transport services and the lower limit could be the demand that must be satisfied at city 8. Bottlenecks that either prevent the demand from being satisfied or require the use of high-cost shipment paths could be identified and a program developed for their elimination. Refinements on the basic model would permit the investigator to take account of the effects of changing prices on supply and demand in surplus and deficit regions or to introduce a wide variety of constraints, noneconomic as well as economic, into the model. Sensitivity analysis could be made to determine the impact of changes in demand, crop mixes, or freight rates. Both the transportation problem and the gravity-model type of study could also be applied to the flow of manufactured goods between the cities in Figure 7.1, using manufacturing production figures and applying average per-capita consumption figures to city populations to obtain surpluses and deficits.

Passenger-flow studies could be based initially on a gravity model using population products (P_iP_j) and distance or transport costs raised to an appropriate power. In addition to modifications involving intervening opportunity and complementarity, the use of demand and abstract mode equations would include the effects of comparative fares, comparative schedules, income, and other factors. Allocation models such as the transportation-problem model could also be applied to passenger traffic. An optimal allocation of vehicles to routes according to the traffic over each route would be one example of a study based on passenger traffic.

Accessibility studies could involve gravity-potential and graph-theoretic models. Potential maps are one sort of accessibility surface, and high points on that surface represent places with a high aggregate proximity to the total population, income, or retail sales, represented by the cities in Figure 7.1. Graph-theoretic measures would be particularly useful in evaluating the accessibility of transportation networks or of points within the network. Aggregate accessibility measures such as alpha and gamma indexes could be applied to the network of linkages connecting the cities. These measures could then be used as a basis for comparison with other networks or for network changes through time. The accessibility of individual nodes or cities in the network could be measured and compared by using techniques such as a T-matrix or a Shimbel distance matrix, which take into account both direct connections and multiple-link connections. A more refined analysis would be possible by using valued graphs in which either the actual interaction between centers or the time-cost impedance to interaction is considered. This could be done for a single network, such as the Interstate Highway System, or for combinations of networks, such as the Interstate, the U.S. and state highway systems, and the older county road systems, by adjusting travel-time over the appropriate linkages. Effects of alternate new highway proposals upon individual cities could be examined, as could changes in the accessibility of these cities relative to each other, as in the example of two plans for additional highways shown in Figures 7.4A and B. Accessibility measures would show that link X (Fig. 7.4A) would be considerably more advantageous for cities 9, 10, and 11; link Y (Fig. 7.4B) would be more advantageous for city 7. The relative advantages of the two plans to the other cities are

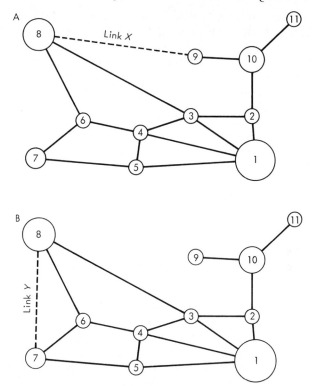

Fig. 7.4. *Alternate Highway Plans. Graph-theoretic measures may be applied to plans for Link X (A) and Link Y (B) to assess the different effects of the two plans upon the relative accessibility of each city in the system.*

less obvious from visual inspection. City 3, for example, would be bene-fited by both but probably more by the construction of link X. Application of different graph-theoretic measures, however, would provide a basis for finer comparison. The changing relative accessibilities of individual cities through time could be measured and related to differing transport tech-nologies or to the different growth rates of the cities in question.

The further examination of hinterland structure might be carried on with all three types of models. The use of a gravity model to determine theoretical divides between cities represents one of its earliest uses. Once divides were identified, a set of hinterlands could be constructed, based on city population, income, retail sales, or some other measure of central-ity. The use of weighted linkages in the form of valued graphs would make it possible to use graph-theoretic measures to identify a set of dominant and subdominant centers and their accompanying linkages. Finally, the transportation problem could be used to identify an optimal set of hinterlands if the objective were to minimize distance or transporta-tion costs. For example, if a set of major medical complexes were to be established at the three large cities in Figure 7.1, an optimal set of hinterlands could be established around them, considering hospital capacities as deficits and some health-weighted population measure of the smaller surrounding areal units as surpluses. Alternate proposals for the location of such medical complexes could then be evaluated in terms of their effects on total travel.

There are many other models, not treated in this text, that are broadly similar in purpose to those selected for discussion. These include the study of network design and geometry by C. Werner, the multivariate procedures for delimiting nodal regions by B. J. L. Berry, W. Reed, and others, and the use of information statistics in measuring accessibility by R. K. Semple, A. Wilson, and others.[1]

Unanswered Questions

The three models presented in this text are in a simplified form for the most part, and further acquaintance with the literature should precede their use in serious research. Even in a ramified and more operational form, however, the application of these and similar models to the analysis of transportation would still leave many important questions unanswered. What sorts of transport patterns exist *within* the cities? What are the effects of different transport innovations on the economic development of regions? To what extent does the movement of goods, people, and ideas reflect actual distance, time-distance, or distance as perceived differently by groups with varying socio-economic backgrounds or life styles? What values are implicit in decisions to provide subsidized rail-passenger service or to build expressways through urban ghettos? None of these questions has been explicitly considered in this text, and most of the models and their variations have not been designed to deal with them.

The first omission is a fairly well-defined and substantive one, consisting simply of certain forms of transportation. This is particularly conspicuous at the two extremes of the geographic scale: intraurban transportation and world shipping. Space limitations simply precluded the treatment of the subjects. To some extent, however, the models discussed in the text are applicable to these forms. Commodity-flow and vehicle-allocation models may be applied to world shipping.[2] Passenger-flow

---

[1] Christian Werner, "The Role of Topology and Geometry in Optimal Network Design," *Papers*, The Regional Science Association, 21 (1968); Brian J. L. Berry, *Essays on Commodity Flows and the Spatial Structure of the Indian Economy*, University of Chicago Department of Geography Research Paper No. 11 (1966); Wallace E. Reed, "Areal Interaction in India: Commodity Flows of the Bengal-Bihar Industrial Area," University of Chicago Department of Geography Research Paper No. 110 (1967); R. K. Semple and L. H. Wang, "A Geographical Analysis of Changing Redundancy in Inter-Urban Transportation Links," *Geografiska Annaler*, 35, Series B, No. 1 (1971), 1–5; Andrew G. Wilson, "Inter-regional Commodity Flows: Entropy Maximizing Approaches," *Geographical Analysis*, 2, No. 3 (July 1970), 255–82; Andrew G. Wilson, "A Family of Spatial Interaction Models and Associated Developments," *Environment and Planning*, 3 (1971), 1–32.

[2] For geographic studies of world trade and world shipping, see John W. Alexander, "International Trade: Selected Types of World Regions," *Economic Geography*, 36, No. 2 (1960), 95–115; Andreas Grotewold, *A Selective Annotated Bibliography of Publications Relevant to the Geographical Study of International Trade*,

models based on gravity- and allocation-model techniques are common in the study of intraurban traffic.[3] In gravity-model applications, attractive forces in destination areas have included employment for journey-to-work studies and floor space devoted to commercial activities for shopping trips. Analogous forces in origin areas have included population, possibly broken down by age, sex, and occupational groups, as well as by auto ownership, which has proven to be a key explanatory variable. The effects of distance have been found to be quite complex within metropolitan areas. There are indications that distance is discontinuous for journey-to-work trips, exerting virtually no effect within four miles, strong effects beyond ten miles, and moderate effects between the two.[4] Allocation-model variations have been used to establish optimal travel patterns for different occupational groups within cities and to demonstrate the relation between transport costs and location rents.[5] Intraurban studies, however, pose so many different problems, such as rush-hour traffic, the need for rapid transit, and the political contexts of expressway building, that it seemed better not to consider them in this brief, introductory work.

IMPACT STUDIES.   Another subject of growing significance in transport study that was omitted might be called impact studies. The overall impact of transportation on economic development, for example, is a matter of particular concern to geographers, economists, and planners. For some time it was simply assumed that improved transportation had almost always preceded development, and it formed an essential early phase in any development scheme. Recent studies, however, indicate a less clearly catalytic role for transportation investment in economic growth.[6] Three possible views of transportation investment have been suggested: positive, neutral, and negative. The positive view is similar to the one expressed in the earlier discussion of the effects of lowered transport costs on regional specialization. Rostow's reference to the critical role played by transportation in bringing about "take-off" is an example of the positive

University of Missouri Department of Geography (1960); G. Alexandersson and G. Norstrom, *World Shipping* (New York: 1963); and Richard S. Thoman and Edgar C. Conkling, *Geography of International Trade*, Foundations of Economic Geography Series (Englewood Cliffs, N.J.: Prentice-Hall, 1967).

[3] There is a vast literature on geography, engineering, economics, and planning in urban transportation. Particularly useful works include Walter Y. Oi and Paul W. Shuldinger, *An Analysis of Urban Travel Demands*, The Transportation Center at Northwestern University (Evanston, Ill.: Northwestern University Press, 1962) and Brian J. L. Berry and Frank W. Horton, eds., *Geographic Perspectives on Urban Systems* (Englewood Cliffs, N.J.: Prentice-Hall, 1970).

[4] Edward J. Taaffe, Barry Garner, and Maurice Yeates, *The Peripheral Journey-to-Work: A Geographic Consideration* (Evanston, Ill.: Northwestern University Press, 1963).

[5] James O. Wheeler, "Occupational Status and Work-Trips: A Minimum Distance Approach," *Social Forces*, 45, No. 4 (June 1967); Benjamin H. Stevens, "Linear Programming and Location Rent," *Journal of Regional Science*, 3 (1961), 15–26.

[6] The following discussion is based on Howard L. Gauthier, "Geography, Transportation and Regional Development," *Economic Geography*, 46 (October 1970), 612–19.

view.[7] The neutral view could be interpreted as assigning a "lag" rather than "lead" role to transportation. According to this view, the transport facilities will expand to meet needs, and will not, themselves, induce new economic activity. The work of several economic historians, for example, has cast doubt on the role of railroads in sparking U.S. economic development.[8] In their view, a similar growth could have taken place if water transportation had remained dominant. According to the negative view, investment in transportation is actually harmful because it diverts funds from other investments more essential to the area's growth. Critics of some of the programs of the Appalachian Development Commission, for example, feel that there has been overinvestment in highway programs at the expense of educational and health programs. In this instance it is also felt that the highway programs may have primary benefits for people driving through the region and that Appalachian manufacturers are as likely to experience increased competition from larger surrounding centers as they are to expand markets for their own products.

Transportation impact may take a variety of forms other than that of overall economic growth. Several studies have been made dealing with the effects of highway improvements. Urban land values have responded to improved highways; cities have been affected by highway bypasses; urban growth has been related to improved accessibility in a network; highway interchanges have become new focal points in changing patterns of spatial organization.[9] Another sort of impact study deals with the political effects of improved transportation system. In a study of Kenya, the role of the transport system in relation to political integration was stressed.[10] Transport connections were closely associated with a complex dual pattern of spatial organization, African and European, both of which pivoted around the single dominant city of Nairobi.

PERCEPTION STUDIES.   Another set of unanswered questions may be associated with the perceptions of spatial organization implicit in any

[7] W. W. Rostow, *The Stages of Economic Growth* (Cambridge: Cambridge University Press, 1964).

[8] See R. W. Fogel, *Railroads and American Economic Growth, Essays in Econometric History* (Baltimore: Johns Hopkins Press, 1964); A. Fishlow, *American Railroads and the Transportation of the Ante-Bellum Economy,* Harvard Economic Papers (Cambridge: Harvard University Press, 1965).

[9] Some examples of studies dealing with these questions are William L. Garrison and Marion E. Marts, *Influence of Highway Improvements on Urban Land: A Graphic Summary* (Seattle: University of Washington, Department of Geography and Department of Civil Engineering, 1958); William L. Garrison and Marion E. Marts, *Geographic Impact of Highway Improvements* (Seattle: University of Washington, Department of Geography and Department of Civil Engineering, 1958); Howard L. Gauthier, "Transportation and the Growth of the São Paulo Economy," *Journal of Regional Science,* 8 (Summer 1968), 77–94; William L. Garrison et al., *A Study of Land Development Problems at Freeway Interchanges* (Seattle: University of Washington, Department of Geography, 1960).

[10] Edward W. Soja, *The Geography of Modernization in Kenya: A Spatial Analysis of Social, Economic and Political Change,* Syracuse Geographical Series, No. 2 (Syracuse: Syracuse University Press, 1968). For a more general treatment of the political aspects of transportation, see Roy I. Wolfe, *Transportation and Politics,* Searchlight Book No. 18 (New York: Van Nostrand, 1963).

transport study. For the most part, we have dealt in this text with distance in its geometric and its economic form. Cost-distance, for example, has been reflected in the freight-rate maps of Chapter 2 and the transport-cost figures used in Chapter 6. Distance may be expressed in a variety of other forms, however. Time-distance is one example. Jet travel isochrones (contour lines of equal travel-time) and Interstate Highway travel isochrones will both show patterns markedly different from each other and from unmodified distance. The air travel-time from Chicago to New York, for example, is less than it is from Grand Rapids, Michigan, to Ashtabula, Ohio, even though the highway driving-time is considerably greater. Within a city there will be a marked difference between the isochrones for rush hour and non-rush hour. Frequency and convenience of service is another basis for expressing distance. The map of jet departures between 7:00 A.M. and 9:00 A.M., for example, is in some ways more meaningful than a map of total flights. To some extent this idea is also expressed in some of the distance surrogates used in the abstract mode equations, such as fares, travel-time, or frequency of service *relative* to that of other modes.

Time and cost relationships may be given quite different interpretations in recreational travel. Each traveler has his own "mental map," or perception, of a specialized and fragmented area containing desirable recreational environments that he views as potential destinations.[11] Such mental maps are also quite significant in the study of intraurban travel behavior. Each urban dweller's perception of the city could be conceptualized as a set of potential destinations for social, shopping, or employment trips, and a set of corridors linking him to these destinations. The term *action space* is sometimes used to describe these corridors and destinations and the way in which they condition urban dwellers' changes in travel behavior or changes in residence.[12]

As we begin to view distance in terms of widely varying perceptions, the close relationships between transportation and communications become evident.[13] Phone calls and the mass media may be expressed in networks of linkages and nodes, and they may show structural and process characteristics similar to those of the transport modes discussed in this text. Phone calls were used in several instances in earlier chapters as indicators of hinterland structure. The mass media also present a number of opportunities for interesting study. The concentration of network television on New York and Los Angeles, for example, is analogous to the

---

[11] There has been considerable recent interest in mental maps as a basis for understanding travel, migration, and other types of behavior in space. See Peter Gould, "On Mental Maps," Michigan Inter-University Community of Mathematical Geographers, Discussion Paper No. 9, mimeographed (Ann Arbor: University of Michigan, Department of Geography, 1966).

[12] For studies of action space and its possible relation to intraurban transportation, see Frank E. Horton and David R. Reynolds, "Effects of Urban Spatial Structure on Individual Behavior," *Perspectives on Urban Spatial Systems*, a special issue of *Economic Geography*, ed. Lawrence A. Brown and Eric G. Moore, 47, No. 1 (January 1971), 36–48.

[13] Ronald F. Abler, "Distance, Intercommunications, and Geography," *Proceedings* of the Association of American Geographers, 3 (1971), 28–31.

concentration of jet air traffic on New York, Los Angeles, and a few other large centers. Both are symptoms of a pattern of spatial organization in which physical distance has little meaning.

It should be noted, however, that the various transformations of distance associated with different perceptions are still within a context of spatial organization even though certain phenomena may be transmitted through a virtually frictionless space. The resultant organizations are often more subtle and complex, but they are still eminently susceptible to study, and in most instances, variants of the basic models discussed earlier may be applied to them.

TRANSPORTATION AND VALUE SYSTEMS.   A final set of questions that have not been considered in this text are those associated with value systems. Is a new transport system worthwhile if it has harmful effects on the environment? Should an expressway be built through an urban ghetto if it will not benefit the local community?

The case of the SST (the supersonic transport) is a classic example of a conflict between technological improvement and environmental quality. Although the SST represented a significant increase in speed over jet aircraft, it also represented an increase in overall noise level and in associated sonic booms. There were also a number of unanswered questions about its effects on the atmosphere. Some scientists felt that the high-altitude injection of pollutants, however small, would have serious consequences on the world's weather. As of winter 1972, the values associated with the environment seem to be stronger than those associated with faster air transport. The incremental value of greater aircraft speed is apparently so weak that the chief arguments of SST proponents were associated with employment and the international competition among aircraft manufacturers. The effects of expanded highway transportation on the environment are also being examined more critically. Conservation groups have opposed the extension of access roads into wilderness areas, and the effects of expressways on the drainage, microclimate, and general ecology of the adjacent countryside are being studied more closely. The resolution of many of these conflicts may lie in more effective impact studies. If we were better able to judge the effects of a transport innovation, we would be in a better position to evaluate the trade-off between the proposed improvement and the environmental side-effects. The problem becomes even more difficult as we become aware of the shortcomings of the traditional cost-benefit studies. Environmental costs to society at large were neglected in such studies, as were the social and political effects, which could be either costs or benefits. Effective means of measuring these have yet to be developed.

Questions of values associated with transportation become even more complex when one moves to intracity study and notes the differing impact of transport improvement on various urban groups. In some instances it is clear that the principal functions of an expressway will be to bring relatively well-to-do suburbanites to work in the central city, while the impact of land acquisitions and the diversion of municipal funds will affect most heavily the low-income, inner-city communities. An interesting series of studies examines the conflict behavior associated with community resistances to expressways. One of the studies deals with the losing battle waged by members of the black community in Nashville in their efforts to prevent a routing of Interstate Route 40, which would displace a considerable number of local homes and businesses and severely disrupt internal circulation patterns of the community.[14] The opposition was unable to organize itself effectively or to produce studies detailing what they felt to be the harmful impact of I-40. Another contrasting study deals with an apparently successful effort by a white, high-income group in the Society Hill area of downtown Philadelphia to successfully bring about a costly alteration in plans for the Delaware Expressway.[15] The Society Hill group claimed that the elevated section of the Expressway running past their community would be an unsightly "Chinese Wall," cutting off the historic parts of Philadelphia from the river, and it should therefore be depressed, covered, and landscaped. Support for this extremely expensive proposal was obtained from the newspapers, the mayor, the Bicentennial Commission, and influential representatives of the federal government. Proponents of the original elevated structure included the state highway department, the Philadelphia Streets Commissioner, and several councilmen, who argued that the funds for the cover could be better expended on low-income housing. After a number of moves and countermoves, after studies produced by both sides, a modified version of the cover was approved. These studies indicate that it is generally easier for a high-income community to exert political influence and have an unwanted expressway changed than it is for a low-income community. In part, however, this question also may be related to the need for more sophisticated impact studies. A clearer picture of the spatial distribution of both the positive and negative effects, social as well as economic, of a given expressway improvement in a metropolitan area would permit a decision for or against the improvement that would bear a closer relationship to the long-run best interest of the city.

Thus, the surface of the large and diverse field of transportation geography has only been scratched in this short volume. We have provided a glimpse of the earlier work in the field as well as a small sample of the investigative models that have been utilized on certain relatively traditional transport problems. Both the models and kinds of problems to which they might be applied have been expanding too rapidly to permit anything but fragmentary coverage. We hope the fragments chosen for presentation here have given the flavor of one of the most exciting and most fundamental subfields of the broad and constantly shifting discipline of geography.

14 John E. Seley, "Spatial Bias: The Kink in Nashville's I-40," *Research on Conflict in Locational Decisions,* Discussion Paper III, Regional Science Department, University of Pennsylvania (September 1970). This is one of a series of studies on conflict in locational decisions, carried on under the guidance of Julian Wolpert at the Regional Science Department of the University of Pennsylvania.

15 James Hinman, "Controversial Facility-Complex Programs: Coalitions, Side Payments, and Social Decisions," *Research on Conflict in Locational Decisions,* Discussion Paper VIII, Regional Science Department, University of Pennsylvania (December 1970).

some statistical considerations

It is helpful in any survey of the research literature in transportation geography if the reader is familiar with certain elementary statistical methods. We have assumed the reader's familiarity with scatter diagrams, regression analysis, and correlation analysis. For those who have had no previous contact with these methods, this Appendix provides a brief and much oversimplified introduction. It should be noted that we make no attempt to provide computational procedures. The emphasis is entirely on the interpretation of regression equations and correlation coefficients as they are used in the text. Further discussion, including computational procedures for these and related measures may be found in any introductory statistics text.

The example here is a comparison between expected passenger traffic and actual passenger traffic from a single city and 15 other cities. Table A.1 lists both the projected and the actual traffic between city A and each of the 15 other cities. Figure A.1 shows the linkages between city A and these cities, with population size indicated by the size of the circle. The traffic expectations might be derived from a number of sources—for example, from a gravity model based on population and distance, or from a model based on an optimal allocation of traffic to different routes, or simply from a transportation planner's expectations based on his knowledge of trends in traffic from his city. Here we will assume expectations derived from a simplified gravity model in which expectations are based on traffic from city A to another city, increasing directly with the population of the other city and inversely with the distance traveled. Thus projected traffic in Table A.1 represents a simple Population/Distance ratio.

Table A.1

To city	Projected passengers from city A (P/D) X	Actual passengers from city A Y
1.	371	339
2.	219	271
3.	300	200
4.	420	299
5.	409	337
6.	185	240
7.	261	238
8.	420	390
9.	189	201
10.	425	400
11.	312	291
12.	440	400
13.	360	270
14.	112	270
15.	150	180

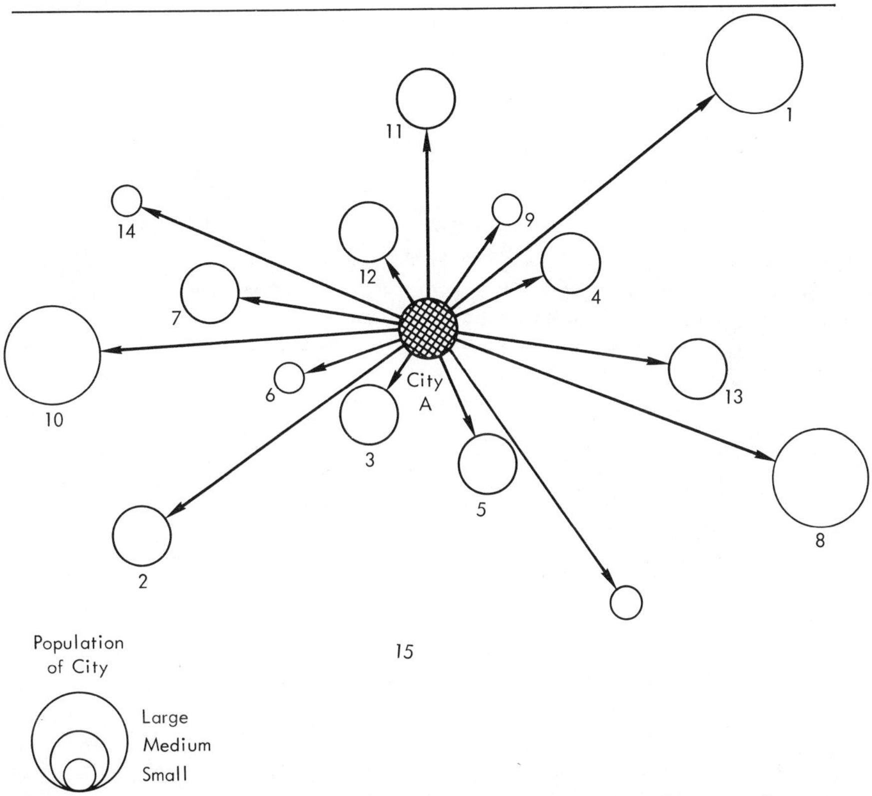

Fig. A.1. Hypothetical Example: City A Linkages. This diagram shows a hypothetical set of linkages between city A and fifteen other cities. The city circles are graded in size according to population.

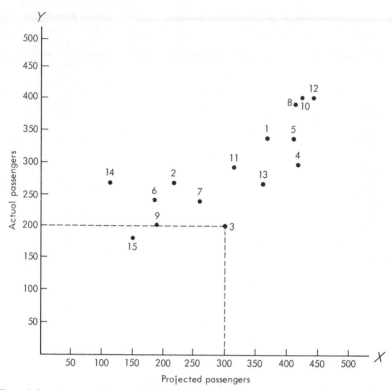

Fig. A.2. Scatter Diagram. This scatter diagram shows the relationship between gravity-model expectations on the X-axis, and actual traffic between each city and city A on the Y-axis. The trend of the scatter indicates a positive relationship between the two.

Figure A.2 is a scatter diagram showing a hypothetical typical relationship between the gravity-model expectations and the actual traffic. For the links between city A and each of the fifteen cities shown on the map, a point is plotted on the scatter diagram with the gravity-model expectation (P_i/D_{ai}) as its X-value, with the actual traffic between city A and that city as its Y-value. For example, city 3 has an expected traffic of 300 passengers and actual traffic of 200 with city A. Thus it is located near the point on the graph where the X-value of 300 intersects the Y-value of 200, as shown by the dotted lines. The general trend of the resultant scatter of dots shows that there is a positive relationship between gravity-model expectations and actual traffic. The dots trend upward and to the right, indicating that actual traffic does increase as expected traffic increases.

Several important measures may be derived from this scatter of points. As shown in Figure A.3, a line may be fitted to the points to give a more precise measure of the functional relation between the actual and expected traffic. This *regression line* may be determined by a procedure

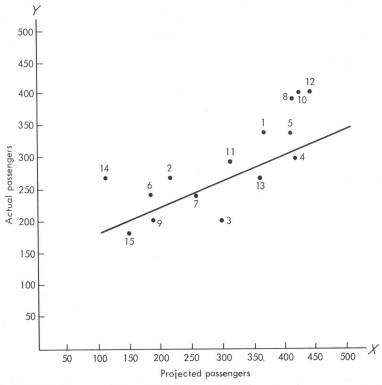

Fig. A.3. Scatter Diagram and Regression Line. A regression line has been fitted to the points in the scatter diagram of Figure A.2 to give a more precise measure of the general relationship between the actual and expected traffic. The regression equation is in the form of the equation for a straight line, $Y = a + bX$, *or in this case,* $Y = 133.7 + .5X$.

designed to minimize its total squared deviations from the plotted points, and it can be expressed in terms of the equation for a straight line, in the form $(Y) = a + b(X)$. The constant (a) locates the Y-intercept, the point on the Y-axis where the line would cross if it were extended back to a value of $X = 0$. The constant (b) indicates the slope of the regression line. If b is positive, it indicates that X and Y are positively related: as X increases, Y increases. In the case of comparing gravity-model expectations with actual traffic, the two constants in the regression equation could be considered as simply variations of the idea of a single constant which expresses the average relation between expected and actual traffic. The equation for the straight line in the hypothetical example used in Figure A.3 is $Y_e = 133.7 + .5X$. These values tell us that the Y-intercept is 133.7 and that .5 is the slope of the line. Thus to compute a more refined expected value for Y (actual traffic) based on the *average* relationship between Y and simple gravity-model expectations (X), you would multiply the X-value by .5 and add 133.7 to it. In the case of city 3 the gravity-model

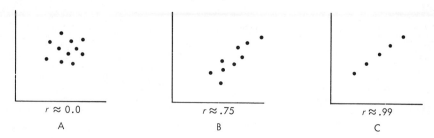

$r \approx 0.0$ $r \approx .75$ $r \approx .99$

A   B   C

Fig. A.4. *Scatter Diagrams and Correlations. The correlation coefficient* (r) *may be regarded as an index of the closeness of relationship between the scatter of points and a regression line. In A, the r would be close to 0 since it would be difficult to choose a regression line that would provide an effective description of the nearby circular pattern of dots. In C, on the other hand, the r would be close to + 1 since most of the dots would fall on or near a straight line. B would fall somewhere between these two extremes, with an r of .7 or .8 for example.*

expectation for traffic with city A was determined to be 300 after dividing the population by distance. The value 300 may be substituted into the regression equation and the computed Y_c will equal $133.7 + .5(300)$. The resultant figure of approximately 284 for Y_c would, of course, fall right on the regression line and would represent an estimate of traffic between city 3 and city A based on an *average* relationship between actual traffic and gravity-model expectations of traffic.

A second important measure associated with the hypothetical example of a relationship between an X and a Y variable is the correlation coefficient, which is an index of the closeness of fit. The correlation coefficient varies from 0 for no correlation (Fig. A.4), to +1 for a perfect fit of a positive regression line to all points on the scatter diagram, to −1 for a perfect fit of a negative regression line to all points on the scatter diagram. The value r^2, the coefficient of determination, indicates the percentage of variation in the original Y-variable that is associated with (statistically "explained" by) the variation in the X-variable. The r^2 measure is referred to frequently in the text as a useful indicator of the closeness of the relationship between two variables.

A third useful measure based on statistical analysis of the relationship between actual and projected traffic comes from an examination of the deviations of actual individual values from those computed by the regression equation. These *residual* deviations may be obtained by subtracting the expected value from the actual value. For example, in the case of traffic between city A and city 3, when the X-value of 300 (based on gravity-model expectations) was put in the regression equation, a computed Y-value of 284 was obtained. The actual number of passengers to city 10 is 200. The residual $(Y - Y_c)$ therefore is −.84. There were −.84 fewer passengers to city 3 than would be expected from the *average relationship* between actual passengers and gravity-model expectations.

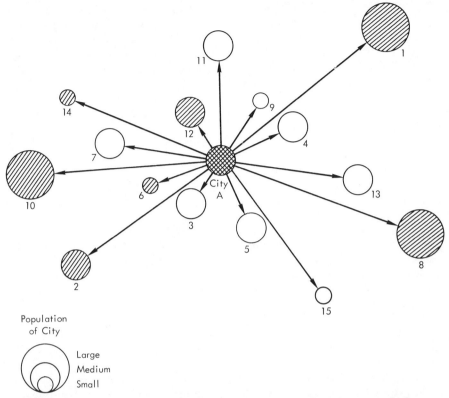

Population
of City

Large
Medium
Small

Fig. A.5. Residuals Map. On this map the cities with positive residuals are lined; the cities with negative residuals are left blank. Cities with positive residuals (Y — Yc > 0) are those at which the actual traffic was greater than would be expected from the average *relationship (as represented by the regression line) between actual traffic and gravity-model ratios.*

Figure A.5 shows some of the highest and lowest residuals as they look on the original map. The cities indicated with a crosshatch pattern are those with positive residuals. Traffic to these cities was greater than would be expected from the average relationship between actual and projected traffic as expressed by the regression line. The cities with the dotted pattern had less traffic than would be expected from this relationship. Examination of these residuals suggests ways in which the simple (P/D) model, as expressed in the regression equation $(PASS) = 133.7 + .5$ (P/D), *fails* to describe the actual traffic. For example, the positive residual of city 14's traffic might be associated with a strong recreational function, as in the case of Miami, where it could be anticipated that passenger traffic to a large northern city would be considerably greater than gravity-model expectations. Thus additional factors influencing traffic, such as city function, might be suggested from the examination of residuals and incorporated into an expanded model. Examination of a map of residuals might also suggest certain consistent spatial relationships. For example, the positive residuals of the large and medium-sized long-haul cities and the negative residuals of the large and medium-sized short-haul cities suggest that the effects of distance on traffic have been over-stated. Passenger traffic doesn't seem to fall off with distance as rapidly as expected since the long-haul cities have more traffic than expected and the short-haul cities have less. Another consistent relationship would be with the size of the city. The largest cities, such as cities 10 and 8, have positive residuals, indicating that their passenger traffic may be less affected by distance than smaller cities.

Modifications of the simple linear regression model may take the form of expansions to include additional variables or departures from the assumed linear relationship. Since most problems involve the effects of more than one factor, a *multiple regression* is commonly used, in which the dependent variable Y is considered dependent on more than a single independent variable X. In the above example, one might include a second independent variable to account for the importance of the recreation function of cities. The equation $Y = a + b_1X_1 + b_2X_2$ might then include (P/D) as X_1 and percent of employment in service industries as X_2. The resultant percentage of "explained" variation would then be expressed as R^2, which would take into account the combined effects of both independent variables. If four factors affecting traffic can be identi-fied, the regression equation could be expressed as $Y = a + b_1X_1 + b_2X_2 + b_3X_3 + b_4X_4$.

Another variation lies in the nature of the functional relationship. The distance relationships in traffic studies, for example, are seldom linear. A common practice is to transform the variables to logarithms, as in Chapter 3 in such gravity-model variations as the abstract mode studies. Other means of incorporating spatial variation into the model by fitting more complex and varied curvilinear relationships are also available, how-ever, and increased attention is being given to the problem of choosing the theoretically appropriate function.[1]

There are, of course, many pitfalls in the use of multiple regression and transformations, although they have been relatively widely utilized in a variety of transportation studies. Discussions of such pitfalls as modifiable units and spatial auto-correlation, are found in texts on statis-tical methods in geography.[2]

[1] N. R. Draper and H. Smith, *Applied Regression Analysis* (New York: John Wiley & Sons, 1966).
[2] See Leslie J. King, *Statistical Analysis in Geography* (Englewood Cliffs, N.J.: Prentice-Hall, 1969).

bibliography

This bibliography is organized according to
the sequence of topics treated in the text,
rather than alphabetically. No entries are repeated.
An asterisk indicates a work particularly relevant to the text.

Chapter 1. Transportation and Spatial Structure

A. THE FUNCTIONAL REGION

* Platt, Robert S. "A Detail of Regional Geography: Ellison Bay Community as an Industrial Organism." *Annals* of the Association of American Geographers 18 (1928); 81–126.
* Philbrick, Allen K. "Principles of Areal Functional Organization in Regional Human Geography." *Economic Geography* 33 (October 1957); 299–336.

B. STRUCTURAL PATTERNS

Becht, Edwin J. *A Geography of Transportation and Business Logistics.* Dubuque, Iowa: Wm. C. Brown, 1970.
* Patton, Donald. "The Traffic Pattern of American Inland Waterways." *Economic Geography* 32 (January 1956); 29–37.
* Ullman, Edward L. "The Railroad Pattern of the U.S." *Geographical Review* 39 (1949); 242–56.
Wallace, William H. "The Freight Traffic Functions of Anglo American Railroads." *Annals* of the Association of American Geographers 53 (1963); 312–31.
Wallace, William H. "The Bridge Line: A Distinctive Type of Anglo-American Railroad." *Economic Geography* 41 (1965); 1–38.
Sargent, A. J. *Seaports and Hinterlands.* Glasgow: A. & C. Black, 1939.
Kant, Edgar. "Umland Studies and Sector Analysis." *Studies in Rural-Urban Interaction.* Lund Studies in Geography, Series B, Human Geography, No. 3, pp. 3–13. Lund, Sweden: C.W.K. Gleerup, 1951.
* Kenyon, James. "Elements in Inter-Port Competition in the United States." *Economic Geography* 46 (January 1970); 1–24.

Patton, Donald. "General Cargo Hinterlands of New York, Philadelphia, Baltimore and New Orleans." *Annals* of the Association of American Geographers 48 (1958); 436–55.

Mayer, Harold M. *The Port of Chicago and the St. Lawrence Seaway.* Department of Geography Research Paper, No. 49. University of Chicago, May 1957.

Hance, William, and Van Dongen, Irene. "Dar Es Salaam: The Port and Its Tributary Area." *Annals* of the Association of the American Geographers 48 (1958); 419–35.

Harris, Chauncy, D. *Salt Lake City: A Regional Capital.* Doctoral dissertation. Chicago: University of Chicago Libraries, 1941.

Sisco, Paul H. "The Retail Function of Memphis." Department of Geography Research Paper, No. 37. University of Chicago, 1954.

Weigend, Guido G. "The Problem of Hinterland and Foreland as Illustrated by the Port of Hamburg." *Economic Geography* 32 (January 1956); 1–16.

* Green, F.H.W. "Urban Hinterlands in England and Wales: An Analysis of Bus Services." *The Geographical Journal* 116 (1950); 64–80.

* Green, F.H.W. "Community of Interest Areas: Notes on the Hierarchy of Central Places and their Hinterlands." *Economic Geography* 34 (July 1958); 210–26.

* Taaffe, Edward J. "The Urban Hierarchy: An Air Passenger Definition." *Economic Geography* 38 (1962); 1–14.

* Burghardt, Andrew F. "A Hypothesis about Gateway Cities." *Annals* of the Association of American Geographers 61 (June 1971); 269–85.

Chapter II.   Transportation and Spatial Processes

A.   TRANSPORT RATES

* Alexander, J. W.; Brown, S. E.; and Dahlberg, R. E. "Freight Rates: Selected Aspects of Uniform and Nodal Regions." *Economic Geography* 34 (January 1958); 1–8.

* Daggett, Stuart, and Carter, John P. *Structure of Transcontinental Rail Rates.* Berkeley and Los Angeles: University of California Press, 1947.

B.   TRANSPORTATION AND DEVELOPMENT

* Taaffe, E. J. "The Transportation Network and the Changing American Landscape." *Geography and the American Environment*, pp. 17–28.

* Taaffe, E. J.; Morrill, R. L.; and Gould, P. R. "Transport Expansion in Underdeveloped Countries: A Comparative Analysis." *Geographical Review* 53 (October 1963); 503–29.

Rimmer, Peter J. "The Changing Status of New Zealand Seaports, 1853–1960." *Annals* of the Association of American Geographers 57 (March 1967); 88–100.

Rimmer, Peter J. "Recent Changes in the Status of Seaports in the New Zealand Coastal Trade." *Economic Geography* 43 (July 1967); 231–43.

Pred, Allan R. *The Spatial Dynamics of U.S. Urban-Industrial Growth, 1800–1914.* The Regional Science Studies Series. Cambridge: The M.I.T. Press, 1966.

Burghardt, Andrew F. "The Origin and Development of the Road Network of the Niagara Peninsula, Ontario, 1770–1851." *Annals* of the Association of American Geographers 59 (September 1969); 417–40.

Taaffe, R. N. "Transportation and Regional Specialization: The Example of Soviet Central Asia." *Annals* of the Association of American Geographers 52 (March 1962); 80–98.

* Gauthier, Howard L. "Geography, Transportation, and Regional Development." *Economic Geography* 46 (October 1970); 612–19.

Owen, Wilfred. "Transportation and Economic Development." *American Economic Review* 49 (1959); 179–87.

Wilson, George, et al. *The Impact of Highway Investment on Development.* Chapters 1, 2, 7 and 8. Washington: The Brookings Institution, 1966.

* Fogel, Robert W. *Railroads and American Economic Growth.* Essays in Econometric History. Baltimore: Johns Hopkins Press, 1964.

Fishlow, Albert. *American Railroads and the Transportation of the Ante-Bellum Economy.* Harvard Economic Papers. Cambridge: Harvard University Press, 1965.

Goodrich, Carter, et al. *Canals and American Economic Development.* New York: Columbia University Press, 1961.

* Pred, Allan R. "Urban Systems Development and the Long Distance Flow of Information Through Pre-electronic U.S. Newspapers." *Economic Geography* 47 (October 1971); 498–524.

C. SELECTED LOCATIONAL IMPLICATIONS OF TRANSPORTATION

Hoover, Edgar M. *The Location of Economic Activity.* Chapters 2 and 3. New York: McGraw-Hill, 1948.

Fulton, Maurice, and Hoch, Clinton L. "Transportation Factors Affecting Locational Decisions." *Economic Geography* 35 (1959); 51–59.

Olsson, R. "Commodity Flow and Regional Interdependence." *Papers* of the Regional Science Association 12 (1964); 225–30.

Isard, Walter. "Distance Inputs and the Space Economy." *Quarterly Journal of Economics* 65 (1954); 181–98.

Berry, Brian J. L. "Recent Studies Concerning the Role of Transportation in the Space Economy." *Annals* of the Association of American Geographers 49 (1959); 328–42.

Orr, Earle W. "A Synthesis of Theories of Location, of Transport Rates, and of Special Price Equilibrium." *Papers and Proceedings* of the Regional Science Association 3 (1957); 61–73.

D. U.S. TRANSPORTATION—SELECTED DESCRIPTIVE STUDIES GENERAL AND HISTORICAL

Pardee, F. S., et al. *Measurement and Evaluation of Transportation System Effectiveness.* RM-5869-DOT. New York: The Rand Corporation, September 1969.

Taylor, George R., and Neu, Irene Dorothy. *The American Railroad Network, 1861–1890.* Cambridge: Harvard University Press, July 1956. 160 pages, 3 six-color maps.

* Isaacs, Arnold. "Traffic Patterns in the Old Northwest, 1815–1860." Unpublished honors paper, Northwestern University Department of Geography, April 1957.

Meyer, Balthasar Henry. *History of Transportation in the United States Before 1860*. Gloucester, Mass.: Peter Smith, 1948.

Jackson, W. Turrentine. *Wagon Roads West: A Study of Federal Road Surveys and Construction in the Trans-Mississippi West, 1846–1869*. New Haven: Yale University Press, 19xx.

Vance, James E., Jr. "The Oregon Trail and Union Pacific Railroad: A Contrast in Purpose." *Annals* of the Association of American Geographers 51 (December 1961); 357–79.

Meinig, D. W. "A Comparative Historical Geography of Two Railnets: Columbia Basin and South Australia." *Annals* of the Association of American Geographers 52 (1962); 394–413.

Davidson, Jack R., and Ottoson, Howard W., eds. *Transportation Problems and Policies in the Trans-Missouri West*. Lincoln: University of Nebraska Press, 1967.

Taylor, George R. *The Transportation Revolution*. New York: Holt, Rinehart & Winston, 1951.

Dodge, William H. *Transportation in the Wisconsin Economy*. Wisconsin Commerce Report, Vol. IV, No. 4. University of Wisconsin, School of Commerce, Bureau of Business Research and Service, August 1955.

Waterway

* Carter, R. E. "A Comparative Analysis of United States Ports and Their Traffic Characteristics." *Economic Geography* 38 (April 1962); 162–75.

Mayer, Harold M. "Great Lakes—Overseas: An Expanding Trade Route." *Economic Geography* (April 1954).

Mayer, Harold M. "Prospects and Problems of the Port of Chicago." *Economic Geography* 31 (April 1955).

Rail

The Association of American Railroads. *American Railroads: Their Growth and Development*. Washington, D.C., 1958.

Fieleke, Norman S. "Toward a More Efficient Railroad System." *New England Economic Review*, Federal Reserve Bank of Boston (March/April 1969), pp. 2–20.

Thomas, Frank H. *The Denver and Rio Grande Western Railroad: A Geographic Analysis*. Studies in Geography, No. 4. Northwestern University, 1960.

Thomas, Frank H. "Evolution of Railroad Route-to-Region Relationship: A Case Study of the Denver and Rio Grande Western Railroad." *Journal of Geography* 62 (1963); 389–97.

Air

Taaffe, Edward J. "Air Transportation and United States Urban Distribution." *The Geographical Review* 46 (April 1956); 219–39.

Caves, Richard E. *Air Transport and Its Regulators*. Cambridge: Harvard University Press, 1962.

Taaffe, Edward J. *The Air Passenger Hinterland of Chicago.* Chicago: University of Chicago Press, 1952.

Taaffe, Edward J. "A Map Analysis of United States Airline Competition. Part I–The Development of Competition." *The Journal of Air Law and Commerce* 25 (Spring 1958); 121–147; "Part II–Competition and Growth." *The Journal of Air Law and Commerce* 25 (Autumn 1958); 402–27.

Highway

Garrison, William L. *Allocation of Road and Street Costs, Part IV.* The Benefits of Rural Roads to Rural Property, State Council for Highway Research, Seattle, Washington, June 1956.

Smith, Wilbur, et al. *Future Highways and Urban Growth.* New Haven; 1961.

* Garrison, W. L., et al. *Studies of Highway Development and Geographic Change.* Seattle: University of Washington Press, 1959.

E.   FOREIGN AND WORLD TRANSPORTATION: SELECTED DESCRIPTIVE STUDIES

World

Wallace, William H. "Railroad Traffic Densities and Patterns." *Annals* of the Association of American Geographers 48 (1958); 352–74.

O'Dell, A. C. *Railways and Geography.* London: Hutchinson 1956. 200 pages, maps.

Jefferson, Mark. "The Civilizing Rails." *Economic Geography* 4 (1928); 217–31.

Sealy, K. R. *The Geography of Air Transport.* Hutchinson University Library Series, 1957.

Alexandersson, G., and Norstrom G. *World Shipping.* New York: John Wiley, 1963.

Foreign Areas

Wheatcroft, S. *The Economics of European Air Transport,* pp. xxii + 358. Cambridge: Harvard University Press, 1956.

Thomas, Benjamin E. *Trade Routes of Algeria and The Sahara.* University of California Publications in Geography, Vol. 8, No. 3, pp. 165–288, plate 21, 36 maps. Berkeley and Los Angeles: University of California Press, 1957.

Patmore, J. Allan. "The British Railway Network in the Beeching Era." *Economic Geography* 41 (1965); 71–81.

Kish, George. "Railroad Passenger Transport in the Soviet Union." *The Geographical Review* 53 (July 1963); 363–76.

Bird, James. "Road and Rail in the Central Massif of France." *Annals* of the Association of American Geographers 44 (1954); 1–14.

Buchanan, Colin D. "Britain's Road Problem." *The Geographical Journal* 130 (December 1964); 470–83.

Chapman, Albert S. "Trans-Europe Express: Overall Travel Time in Competition for Passengers." *Economic Geography* 44 (1968); 283–95.

Appleton, J. H. *The Geography of Communications in Great Britain.* London: Oxford University Press, 1962.

Smith, Robert H. T. "Transport Competition in Australian Border Areas: The Example of Southern New South Wales." *Economic Geography* 39 (January 1963); 1–13.

Chapter III.   The Gravity Model

* Carrothers, G. "An Historical Review of the Gravity and Potential Concepts of Human Interaction." *Journal of the American Institute of Planners* 22 (1956); 94–102.

* Godlund, S. "The Function and Growth of Bus Traffic Within the Sphere of Urban Influence." *Lund Studies in Geography*, Series B, No. 18 (1956); 59–72.

* Harris, C. "The Market as a Factor in the Localization of Industry in the U.S." *Annals* of the Association of American Geographers 44 (December 1954); 315–48.

* Isard, W. *Methods of Regional Analysis.* Chapter II. Cambridge: M.I.T. Press, 1959.

Taaffe, E. J.; Garner, B. J.; and Yeates, M. H. *The Peripheral Journey to Work.* Chapter III. Evanston: Northwestern University Press, 1963.

* Alcaly, Roger E. "Aggregation and Gravity Models: Some Empirical Evidence." *Journal of Regional Science* 17 (1967); 61–73.

Belmont, David M. "A Study of Airline Interaction Traffic." *Journal of Air Law and Commerce* 25 (1958); 361–68.

Bergsman, Joel. "Comments on Quandt and Baumol's Demand Model for Abstract Transport Modes." *Journal of Regional Science* 7 (1967); 83–86.

Bucklin, Louis P. "Retail Gravity Models and Consumer Choice: A Theoretical and Empirical Critique." *Economic Geography* 47 (October 1971); 489–97.

Clark, C., and Peters, G. H. "The 'Intervening Opportunities' Method of Traffic Analysis." *Traffic Quarterly* 19 (1965); 101–19.

Ellis, J., and Van Doren, C. "A Comparative Evaluation of Gravity and Systems Theory Models of Statewide Recreational Traffic Flows." *Journal of Regional Science* 6 (1966); 57–70.

Harris, Britton. "A Note on the Probability of Interaction at a Distance." *Journal of Regional Science* 5 (1964); 31–35.

* Heggie, I. G. "Are Gravity and Interactance Models a Valid Technique for Planning Regional Transportation Facilities." *Operational Research Quarterly* 20 (1969); 93–110.

* Howrey, E. P. "On the Choice of Forecasting Models for Air Travel." *Journal of Regional Science* 9 (1969); 215–24.

Huff, David L. "A Topographic Model of Consumer Space Preference." *Papers and Proceedings,* Regional Science Association 6 (1966); 159–74.

* Huff, David L. "A Probabilistic Analysis of Shopping Center Trade Areas." *Land Economics* 34 (February 1963); 81–90.

* Huff, David L., and Jenks, George F. "A Graphic Interpretation of the Friction of Distance in Gravity Models." *Annals* of the Association of American Geographers 58 (December 1968); 814–24.

Huff, David L. "A Computer Program for Locational Analysis," *Science, Technology and Marketing.*

* Illeris, Sven. "Functionelle Regionen in Danmark, Omkring, 1960." *Geografisk Tijdskrift* 66 (1967).

"Land Use and Traffic Models, Progress Report." *Journal of the American Institute of Planners* (May 1959).

Kolars, John, and Malin, R. "Population and Accessibility: An Analysis of Turkish Railroads." *Geographical Review* 60 (April 1970); 229–46.

Niedercorn, J. H., and Bechdolt, B. V., Jr. "An Economic Derivation of the 'Gravity Law' of Spatial Interaction." *Journal of Regional Science* 9 (1969).

* Olsson, Gunnar. *Distance and Human Interaction: A Review and Bibliography.* Philadelphia: Regional Science Research Institute, Bibliography Series No. 2, 1965.

Olsson, Gunnar. "Explanation, Prediction and Meaning Variance: An Assessment of Distance Interaction Models." *Economic Geography* 46 (Supplement) (June 1970). Proceedings International Geographical Union Commission on Quantitative Methods.

* Porter, Herman. "Application of Intercity, Intervening Opportunity Models to Telephone, Migration and Highway Traffic Data." Unpublished Ph.D. Dissertation, Northwestern University, Department of Geography, 1964.

Quandt, Richard E., and Baumol, W. J. "The Demand for Abstract Transport Modes: Theory and Measurement." *Journal of Regional Science* 6 (1966); 13–26.

Quandt, Richard E., and Young, Kan Hua. "Cross-Sectional Travel Demand Models: Estimates and Tests." *Journal of Regional Science* 9 (1969); 201–14.

Reilly, W. J. "Methods for the Study of Retail Relationships." Bulletin No. 2944, University of Texas, November 1929.

Richmond, Samuel B. "Interspatial Relationships Affecting Air Travel." *Land Economics* 33 (1957); 65–73.

Ruiter, E. R. "Toward a Better Understanding of the Intervening Opportunities Model." *Transportation Research* 1 (1967); 47–56.

Stouffer, S. A. "Intervening Opportunities: A Theory Relating Mobility and Distance." *American Sociological Review* 5 (1940); 445–67.

* Smith, Robert H. T. "Toward a Measure of Complementarity." *Economic Geography* 40 (1964); 1–8.

* Smith Robert H. T. "Concepts and Methods in Commodity Flow Analysis." *Economic Geography* 46 (Supplement) (June 1970). Proceedings International Geographical Union Commission on Quantitative Methods.

* Warntz, W. "Contribution Toward a Macroeconomic Geography: A Review." *Geographical Review* 47 (1957); 42x–24.

* Warntz, W. "A New Map of the Surface of Population Potentials for the United States, 1960." *Geographical Review* 54 (1964); 170–84.

Zipf, G. K. "The PP/D Hypothesis: On the Intercity Movement of Persons." *American Sociological Review* 11 (1946); 677–86.

Black, William R. "The Utility of the Gravity Model and Estimates of its Parameters in Commodity Flow Studies." *Proceedings* of the Association of American Geographers 3 (1971); 28–32.

Black, William R. "Substitution and Concentration: An Examination of the Distance Exponent in Gravity Model Commodity Flow Studies." Discussion Paper No. 1, Indiana University Department of Geography, Bloomington, Indiana.

Brush, John E., and Gauthier, Howard L. *Service Centers and Consumer Trips: Studies on the Philadelphia Metropolitan Fringe.* Department of Geography Research Paper #113, 182 pp. Department of Geography, University of Chicago, Chicago, 1968.

* Ullman, Edward L. "The Role of Transportation and the Bases for Interaction." In *Man's Role in Changing the Face of the Earth,* edited by William L. Thomas, Jr., et al. Chicago: The University of Chicago Press, 1956.

* Ullman, Edward L. *American Commodity Flow.* University of Washington Press, 1957.

Chapters IV and V.   Structural Analysis of Transport Networks

A.   APPLICATIONS

* Garrison, W. L. "Connectivity of the Interstate Highway System." *Papers and Proceedings* of the Regional Science Association 6 (1960); 121–37.

* Burton, Ian. "Accessibility in Northern Ontario: An Application of Graph Theory to a Regional Highway Network." *Report for Ontario Department of Highways,* 1962.

* Garrison, W. L., and Marble, D. "Factor-Analytic Study of the Connectivity of the Transportation Network." *Papers of Regional Science Association,* Lund Congress 12 (1964); 231–39.

* Nystuen, J., and Dacey, M. "A Graph Theory Interpretation of Nodal Regions." *Papers of the Regional Science Association* 7 (1961); 29–42.

* Kansky, K. *Structure of Transport Networks.* Department of Geography Research Papers 84, University of Chicago, 1963.

* Gauthier, H. "Transportation and the Growth of the Sao Paulo Economy." *Journal of Regional Science* 8; 77–94.

* Gauthier, H. "Least Cost Flows in A Capacitated Network." *Geographic Studies of Urban Transportation and Network Analysis.* Edited by F. Horton. Northwestern University Studies in Geography, No. 16, 1968.

Gauthier, H. "Potential of Graph Theory in Evaluation of Logistics Systems." In *Science, Technology and Marketing,* edited by Raymond Haas, pp. 359–70 (1966).

* Chorley, R., and Haggett, P. *Models in Geography.* Chapter 15. London: Methuen, 1967.

* Kissling, C. C. "Linkage Importance in a Regional Highway Network." *Canadian Geographer* 13 (1969); 113–27.

* Reed, Wallace. "Indirect Connectivity and Hierarchies of Urban Dominance." *Annals* of the Association of American Geographers 60 (December 1970); 770–85.

B.   BACKGROUND

Haggett, P., and Chorley, R. *Network Analysis in Geography.* New York: St. Martin's Press, 1970.

Harary, F. *Graph Theory*. Reading, Mass.: Addison-Wesley, 1969.

Ford, L. K., and Fulkerson, D. R. *Flows in Networks*. Princeton: Princeton University Press, 1962.

Berge, C. *The Theory of Graphs and Its Applications*. New York: John Wiley, 1962.

Busacker, R., and Saaty, T. *Finite Graphs and Networks*. New York: McGraw-Hill, 1965.

Avondo-Bodino, G. *Economic Applications of the Theory of Graphs*. New York: Science Publishers, 1962.

Flament, C. *Applications of Graph Theory to Group Structure*. Englewood Cliffs, N.J.: Prentice-Hall, 1963.

Harary, F., Norman, R., and Cartwright, D. *Structural Models: An Introduction to the Theory of Directed Graphs*. New York: John Wiley, 1966.

Harary, F., ed. *A Seminar on Graph Theory*. New York: Holt, Rinehart and Winston, 1967.

Ore, O. *Graphs and Their Uses*. New York: Random House, 1963.

Poustein, J. *Matrices in Graph and Network Theory*. Assen, Netherlands: Van Gorum and Comp. N.V., 1966.

Seshu, S., and Reed, M. B. *Linear Graphs and Electrical Networks*. Reading, Mass.: Addison-Wesley, 1961.

Berge, C., and Ghouila-Houri, A. *Programming, Games and Transportation Networks*. London: Methuen, 1962.

Beckenback, E., ed. *Applied Combinatorial Mathematics*. New York: John Wiley, 1964.

Dantzig, G. *Linear Programming and Extensions*. Princeton: Princeton University Press, 1963.

Smythe, W., and Johnson, L. *Introduction to Linear Programming With Applications*. Englewood Cliffs, N.J.: Prentice-Hall, 1966.

Chapter VI. Allocation Models

* Cox, K. "The Application of Linear Programming to Geographic Problems." *Tijdschrift voor Economische en Sociale Geografie* 56 (November/December 1965); 228–35.

Garrison, W. L. "The Spatial Structure of the Economy, II and III." *Annals of the Association of American Geographers* 49 (December 1959); 471–82 and 50 (1960); 357–73.

* Morrill, R., and Garrison, W. L. "Projections of Interregional Patterns of Trade in Wheat and Flour." *Economic Geography* 36 (1960); 116–26.

* Casetti, E. "Optimal Location of Steel Mills Serving the Quebec and Southern Ontario Steel Market." *Canadian Geographer* 10 (1966); 27–38.

* Yeates, M. "Hinterland Delimitation: A Distance Minimizing Approach." *Professional Geographer* 15 (1963); 7–10.

Enke, S. "Equilibrium Among Spatially Separated Markets: Solution by Electric Analogue." *Econometrica* 19 (1951); 40–47.

Fox, K. A., and Taeuber, R. C. "Spatial Equilibrium Models of the Livestock-Feed Economy." *American Economic Review* 45 (1955); 584–608.

Samuelson, P. A. "Spatial Price Equilibrium and Linear Programming." *American Economic Review* 42 (1952); 283–303.

Takayama, T., and Judge, G. G. "Spatial Equilibrium and Quadratic Programming." *Journal of Farm Economics* 46 (1964); 67–93.

Vidale, M. L. "A Graphic Solution of the Transportation Problem." *Journal of Operation Research* 4 (1956); 193–203.

Scott, A. J. "Programming Models of An Integrated Transport Network." *Papers and Proceedings* of the Regional Science Association 19 (1967); 215–22.

Orden, A. "The Transshipment Problem." *Management Science* 3 (1956); 276–85.

* Henderson, J. *The Efficiency of the Coal Industry: An Application of Linear Programming.* Cambridge: Harvard University Press, 1958.

Miller, R. E. *Domestic Airline Efficiency: An Application of Linear Programming.* Cambridge, Mass.: M.I.T. Press, 1963.

Beckman, M. J., and Marschak, T. "An Activity Analysis Approach to Location Theory." *Kyklos* 8 (1955); 125–41.

Dorfman, R.; Samuelson, P.A.; and Solow, R. M. *Linear Programming and Economic Analysis.* New York: McGraw-Hill, 1958.

Fox, K. A. "A Spatial Equilibrium Model of the Livestock Feed Economy of the U.S." *Econometrica* 21 (1953); 547–66.

Garrison, W. L., and Marble, D. F. "Analysis of Highway Networks: A Linear Programming Formulation." *Proceedings of the Highway Research Board* 37 (1958); 1–17.

* Goldman, T. A. "Efficient Transportation and Industrial Location." *Papers and Proceedings* of the Regional Science Association 4 (1958); 91–106.

Gould, P. R., and Leimbach, T. R. "An Approach to the Geographical Assignment of Hospital Services." *Tijdschrift voor Economische en Sociale Geografie* 57 (1966); 203–6.

Heady, E. O., and Egbert, A. C. "Programming Models of Interdependence Among Agricultural Sectors and Spatial Allocation of Crop Production." *Journal of Regional Science* 4 (1962); 1–20.

Hitchcock, F. L. "The Distribution of a Product from Several Sources to Numerous Localities." *Journal of Mathematical Physics* 20 (1941); 224–30.

* Isard, W. "Interregional Linear Programming: An Elementary Presentation and a General Model." *Journal of Regional Science* 1 (1958); 1–59.

Moses, L. N. "A General Equilibrium Model of Production, Interregional Trade and Location of Industry." *Review of Economics and Statistics* 62 (1960); 373–99.

Ridley, T. M. "Reducing the Travel Time in a Transport Network." In *Studies in Regional Science,* pp. 72–87, edited by A. J. Scott. London: Pion Ltd., 1969.

Scott, A. J. "Combinatorial Programming and the Planning of Urban and Regional Systems." *Environment and Planning* 1 (1969); 125–42.

Scott, A. J. "Location-Allocation Systems: A Review." *Geographical Analysis* 2 (1970); 95–119.

Scott, A. J. *Combinatorial Programming, Spatial Analysis, and Planning.* London: Methuen, 1971.

Stevens, B. H. "An Interregional Linear Programming Model." *Journal of Regional Science* 1 (1958); 60–98.

° Stevens, B. H. "Linear Programming and Location Rent." *Journal of Regional Science* 3 (1961); 15–25.

Wagner, H. M. "On a Class Management of Capacitated Transportation Problems." *Science* 5 (1959); 304–18.

° Scott, Allen J. *An Introduction to Spatial Allocation Analysis.* Commission on College Geography, Resource Paper No. 9. Washington, D.C.: Association of American Geographers, 1971.

King, L., et al. "Optimal Transportation Patterns of Coal in the Great Lakes Region." *Economic Geography* (July 1971); 401–13.

Chapter VII.   Other Selected Aspects of Transportation Geography

Werner, Christian. "The Role of Topology and Geometry in Optimal Network Design." *Papers and Proceedings* of The Regional Science Association 21 (1968). Morgan D. Thomas, editor.

Semple, R. K., and Wang, K. H. "A Geographical Analysis of Changing Redundancy in Inter-Urban Transportation Links." *Geografiska Annaler* 25, Series B (1971); 1–5.

Wilson, Andrew G. "A Family of Spatial Interaction Models and Associated Developments." *Environment and Planning* 3 (1971); 1–32.

Wilson, Andrew G. "Inter-regional Commodity Flows: Entropy Maximizing Approaches." *Geographical Analysis* 2 (July 1970); 255–82.

° Berry, Brian J. L. *Essays on Commodity Flows and the Spatial Structure of the Indian Economy.* Department of Geography Research Paper No. 111, University of Chicago, 1966.

Appleyard, Donald; Lynch, Kevin; and Myer, John R. *The View from the Road.* Cambridge: M.I.T. Press, 19xx.

Murdie, Robert A. "Cultural Differences in Consumer Travel." *Economic Geography* 41 (July 1965); 211–33.

Abler, Ronald F. "Distance, Intercommunications, and Geography." *Proceedings* of the Association of American Geographers 3 (1971); 28–31.

Brown, Lawrence A. "Migration, Functional Distance and the Urban Hierarchy." *Economic Geography* 46 (1970); 472–85.

Gould, Peter. *On Mental Maps.* Michigan Inter-University Community of Mathematical Geographers, Discussion Paper No. 9, (mimeo). Department of Geography, University of Michigan, Ann Arbor, 1966.

Horton, Frank E., and Reynolds, David R. "Effects of Urban Spatial Structure on Individual Behavior." *Perspectives on Urban Spatial Systems,* edited by Lawrence A. Brown and Eric G. Moore. Special issue of *Economic Geography* 47 (January 1971); 36–48.

Hinman, James. "Controversial Facility-Complex Programs: Coalitions, Side Payments, and Social Decisions." Research on Conflict in Locational Decisions. Discussion Paper VIII, Regional Science Department. University of Pennsylvania, December 29, 1970.

* Seley, John E. "Spatial Bias: The Kink in Nashville's I-40." Research on Conflict in Locational Decisions. Discussion Paper III, Regional Science Department. University of Pennsylvania, September 1970.

Wolfe, Roy I. *Transportation and Politics*. Searchlight Book #18. New York: Van Nostrand, 1963.

index

Abler, Ronald F., 201n
Abstract mode, 82, 98, 99, 196, 201
Accessibility, 2, 11, 12, 66, 73, 92, 98, 99, 116–58, 194, 196, 197, 200
Accessibility matrix, 124m, 125–26, 127m, 129
Action space, 201
Adams, Russell B., 118m, 119n
Agglomeration economies, 34, 36, 45–48, 55, 60, 67, 69
Airlines, 41, 60, 65, 66, 69–71, 118m, 120m, 127, 152
Air-passenger traffic, 30, 32m, 33, 69, 70m, 71m, 75–82, 87, 88m, 89m, 152, 155, 156m, 157m, 193
Alcaly, Roger E., 82
Alexander, John, 38m
Alexandersson, G., 199n
Allocation model, 159–91, 194, 196, 198, 199
Alpha index, 102, 104–8, 113, 114, 196
American manufacturing belt, 3, 7, 13, 16, 60, 61, 70, 71, 82, 87, 92, 119, 120, 143, 144m, 145m, 146m, 147m
Amtrak, 66, 68m, 69
Association of American Railroads, 6m, 58m, 59m

Back-haul, 170, 188
Barr, Brenton, 169, 170n, 171m, 172m
Berry, Brian, 67n, 112, 198, 199n
Bigham, Truman, 54n
Black, William R., 83, 84

Boolean Rules, 141, 158
Bottleneck, 182, 183, 191, 196
Break-of-bulk, 13, 42, 43, 44m, 45, 57, 60
Bridge line, 7, 11, 16, 33
Brown, Lawrence A., 201n
Brown, S. Earl, 38m
Brush, John, 24m, 28m, 85
Burghardt, Andrew, 11n
Busacher, R., 101n

Canals, 52, 54, 55, 56m
    Chesapeake & Ohio, 54
    Erie, 52–55
    Ohio & Erie, 55, 56
    Pennsylvania Public Works, 54
Capacitated network, 159, 175–86
Carrothers, Gerald, 76n
Carter, Richard, 64m
Casetti, Emilio, 185, 187m, 188, 190
Chorley, Richard, 101n
Circular causation, 45, 46
Class rates, 37, 38m
Commodity flows, 83–85, 94–96, 99, 193–95, 198
Commodity rates, 37, 38m, 44, 60, 95
Complementarity, 54, 55, 60, 73, 93–95, 194, 196
Conflict resolution, 202, 203
Conkling, Edgar, 199n
Connectivity, 101–6, 109m, 114, 118m, 119
Connectivity matrix, 119, 120, 122, 123–25, 128, 133–35, 138, 139, 152, 158

Consumer movement, 85, 86
Containerization, 65
Cross-haul, 170

Dacey, Michael, 149, 153t, 154m, 155m
Dahlberg, Richard, 38m
Dantzig, George, 160n, 182n
Dominance, 2, 20, 21, 26, 30, 33, 67m, 69, 70m, 71m, 87, 88m, 89m, 116, 149, 152–55, 194, 197
Dominant flow analysis, 152, 154, 155, 156m, 157m
Draper, N., 210n
Durbin, E., 180n

Equilibrium price, 164, 190

Fair, Marvin, 37n
Feeder lines, 7, 10, 13, 16, 33, 47, 56, 61, 106, 193
Fields of influence, 17, 33, 86–90, 95–97
Fieleke, Norman, 66m, 67m
Fishlow, A., 200n
Flows, 1, 2, 5, 16, 28, 29m, 30, 33, 34, 53, 57, 61, 63, 64, 66, 73, 93, 98, 116, 159, 162, 171m, 175, 183, 185, 193
Fogel, R., 200n
Fulkerson, D. R., 179, 182n
Functional Region, 2, 3, 4m, 5, 34, 36, 69, 150–55

Gamma index, 102–4, 106, 108, 109, 110, 113, 114, 196
Garner, Barry, 199n
Garrison William, 112, 113t, 126, 127, 128, 129m, 130, 131n, 200n
Gateway, 11, 13, 16, 17, 33, 37, 60, 106, 193
Gauthier, Howard, 24m, 28m, 85, 183n, 184m, 199n, 200n
General transportation problem, 175–86, 190
    capacity constraints, 175, 177, 178m, 179, 180, 181m, 182m
    flow augmentation, 178m, 180
    max flow-min cut theorem, 182n
Godlund, Sven, 17n
Goldman, T. A., 188
Gould, Peter, 47n, 48m, 51m, 201n
Graph theory, 100–58, 159, 194, 196, 197
    circuit, 104, 105, 110, 111, 113
    connected graph, 102
    degree of a node, 119
    diameter, 113, 124, 125, 128, 131, 135, 136m

Graph theory (*cont.*)
    directed graph, 149
    edges, 101–3, 108, 113
    planar graph, 103, 105, 107m
    redundancy, 125, 128m, 131, 133, 138, 158
    scalar, 131, 132t, 133m, 134t, 138
    vertices, 101–3, 108, 113
Gravity model, 73–99, 159, 194, 196, 197, 199, 204, 206, 207, 210
    distance exponent, 78–80, 83, 84, 87, 88, 90, 98, 194
    impedance factor, 82, 92, 93, 98, 99, 194
Green, F. H. W., 24, 30, 31m

Haggett, Peter, 101n
Harris, Chauncy, 21, 90, 91m, 92
Heggie, I. G., 97n, 98n
Hierarchy, 1, 25–34, 52, 69, 73, 99, 119, 130t, 131, 132t, 137, 138, 149–55
Highways, 5, 7, 10m, 17, 51, 60–62, 105, 106m, 127, 183, 184m, 185, 193, 196, 197m, 202
Hinman, J., 203n
Hinterland, 1, 17–28, 33, 34, 47, 52, 73, 86–90, 99, 152, 155, 173–75, 193, 194m, 197
Horton, Frank, 199n, 201n
Houthakker, H. S., 95n
Howrey, E. P., 82n
Huff, David, 85, 87n, 90

Illeris, Sven, 90
Impact studies, 199, 200
Indirect connectivity, 120–26
Intercity passenger traffic, 26, 28, 65, 67m, 70, 71, 99, 196, 198, 199, 204–7
Interstate highway system, 7, 11, 12m, 16m, 17, 61, 62m, 69, 105, 106m, 119, 120, 123, 125, 126, 128, 129m, 130t, 131, 132t, 133m, 134t, 137, 143, 144m, 147m, 148t, 151m, 196
Intervening opportunity, 73, 93, 95–97, 194, 196
Intracity transportation, 198, 199, 202
Isaacs, Arnold, 53m, 56m, 57m
Isard, Walter, 45n, 97n

James, Preston, 5n
Jones, Clarence, 5n

Kansky, Karl, 113n, 114
Kant, E., 28m

Kenyon, James, 21, 22m
King, Leslie J., 32m, 70m, 71m, 74m, 88m, 185, 187m, 190, 210n
Kroenke, D. M., 180n

Line-haul costs, 37–39, 41
Linnemann, H., 84n
Location of economic activity, 41–45, 66, 67
Locklin, D. P., 37n
Long-haul traffic, 40, 41, 60, 65, 210

Magee, S. P., 95n
Marble, Duane, 112, 113t
Marts, Marion, 200n
Matrix multiplication, 121–25, 130, 131, 139, 141, 152
Maximal connectivity, 103m, 104, 108, 110
Maximum flow, 175–179, 181m, 190
McConnell, James, 84n
Minimal connectivity, 102, 108, 110
Minimal cost path, 176, 177m
Minimal distance, 173, 174, 197
Minimal transport costs, 92, 98, 159–70, 175–79, 181m, 186, 188–91, 195, 197
Miyagi, M., 152, 154, 156m
Moore, Eric, 201n
Morrill, Richard, 47n, 48m, 51m, 165n
Myrdal, Gunnar, 45, 46n

National road, 53, 54
Net linkage cost, 179, 181m, 183
Net social payoff, 189
Network configuration, 108–11, 113
Network development, 47–69, 105–7, 110–11, 194
Nodal region, 5
Normative model, 159, 160, 190, 191
Norstrom, G., 199n
Nourse, H., 45n
Nystuen, John, 149, 153t, 154m, 155m

Objective function, 168, 169, 173, 175, 179
Odland, John, 185, 187m, 190
Oi, Walter Y., 199n
Olsson, Gunnar, 97n
Opportunity cost, 164, 165, 166m, 167
Optimality, 92, 159–62, 175, 179, 190, 195
  optimal flow, 170, 172m, 183, 185, 187m, 188, 189, 195, 196, 204
  optimal hinterland, 173, 197
Out-of-kilter algorithm, 179–86

Pardee, F. S., 41t, 65t
Path, 104, 108, 110, 122, 123, 125, 126, 131, 133, 135m, 182, 196
Patton, Donald, 63m
Perception studies, 192, 200–202
Phantom region, 186–88
Philbrick, Allen, 25m, 154n
Pipeline, 65
Platt, Robert, 2
Port concentration, 47–49, 50m, 54m
Porter, H., 95, 96m
Ports, 11, 12, 20–22, 52, 53, 54m, 64m
Potential maps, 73, 90, 91m, 92, 196
Pred, Allan, 46, 54m
Price differentials, 36, 53, 95, 164–66, 169, 170

Quandt, R. E., 82n

Railroads, 5, 6m, 7, 8m, 9m, 10, 11, 13, 14m, 15m, 16, 40, 41, 55–57, 58m, 59m, 65, 66, 68, 127, 131, 133m, 134t, 143, 148t, 151m, 200
  Baltimore & Ohio, 55
  Boston & Maine, 14, 16
  Canadian National, 13, 16
  Canadian Pacific, 13, 16
  Delaware & Hudson, 14, 17
  Erie, 55
  Lehigh & Hudson, 14, 17
  New York Central, 55
  Penn Central, 14, 16
  Pennsylvania, 55
  Richmond, Fredericksburg & Potomac, 7, 11
Rate-break point, 13, 60
Reed, Wallace, 198
Reese, P., 4m
Regional specialization, 34–36, 45, 47, 52, 54, 57, 60, 66, 67, 69, 93, 199
Regression, 76–80, 81t, 94, 96–98, 112–14, 194, 204–10
  correlation coefficient, 77, 113t, 208, 210
  multiple regression, 210
  residual values, 208–10
  scatter diagram, 76, 77, 78m, 80m, 204, 206, 207m, 208m
Reilly, W. J., 87
Reynolds, David, 201n
Rimmer, Peter, 49, 50m
Roberts, M. J., 54n
Rostow, W. W., 199, 200n

Saaty, T., 101n
Sargent, A. J., 21n
Schroeder, W., 86m

Scott, Allan, 165n
Seley, J. E., 203n
Semple, R. K., 185, 187m, 190, 198
Sensitivity analysis, 189, 190
Shimbel, A., 133, 137, 141, 143, 158, 196
Short-haul traffic, 40, 41, 60, 61, 65, 210
Shortest-distance path, 125, 133, 135,
    136m, 137, 138, 145t, 146t, 158, 159
Shortest path matrix, 131–38, 143, 196
Shuldiner, P. W., 199n
Sisco, Paul, 21, 23m
Slack variable, 186
Smith, David A., 76t, 80, 81t
Smith, H., 210n
Smith, Robert H. T., 83, 84m, 94
Soja, Edward, 200n
Spatial organization, 1, 5, 10, 13, 24, 30,
    33, 36, 55, 57, 69, 138, 148, 152,
    155, 156m, 157m, 159, 173, 193,
    200, 202
Spatial price equilibrium, 189
Spatial structure, 1, 2, 5, 33, 69, 106,
    111, 143
Stevens, Benjamin, 199n
Stewart, J. Q., 90n
Stouffer, S., 95
Supersonic transport, 202

Taaffe, Edward J., 28m, 32m, 47n, 48m,
    51m, 52n, 70m, 71m, 74m, 88m,
    199n
Tapered rate structure, 37–41, 42, 43,
    47, 60, 69
Telephone calls, 86m, 149, 152, 153t,
    193, 201
Terminal costs, 37, 39–41
Thoman, Richard, 199n
Thomas, Frank, 10n
Tinbergen, J., 84n
Topological structure, 100, 101, 111, 113
Traffic analysis, 73, 75–85
Transferability, 93
Transportation costs, 17–20, 34, 36–44,
    45t, 53, 54, 60, 65t, 66, 95, 98, 193,
    194

Transportation costs (*cont.*)
Transportation problem, 160–75, 190,
    195–97
    constraints, 162, 167m, 168, 169, 173,
        175, 179, 186, 189, 190
    dual, 164, 166, 167, 169, 179, 180,
        181m, 190
    feasible solution, 162–64, 179
    primal, 164, 166, 169, 170, 179, 180,
        190
    shadow prices, 164–67, 169, 170, 179,
        180, 183, 190
Truck transportation, 40, 41, 60, 61, 65
Trunk lines, 5–7, 10, 13, 17, 26, 33, 47–
    49, 53, 54, 56, 60, 61, 127, 148, 193

Uniform region, 2, 3, 4m, 34, 36, 69
Ullman, Edward, 7, 9m, 93
U.S. transportation development, 52–69

Valued graph, 138–48, 151m, 158, 196,
    197

Wallace, William, 10n
Warntz, William, 90n
Waterways, 5, 40, 41, 60–62, 63m, 64,
    200
    Great Lakes, 13, 55–57, 61, 185, 186,
        187m, 188, 190
    Mississippi River, 52, 56, 61, 63
    Ohio River, 37, 52, 53, 55–57, 61, 63
Werner, Christian, 198
Wheeler, James, 199n
Whittlesey, D., 5n
Williams, Ernest, 37n
Wilson, Andrew, 198
Wolfe, Roy I., 200n
Wolpert, Julian, 203n

Yeates, Maurice, 173, 174m, 199n

(m—map; n—footnote; t—table)